IN THE SHADOW OF THE MAMMOTH
Italo Svevo and the Emergence of Modernism

IN THE SHADOW OF THE MAMMOTH

Italo Svevo and the Emergence of Modernism

Giuliana Minghelli

UNIVERSITY OF TORONTO PRESS
Toronto Buffalo London

© University of Toronto Press Incorporated 2002
Toronto Buffalo London
Printed in Canada

ISBN 0-8020-3638-4

Printed on acid-free paper

Toronto Italian Studies

National Library of Canada Cataloguing in Publication

Minghelli, Giuliana
　In the shadow of the mammoth : Italo Svevo and the emergence of
modernism / Giuliana Minghelli

　Includes bibliographical references and index.
　ISBN 0-8020-3638-4

　1. Svevo, Italo, 1861–1928 – Criticism and interpretation.
2. Symbiosis (Psychology) in literature.   3. Modernism (Literature) Italy.
I. Title.

PQ4841.V4Z754 2002   853'.8   C2002-902951-1

University of Toronto Press acknowledges the financial assistance to its publishing program of the Canada Council for the Arts and the Ontario Arts Council.

University of Toronto Press acknowledges the financial support for its publishing activities of the Government of Canada through the Book Publishing Industry Development Program (BPIDP).

All'ombra di mio padre

Contents

ACKNOWLEDGMENTS ix

ABBREVIATIONS xi

Introduction 3

chapter one
Between Darwinian Origins and Modernist Ends:
Svevo's Allegory of Symbiosis 15

chapter two
Of Artists, Women, and Jews:
Svevo and the Modernist Contamination 46

chapter three
Between Darwinism and Dreams:
The Stories of Alfonso and Annetta in *Una vita* 73

chapter four
The Crying of the Statues: Art and Women in *Senilità* 102

chapter five
Leading the Pedagogue by the Hand 127

chapter six
Out of the Shadow of the Mammoth:
Zeno and the Story of the Other 161

Conclusion 204

NOTES 207

BIBLIOGRAPHY 223

INDEX 233

Acknowledgments

For the three novels I used the volume *Romanzi*, general editor Mario Lavagetto (1993). The text of *Una vita* was edited by Ferdinando Amigoni, the text of *Senilità* by Nunzia Palmieri, and the text of *La coscienza*, as well as that of the 'fourth novel' organized under the heading 'Continuazioni,' by Arrigo Stara. All translations are mine, except for *Senilità* and *La coscienza di Zeno*. For these I have occasionally consulted Beryl de Zoete's English translations: *As a Man Grows Older* (London: Secker and Warburg, 1980); and *Confessions of Zeno* (New York: Vintage Books, 1989).

An earlier version of chapter 6 appeared in *Modern Language Notes* in 1994, and the final section of chapter 5, 'The Death of the Pedagogue,' appeared in 1996 in *Gendered Contexts: New Perspectives in Italian Cultural Studies*, edited by Laura Benedetti, Julia Hairston, and Silvia Ross.

I would like to thank Eduardo Saccone, who first introduced me to the work of Italo Svevo; Elaine Marks and Joseph Buttigieg for reading the manuscript at different stages and offering encouragement and helpful criticism; Alice Jardine for supporting my research with her offer of a position as visiting scholar in the Women's Studies Program at Harvard University; and Silvestra Mariniello for her friendship and insights. With a great sense of loss, I would like to remember the late Robert Dombroski. His intellectual generosity and enthusiasm were essential to the publication of this book. A special thanks goes as well to the readers at the University of Toronto Press for their kind words and insightful comments, and to editor Ron Schoeffel for his support and patience. I would also like to thank Dr Franco Caramanti at Edizioni Mediterranee for his help in clearing copyrights. Finally, this book would not have come into existence without the critical eye, hard work, and enthusiasm of my most demanding editor, Harris Gruman.

Abbreviations

CA   'La corruzione dell'anima'
CdZ *La coscienza di Zeno*
M   'La morte'
NB   'La novella del buon vecchio e della bella fanciulla'
Pds 'Pagine di diario e sparse'
S   *Senilità*
SeS Giacomo Debenedetti, 'Svevo e Schmitz'
UT   'L'uomo e la teoria darwiniana'
UV   *Una vita*

IN THE SHADOW OF THE MAMMOTH
Italo Svevo and the Emergence of Modernism

Introduction

The year is around 1910. During the pauses in his work at the Veneziani paint factory, the Triestine businessman Ettore Schmitz escapes the jungle of prices and profits, even if only briefly and surreptitiously, into the haven of literature that he had abandoned years earlier. After the critical and commercial failure of *Senilità* (an even greater flop than his first novel, *Una vita*, which had appeared six years before, in 1892) Ettore had sworn to leave behind 'quella ridicola e dannosa cosa che si chiama letteratura' [that ridiculous and damaging thing called literature (Pds, 1968: 818)]. The life of commerce he has embraced leaves no time for writing novels or stories, but in the silence of the night his alter ego, Italo Svevo, can still satisfy the secret vocation by diving into reading (Ghidetti 1992: 48).

Among the books which may have caught Svevo's attention in this period is *La guerre du feu* (1909), an adventure story set in prehistoric times. Its author, J.H. Rosny ainé, a popular Franco-Belgian writer, was an early practitioner of that hybrid genre known as science fiction, or 'merveilleux scientifique,' which much attracted Svevo's own cultural eclecticism. At the core of the story stands 'l'alliance entre l'homme et le mammouth,' a pact between the colossal animal and that more fragile creature which allows the weaker to survive. The image of Naoh, the head of the tribe, who 'fait alliance avec le mammouth' and becomes 'le plus puissant des hommes' (Rosny 1994 [1911]: 122), struck a cord in Svevo's imagination to the point of inspiring him to undertake the writing of his own anthropological reflection on the birth of man, in an essay titled 'L'uomo e la teoria darwiniana' (Man and Darwinian Theory).[1]

This fragmentary piece, heterogeneous in form and inspiration, champions the aspirations of Italo Svevo, the unknown writer, against those of the 'successful' Ettore Schmitz. Success in the struggle for life, argues Svevo, means nothing more than crystallization. The man of the future, on the other hand, displaces the struggle to an existential level: he is unfinished, constantly changing, a man who 'waits knowing that he is nothing else than a sketch' (UT, 638) – (*un abbozzo*), a 'uomo in abbozzo.'

Then, in the second part of the essay, with a jolting movement, Svevo precipitates his virtual man, the last embodiment of a modernity yet to come, into a primitive setting inspired by Rosny's story. Man as such would not have survived on earth, narrates Svevo, if it had not been for his encounter with the strong and gentle mammoth, to whom he offered himself as slave in exchange for protection from a hostile environment. Hidden next to the huge animal – *in its shadow*, as it were – man developed his weapons and tools in order to eventually move in the world alone. Read metaphorically, the shadow of the mammoth is the space in which the subject escapes the contingencies of history and nature and projects his desire into the future. The shadow defines both the space from which man emerges and the time required for his adaptation, the pause in the struggle. But, more importantly, this fable identifies the birth of man with the community and with an 'other.' Hiding like his imagined ancestor, in the shadow of Rosny's feuilleton, Italo Svevo – the writer who feels his survival threatened – refined his artistic tools, transforming an entertaining plot for travellers and businessmen into a true intellectual adventure.

This study enters the 'shadow of the mammoth' to demonstrate how Svevo's allegory of symbiosis is the crucial poetic and philosophical moment in his writing. Contrary to what might be expected, the 'uomo in abbozzo,' seemingly the highest embodiment of both primitive and modern man, is not the hero of our fable. But neither is the mammoth, of whom we know only its shadow and animal silences.

What this study investigates is the shadow itself, that is, the *bond*, the *pact*, that ties two actors, the 'weak' male protagonist of Svevo's novels – failed artist, dreamy businessman, listless bourgeois, and uncertain revolutionary – and 'the woman.' But it should be clarified immediately that not only women are mammoths, and the condition *abbozzo* is not the sole prerogative of man. The story of the bond is not a story of a reflection, but of a becoming through mutual contamination, one that unfolds between the active voice of the verb *tutelare* – to protect – and the passive one, *essere tutelati* – to be protected – *between* strength and weakness, altruism and self-interest, animal and human, silence and language, and *beyond* any logic of identity and opposition.

The reading of 'L'uomo e la teoria darwiniana' and its companion fable 'La corruzione dell'anima' [The Corruption of the Soul] leads to a reassessment, in chapter 2, of Svevo's position within the modernist movement and a comprehensive interpretation of his major works: his first novel *Una vita* [*A Life* (1892)] in chapter 3; *Senilità* [*As a Man Grows Older* (1898)] in chapter 4; Svevo's late short fiction, namely, 'La novella del buon vecchio e della bella fanciulla' ['The Story of the Good Old Man and the Beautiful Girl' (1926)], 'Corto viaggio sentimentale' ['Short Sentimental Journey' (1925)], and 'La morte' ['Death' (1928)] in chapter 5; and his last and more famous novel *La coscienza di Zeno* [*Confessions of Zeno* (1923)] in chapter 6.

In the tradition of Svevo studies, much attention has been given to what one critic called 'Zeno and his brothers' (Jeuland Meynaud 1985), while the women characters have received only indirect treatment as objects of the desires and frustrations of these men, and virtually no attention has been paid to the intersubjective contamination between sexes. One of the early critics of Svevo, Giacomo Debenedetti (1945), however, unwittingly indicated the direction of this study by attacking the complicity that ties Svevo's 'inetti' (misfits) to a vaguely identified 'feminine essence': these characters, he says, are failed heroes because of their 'feminine' ineptitude for action and self-affirmation. Borrowing from Otto Weininger's metaphysics of gender, expounded in *Geschlecht und Charakter* (*Sex and Character* [1906]), Debenedetti stigmatized Svevo because of his inability to purge himself of the other, the woman, and the feminized Jew.

It is this anxiety over contamination, dreaded by Debenedetti and Weininger, that Svevo embraces, thus placing himself at the forefront of the modernist project. In fact, modernism as a movement could be defined as a programmatic unfolding of contaminations – between tradition and future, realist writing and experimental writing, male and female subjects. In this fable, woman is the 'other' par excellence, the sought for and dreaded symbiont of Svevo's 'anxious hope' for change and the 'not yet,' and at the same time an irrepressible remainder that points to a forgotten tale of human origin: the story of the bond with an other. As a story that attempts to project the final horizon of the human parable while pursuing the construction of its remotest past, the fable of the man and the mammoth stages a fundamental movement of modernism. Woman occupies the modernist site of this temporal and existential contamination.

It is in this context that Svevo's unfinished man – a subject that defines itself through potentiality and change and the questioning of limits – affords a new insight into the modernist effort to rethink subjectivity and otherness beyond the institutional borders drawn by gender, race, and nationality. Trieste, a city inscribed within a myriad of contaminations that break through the borders set up by passports and maps, is the stage where Ettore Schmitz-alias-Italo Svevo experienced this ethic of symbiosis in his everyday historical and cultural reality. Like a legend inspired by an ancient genius loci, it is to the streets of Trieste that the fable of the man and the mammoth belongs.

* * *

*Intorno
circola ad ogni cosa
un'aria strana, un'aria tormentosa,
l'aria natia.*

*[All around
all through everything there turns
a strange air, a tormenting air,
the air of home.]*

Umberto Saba, *Trieste*

In 1861, together with the kingdom of Italy, Ettore Schmitz – son to Francesco Schmitz, a well-to-do Jewish merchant, and the Italian-Jewish Allegra Moravia – is born in Trieste, a thriving port of the Hapsburg empire and a city tightly bound historically and culturally with the recently formed Italian nation. Within this telegraphic biography alone, the tensions of Trieste find expression. A Jewish past rooted in the history of Eastern Europe, an everyday reality as a subject of the Austrian empire, and a longing for Italy and its culture mingle in the anagraphical name of Ettore Schmitz.

It was perhaps this centrifugal tension that the Triestine writer tried to contain and correct in the string of pseudonyms he adopted: Erode, Ettore Samigli, and finally Italo Svevo. Observing how the pen name is a means to 'rinascere in un nuovo ordine, risacralizzare un'origine o rendere legale un nuovo status' [be reborn in a new order, to re-sacralize an origin, to render legal a new status (1979:13)], Marina Beer reads Svevo's effort as a wish to assimilate progressively a German-Jewish origin into a desired Italian identity. But the pureness of the latter may not have been Svevo's true goal, as the passage from the second and seamless Ettore Samigli to the final and oxymoronic Italo Svevo (literally Italian Swabian [i.e., German]) testifies. The pseudonym *Italo Svevo* evokes a border that both severs and joins two pure and separate elements. But behind its orderly facade lurks the now hidden, yet defiant, code name 'Erode' to remind us of a subterranean contamination within the asserted hybrid of Italian and German identities. Our journey through the artist's poetics finds a necessary point of departure in the ambiguous symbiosis expressed by the writer's names, the 'from where he speaks,' namely turn-of-the-century Triest.

'And trieste, ah trieste ate I my liver,' writes James Joyce – Svevo's former English instructor – in *Finnegans Wake*. This exclamation can be read as a pun on the French 'ah trieste était mon livre' (Cary 1993: 10), an interpretation that stresses the textual nature of the city. Trieste, like all cities, is a text waiting to be read carefully, and a text that in turn writes itself in and through the reader. A literary excursion through Trieste will further an intertextual understanding of what Henri Lefebvre (1991) calls the 'espace vécu,' a lived space that inhabits, like Saba's 'strange tormenting air,' the space of writing, Joyce's as well as Svevo's.

Visible and oppressive in the first novel (*Una vita*), Trieste fades in Svevo's later work into an invisible mise en scène, more an atmosphere, a suspension, than a place (Biondi 1990). In *Senilità*, Emilio, during a walk up the Karstic hills with Angiolina, gives a bird's-eye view of the city that expresses a condensed allegory of the place:

> l'arsenale che giaceva sulla riva, tutta una città, in quell'ora, morta. – La città del lavoro! – disse egli sorpreso d'essere venuto là ad amare. (S, 361)
>
> [the arsenal that was lying on the beach, the whole city, at that hour, dead – The city of work! – he said, surprised at having come there to love.]

Trieste is 'la città del lavoro,' but a dead city, a flat stage set, beside the living presence of he and Angiolina, the two actors of the story. The opposition evoked here, by no means unique to Svevo, is an often repeated refrain in the voluminous literature dedicated to the city: Trieste is a city of commerce, full of life and activity, *and* a city devoid of the true life, the life of art, love, and culture – *the life that marks time* (CA, 641).

Already, in 1824, Niccolò Tommaseo, the eminent Italian philologist, writer of the unsurpassed *Dizionario dei sinonimi* and native of nearby

Dalmatia, expressed similar impressions during a forced stop in Trieste en route to Italy:

> Di nuovo a Trieste risospinto dal tempo ... *nella barbara terra di Trieste*. [...] Una moltitudine affaccendata che inonda le vie, un andazzo di mercanti e meretrici, un bisbigliare di varie lingue, un misto di vari costumi, *molta industria, poco impegno, molta arte, poco studio, molto moto, poca vita, tale è Trieste*... (cited in Pittoni 1968: 45-6; emphasis mine)

> [Again in Trieste held over by bad weather ... *in the barbarous land of Trieste*. ... A busy multitude that floods the streets, a traffic of merchants and prostitutes, a whispering of many languages, a mixture of various customs, *much industry, little commitment, much artistry, little study, much movement, little life, this is Trieste* ...]

In Tommaseo's misanthropic portrayal, Trieste is a 'barbarian' land, a modern Tower of Babel, where the evils of cultural and linguistic contamination reign supreme.

In 1909 Scipio Slataper, the Slavic-Italian writer of *Il mio Carso*, will reiterate Tommaseo's verdict: 'Trieste non ha tradizioni di cultura. [...] Trieste ha un tipo triestino, deve volere un'arte triestina. [...] Trieste era fuori della storia' [Trieste does not have cultural traditions. ... Trieste has a Triestine type, it must strive for a Triestine art. ... Trieste was outside history (1954: 8)]. And again, eighty years later, Magris and Ara will reach this same conclusion in *Trieste. Un'identità di frontiera* [*Trieste: A Frontier Identity*]:

> Città senza la continuità di un passato, essa era una città borghese per eccellenza, nata, cresciuta ed esistente – sul piano economico e su quello spirituale – soltanto in questa dimensione mercantile. Priva di una storia illustre, Trieste aveva alle proprie spalle solo *una recente preistoria minimale*, le ramificate ascendenze dei suoi cittadini provenienti dalle piú diverse contrade ... (1982: 33; emphasis mine)

> [City without the continuity of a past, it was a bourgeois city par excellence, born, grown and existing – on the economic as well as the spiritual plane – only in this mercantile dimension. Deprived of an illustrious history, Trieste had behind it only *a recent minimal prehistory*, the complex ancestries of its citizens deriving from the most diverse regions ...]

Trieste has no history, or at best a 'minimal prehistory.' But as these writers know, a history, no matter how 'minor' – a history of colonizations, of dependence, perhaps a history about which it is difficult to boast, but nonetheless a history – must exist.

Located at the northern reach of the Adriatic Sea, naturally separated from the interior by the Karstic plateau, Trieste marked since Roman times the end of a territory and the beginning of an uncharted land. First a Roman military camp and then a colony after 60 BC, Trieste emerged in the eleventh century as an independent city state. Its position, however, was weakened by the powerful presence of the nearby Venetian Republic, so in 1382, while ostensibly keeping its autonomy, Trieste placed itself under the protection of the House of Austria. For almost four centuries the city, protected but excluded from the main commercial routes, stagnated. Then, in 1748, Maria Theresa extended free port status to the city, thus inaugurating the economic fortunes of what had been up to then a sleepy fishing town.

'Con uno scatto imprevedibile dalle comuni regole storiche, Trieste si presenta improvvisamente "nuova"' [With a leap unpredictable according to common historical norms, Trieste suddenly appears as 'new' (1968: 14)]; so Anita Pittoni describes this founding moment in the history of Trieste. Thus history gives way to myth, the myth of Trieste as a 'new' virgin space, one whose geography is its true destiny. Swarmed over by hosts of émigrés and immigrants attracted by the economic opportunities and civic protections it offered – people from all over Europe escaping poverty, the law, revolutions, and counter-revolutions – Trieste becomes a little 'New World' in the heart of the old, a 'Philadelphia in Europe' to which refugees come 'con un sogno da Robinson Crusoe: edificare una città' [with a Robinson Crusoe dream: to build a city (Pittoni 1968: 20)]. 'Il passato è morto' [The past is dead (1968: 25)], writes the French aristocrat Charles Albert de Moré about Trieste, where his brother took refuge. 'I sopravvissuti devono cominciare a costruire ogni cosa dalla base, come i pionieri che furono subito all'opera in America' [the survivors must start to build everything from the foundations, like the pioneers who immediately set to work in America (25)]. Trieste, a city of survivors, is the sum of many historical deaths. From the death of the past, not least its own modest one, Trieste is born.

The leap that marked Trieste's development is commonly assumed to embody the peculiarity of the city. For this reason, Trieste has been compared to St Petersburg, Dostoyevski's 'premeditated city,' 'cresciuta per decisione di un sovrano anziché per un processo di sviluppo organico' [grown by the decision of a sovereign rather than by a process of organic development (Ara and Magris 1982: 4)]. But Trieste's existence, though incubated, predates this decree. Since its earliest beginnings, Trieste's peculiarity lies instead in an independence and resulting vulnerability that forces it to find definition in relation to a more powerful country: to Austria from 1348, and, later, after both the First and Second World Wars, to Italy. As in the Svevian fable of the primitive man, Trieste lived in the shadow of a stronger other, and it is out of the *pause* granted by the other – its economic and political protection – that it could emerge and thrive.

In Svevo's lifetime Trieste grew and expanded in the shadow of Austria-Hungary. But in this shadow the different ethnic communities that made up its fabric looked – like the 'malcontento uomo' [the unhappy man] in the shadow of the mammoth – towards a farther horizon, the dream of a unified homeland (Ara and Magris 1982: 9). The delicate sociopolitical equilibrium on which the city rested at the turn of the century is well summarized by a Triestine native, Bobi Bazlen, the man of letters and talent scout who 'smuggled' Svevo into the Italian literary scene:

> ... una città che parla un dialetto veneto, circondata da una campagna nella quale non si parla che una lingua slava, la parte piú intellettuale della borghesia, che si sente staccata dal paese cui crede di appartenere per lingua e cultura [...] l'altra parte della borghesia, quella meno colta, continua a fare i suoi affari [...] dunque questa città [è] affidat[a] a una burocrazia austriaca ineccepibile, ma che parla il tedesco. (1970: 137-8, 141)

> [... a city that speaks a Venetian dialect, surrounded by a countryside in which only a Slavic language is spoken; the most intellectual part of the bourgeoisie who feel separated from the country [Italy] to which they believe they belong by language and culture ... the other part of the bourgeoisie, the less cultured one, minding its business ... then this city is entrusted to an impeccable Austrian bureaucracy, but one that speaks German.]

Divided by different linguistic and cultural identities, but still held together by common commercial pursuits and political organization, Trieste's human geography constitutes a host of possibilities, a net of connections, a space akin to Foucault's 'heterotopia': 'the juxtaposing in a single real place of several spaces, several sites that are in themselves incompatible' (1986: 25). The momentous challenge for the people of Trieste would be to recognize, beyond the differences, the thread of a common history.

Under Austrian rule, mutual contamination between the ethnic groups, even if resisted, was the reality of everyday life. Perhaps to deflect the potentially explosive political dimension of this contamination, Trieste has been described in terms borrowed from the language of natural history. For example Anita Pittoni speaks of the city as 'un insetto strano che per difetto di nozione scientifica non trova un posto definitivo di catalogazione' [a strange insect that for lack of a scientific notion cannot find a definite place in the catalogue of species (Pittoni 1968: 11)]. The human and cultural exchanges the city is built upon resemble the unpredictable *mélanges* Darwin saw unfolding in prehistoric times; as with the products of nature there is a certain 'unfinishedness' and tentativeness in the human geography of Trieste, a condition at the same time threatening and full of potentiality.

'Cosa sono questi triestini, questa cultura triestina, questa città di cui si diceva, ed i triestini non si offendevano, anzi, che è un crogiuolo?' [What are these Triestine people, what is this Triestine culture, this city that was called – and the Triestine people did not get offended, in fact, quite the contrary – a crucible?], wonders Bobi Bazlen (1970: 143). Against the opinion of Umberto Saba who coined this description, Bazlen replies:

> A occhio e croce, direi che Trieste è stata tutto meno che un crogiuolo: il crogiuolo è quell'arnese nel quale metti dentro tutti gli elementi più disparati, li fondi, e quello che salta fuori è una fusione, omogenea, con una distribuzione uguale di tutte le componenti, e con caratteristiche costanti – ora, a Trieste, che io sappia, un tipo fuso non s'è mai prodotto, o un tipo con caratteristiche costanti [...] c'erano le possibilità di quello che gli italiani chiamano 'dialoghi' (quando sono chic), di molti incontri, di accostamenti tra elementi che normalmente non si avvicinano, ma saltavan fuori dei *tentativi*, delle *approssimazioni, figure mai completamente definitive, esperimenti di Dio giunti fino a un certo punto.* (1970: 143; emphasis mine)

[At first sight, I would say that Trieste has been everything but a crucible: the crucible is that instrument inside which you put all the most disparate elements, melt them, and what comes out is a fusion, homogenous, with an equal distribution of all the components, and with constant characteristics. Now, in Trieste, as far as I know, a fusion was never produced, or a type with constant characteristics ... There was the possibility of what the Italians call 'dialogues' (when they are chic), of many encounters, of meetings between elements that usually do not come together, but what came out were *attempts, approximations, figures never quite completed, experiments of God that reached only a certain point.*]

It is impossible not to detect in Bazlen's conclusion a negative verdict on the outcome of this experiment called Trieste. Quite unexpectedly, coming from a cosmopolitan intellectual who strenuously opposed any kind of formal closure like those imposed by ideas and texts, Trieste is judged for its failure to express a cohesive unity. By speaking of an 'attempt,' an 'approximation,' a 'figure never quite completed,' Bazlen presupposes an ideal (if itself no more clearly defined) that the city failed to achieve. By falling short of this hypothetical figure of perfection, Trieste is left as an intriguing yet unfinished sketch, a city *in abbozzo*. Thus, forgetful about her past, Trieste fails as well to meet her future.

Left an orphan, without a cohesive and unified history, Trieste, the city of contaminations and experiments, becomes a fertile ground for the creation of many 'natural histories.' If at best such chronicles succeed in comprehending the city's diverse and rich composition, at worst they end up levelling Trieste's past and future within a stark Social Darwinist eschatology. Although symbiosis and reciprocal adaptation might be imagined as a possible outcome of the 'melting pot,' Triest's present and future is consistently cast within the rhetoric of struggle and selection. Once again Slataper's reflection exemplifies this tension. 'Trieste è un posto di transizione,' he writes, '*cioè di lotta*. Ogni cosa è duplice e triplice a Trieste, cominciando dalla flora e finendo con l'etnicità' [Trieste is a place of transition, *that is of struggle*. Everything is double and triple in Trieste, starting from the flora and ending with ethnicity (Slataper 1954: 93; emphasis mine]). On the eve of the First World War, Slataper and his Trieste would embrace this myth of a decisive and cleansing struggle. Soon thereafter, however, the promise contained in Trieste's 'double triple nature' was shot down on the Karstic plateau, as Slataper and much of the Trieste's youth died there for the 'redemption' of the city.

The tendency to an ideal purity, to a unity of character, to the closure promised by belonging to an idealized fatherland, suffocated Trieste's rich and fertile 'imperfection' in the unhappiness of an imperfect belonging. After 1918 the idea of a redeemed Italian Trieste was co-opted by a Fascist rhetoric of racial purity, one which found fertile ground in the hostility towards the Slavs, and which in turn led to the harbour being cut off from its northern and eastern hinterland, a useless appendage to the Italian peninsula. The history of Italian Trieste in the twentieth century can be understood as a search to attain Bazlen's coherent ideal, an attainment which, once it supposedly took place, sent the city into steady decline.

'What the map cuts up, the story cuts across,' writes Michel de Certeau (1988: 129). Deprived of political expression, the anomalous situation of Trieste has found its truest representation in the texts of its major writers: Svevo, Saba, and Slataper. Theirs is an arduous and self-deprecatory conquest, and thus truly Triestine, since stylistically and linguistically, as already historically and geographically, all of these writers felt less than whole, improper, and 'impure.' Their language, in their own judgment, as well as in the eyes of their Italian critics, seemed unnatural, 'avventizia' [literally translated as 'coming from outside' (Debenedetti 1945: 71)]. Slataper prefaces one of his articles in the Florentine journal *La voce* with the admission: 'Il nostro stile è peso. E' plasmato sulla convenzione letteraria non animato dalla vita' [Our style is heavy. It is molded on literary convention, not animated by life (Slataper 1954: 151)]. Similarly Svevo endlessly apologizes for his 'linguetta' (little language). The very composition of *La coscienza di Zeno* is presented by its author as a direct result of the political redemption of Trieste. 'È' poi certo,' he writes in 1923 to his editor, Attilio Frescura, 'che se l'Italia non fosse venuta a me io non avrei neppur pensato di poter scrivere' [It is quite certain that if Italy had not come to me, I would not have thought myself able to write (1993: 1178)]. It is in the venerable shadow of Florence and its projected ideal of a Tuscan language that Italo Svevo and his contemporaries wrote. And from within that shadow, they forever changed the physiognomy of the Italian literary tradition.

'Se qualcuno volesse o dovesse raccontare la storia della letteratura italiana del Novecento,' speculates Lavagetto, 'potrebbe incominciare il proprio racconto dall'Austria: piú precisamente da Trieste' [If somebody wanted or had to tell the story of the Italian literature of the twentieth century, he could start his story with Austria: more precisely with Trieste (1989: 239)]. The 'arte impura' [impure art (1989: 237)] of Svevo, Saba, and Slataper contains all the disruptive and innovative force of what Deleuze and Guattari (1986) theorized as 'minor literature,' a force that opens Italian Literature to modernist experimentation and contamination, making of it *something other*.

Svevo's narrative and Saba's poetry are powerful statements of *belonging through difference*. Trieste is a city of commerce, as whole generations of Triestine artists have lamented. But what this multicultural city embodies is rather that 'logic of ambiguity' that de Certeau identifies as the trademark of stories, a logic that '"turns" the frontier into a crossing [...] it recounts inversions and displacements' (de Certeau 1988: 128). From this perspective, Trieste was the ideal city for literature. As Ara and Magris rightly observed: 'Trieste, forse piú di altre città, è letteratura, è la sua letteratura' [Trieste, perhaps more than other cities, is literature, is its literature (1982: 8)]. Thus Trieste has not been simply 'un sismografo sensibile' [a sensitive seismograph (Lavagetto 1989: 214)] of the literary earthquake that shook up Europe in those first astounding years of the last century; nor is it only an 'ottima cassa di risonanza' [excellent sounding board (Bazlen 1970: 144)] of faraway tunes. Trieste created the music itself. Humbly, unpretentiously, subterraneously, Italian modernism initiated itself in Trieste.

Finally, to correct Scipio Slataper's statement, we can agree that the city 'ha un tipo triestino' [has a Triestine type] – a historical 'uomo in abbozzo,' as it were. But we must insist as well that 'ha un'arte triestina' [it has a Triestine art], an art that paradoxically gives form to precisely what existentially and linguistically subverts containment in a form, figure, or style. It is an art of contamination, born from the space of symbiosis.

chapter one

Between Darwinian Origins and Modernist Ends: Svevo's Allegory of Symbiosis

Coloro che guardano con occhio critico il progresso umano possono accorgersi di una massima evidente: La difficoltà di scoprire è grande, ma la seconda e maggiore difficoltà è di sapere quello che si è scoperto. [Those who look with a critical eye on human progress can take note of a self-evident truth: the difficulty of discovering is great, but the second and greatest difficulty is knowing what one has discovered.]

Italo Svevo, 'L'uomo e la teoria darwiniana'[1]

Italo Svevo wrote these opening lines of 'L'uomo e la teoria darwiniana' sometime between 1909 and the outbreak of the First World War, at a time of apparently unbounded progress, of daring exploratory trips to the still mysterious corners of the earth, and even more momentous explorations of the invisible geographies of matter. In the wake of these discoveries that are restlessly changing the face of his time, Svevo, like other modernist writers, feels the need to undertake his own expedition, less spectacular, more obscure, but no less challenging: the mapping – through storytelling – of the existential meaning of such discoveries.

The two fables 'La corruzione dell'anima' and 'L'uomo e la teoria darwiniana' are half-parodic, half-serious explorations of the Darwinian theory of evolution and modernity's concomitant myth of progress propelled by an autonomous self-improving humanity. With these fables Svevo elaborates two myths of origins that pose alternatives to the Darwinian narrative: the birth of humanity out of restless unhappiness and weakness – the survival of the unfittest; and the invention of self and the other through symbiotic interdependency as represented in the fable of man's encounter with the silent Mammoth.

Svevo's own brand of modernism resonates with Astradur Eysteinsson's definition of the movement 'as an attempt to *interrupt* the modernity that we live and understand as a social if not "normal" way of life' (Eysteinsson 1990: 6). The two fables are organized around such interruption, first defined as 'resistance' to evolutionary temporality, and then as the search for a pause, gained in the allegorical shadow of the other. Beyond the solitary Darwinian striving in nature or the pursuit of a technological future outside the body, Svevo's allegiance to the future unfolds at the moment of the encounter with the other. The creation of an intersubjective space of symbiosis, what Deleuze and Guattari defined as a moment of 'creative involution,' is both a hermeneutically charged blockage of time – the possibility of pausing and looking back upon older, established fictions of origin and recovering the traces of an unexplored and untold future – and the staging of subjectivity as an endless invasion and contamination between self and other: to borrow a Deleuzian expression, 'a becoming-wasp of the orchid and a becoming-orchid of the wasp' (Deleuze and Guattari 1987: 10). It is in this space and time that Svevo, defined by Claudio Magris in the rhetoric of heroic modernism as 'the poet of the Nietzschean twilight of the subject, of the "over-man" ... of the "I" that lives a present of transition and mutation,' reaches 'towards a new anthropological epoch,' thus pursuing his promise, the 'anxious hope' of a future, of a trans-human condition (Magris 1988: 298).

The present study is a reflection on the figure of the woman in Svevo's narrative as the site of such a promise. Besides being obviously indebted to recent feminist and post-colonial theories that move beyond simplistic notions of identity, autonomy, and genealogical becoming, this opening chapter moves in the context of an emerging theoretical discourse about symbiosis as the 'communication' between the heterogeneous categories of human, animal, and machine that allow a rethinking of the human actor and his story.

From this perspective, Svevo's man is not just a hybrid, a mixture of pre-existing pure elements – Jew and Italian, male and female, realist and modernist – but can be read rather as 'contaminated,' or, to borrow a term from the biological discourse that finds such a rich resonance in Svevo's rhetoric of sickness and health, as a 'diseased' subject. He becomes a site where one can witness an ongoing synthesis of heterogeneities, an ongoing invention of consciousness as an experiment in reactions and counter-reactions, in the assimilation and rejection of 'foreign' objects. The encounter of the man and the Mammoth, the human and the animal, of 'soul' and body, stages allegorically what I believe to be the defining contamination of Svevo's subject, the one taking place between man and woman. This fable foreshadows the story, told over and over in Svevo's texts, of a life-giving disease: the impossible but unavoidable association with the other. As Svevo reminds us: 'In complesso abbiamo il bisogno di tutelare o di essere tutelati. Altrimenti la nostra mente non vede uno scopo della vita' [In the end, we need to protect or to be protected. Otherwise our mind does not see an aim to life (Pds, 828)].

Modernism has been characterized by Fredric Jameson as a representation of life through 'sealed subjective worlds' whose interaction is similar to 'a passage of ships in the night' (Jameson 1988: 350). Robert Dombroski, in the wake of this interpretation, has described the consciousness of Zeno – to me, Svevo's most open and 'contaminated' character – as 'a closed world,' impermeable to the challenge of other voices, other points of view, stable in its systematic instability. Nevertheless, at the same time he has spoken of Svevo's last novel as staging the *production* of consciousness through writing (Dombroski 1995: 139–47). I find that Svevo's contribution to the modernist project lies in the 'discovery' that such production – of consciousness, of the work of art, of language – while it might be described as a hermetically sealed, autonomous, solitary moment, is at the same time an encounter of worlds, of perspectives, of subjectivities, a sea of otherness that keeps the self afloat. The woman is the catalyst for Svevo's experiment with life and consciousness. The discovery that the story of the restless man is molded by the story of the other – the Mammoth or the woman – suggests that the future is not far away, somewhere outside us, but rather right in-between, in the translation of self and other, in the subtle contamination of an allegedly monological text by the silent existence of a differently-voiced story. This gendering of time, space, and the invention of the self through narrative defines the extent of Svevo's rethinking of modernity.

It is a fitting irony that in these two fables Svevo's writer – like the Norsemen who arrived in America without discovering it (UT, 637) – seems to overlook the full import of his own reflection. In fact, even though the allegory of origins, featuring a weak, unhappy, restless man and a strong, well-adapted, silent Mammoth, bears indirect yet important consequences for the understanding of the figure of the woman *as other* in the whole of Svevo's work, any explicit consideration of gender remains repressed in Svevo's theory of origins. If the question of man is, in Darwin's words, 'a frontier instance,'[2] the question of woman seems to remain out of bounds. In both Darwinian theory and in Svevo's speculative fables, the woman is latent. Nonetheless it is precisely her absence that unexpectedly throws a shadow on the text and its writer.

The Unhappiness of Origin

When we reflect on [the struggle for life], we may console ourselves with the full belief, that the war of nature is not incessant, that no fear is felt, that death is generally prompt, and that the vigorous, *the* healthy, *and the* happy *survive and multiply (emphasis mine).*

Charles Darwin, The Origin of Species

Finally, the great question would still remain whether we can really dispense with illness – even for the sake of our virtue – and whether our thirst for knowledge and self-knowledge in particular does not require the sick soul as much as the healthy, and whether, in brief, the will to health alone, is not a prejudice, cowardice, and perhaps a bit of very subtle barbarism and backwardness.

Friedrich Nietzsche, The Gay Science

Svevo asked himself, how could the weakest, the most unhappy of all animals have come into being and then survived? In the two fables 'La corruzione dell'anima' and 'L'uomo e la teoria darwiniana,' Svevo takes this question as his point of departure and creates an allegory of human origins that, while it upholds Darwin's secularization of nature and naturalization of humanity, still strives to articulate, as Nietzsche did before him, human specificity in a world voided of subjective purpose.

'Therefore, fable: an allegory saying ironically the truth of the allegory that it actually is ...'[3] – so Derrida defines the self-referentiality of this genre. Though light and entertaining, Svevo's unfinished *divertissements* use a playful awareness of the narrative and allegorical continuity between religious and scientific discourses to question the theory of human origins and progress. In so doing they articulate an alternative evolution whose focus is no longer the individual or the species but a *relation* through which what is human is at the same time constituted and challenged in its claim of unity, indivisibility, and mastery. The first fable, 'La corruzione dell'anima,' lays out the context and setting of Svevo's allegory of symbiosis. Here Svevo parodically combines the oldest story of origin – the book of Genesis – with its modern day counterpart – the Darwinian theory of evolution – in order to tell a secularized myth of a weak humanity that survived and put a strong claim on the future precisely by resisting the demands of nature.

God, having separated the elements and created the various organisms, got tired of his work and decided to endow each with a soul that could carry on the business of creation independently. These souls, because they contained the very principle of creativity and restlessness, were still as chaotic as the universe was before divine intervention, and thus were unhappy with both the organisms in which they had been enclosed and the created universe in which they dwelled.

> ... l'anima era in primo luogo malcontento. [...] E lentamente causa tale malcontento l'organismo si trasformava accordando all'anima brevi intervalli di soddisfazione. (CA, 641)

> [... the soul was first of all discontent ... and slowly because of this discontent the organism transformed itself, granting the soul brief intervals of satisfaction.]

Because of this unhappiness, each organism restlessly continued its own work of creation. But inventing oneself meant a constant confrontation with one's own limits, meant unhappiness and a yearning for a satisfaction always deferred to a far distant future. For this reason 'non da tutti gli animali il processo continuò' [not in every animal did the process continue (CA, 641)].

Some creatures, desiring above all the contentedness of successful adaptation, renounced the restless yearning of the soul in order to live in the present of one chosen environment.

> Intanto qualcuno di essi appena uscito dalle mani del Creatore, proprio come era, piccolo e tuttavia un'immagine dello stesso caos [...] si sprofondò nell'acqua, nel fango o nell'aria e si disse soddisfatto. (CA, 641)

> [As soon as they came out from the hands of the Creator, some animals plunged themselves – as they were, small and still an image of chaos – ... in the water, in the mud or in the air and pronounced themselves satisfied.]

One after another, each animal took shelter in a home where it lived limited by the laws of the elements and the rhythm of the seasons. For the sake of an immediate fulfillment, most animals ended up living a lower but happier existence.

> I piú forti fra gli animali sorrisero alla vita si nutrirono liberamente di piante ed animali e corsero da padroni i mari e le terre. [...] I piú deboli inventarono la difesa e s'acquietarono anch'essi quando parve loro efficace abbastanza. [...] E fu una gioia sulla terra e un grande ordine imperocché l'anima vi mancava. [...] E tutti costoro vissero lieti non accorgendosi di aver perduta la vera vita. (CA, 642)

> [The strongest among the animals smiled at life, fed themselves freely on plants and animals, ran like masters over land and sea. ... The weakest invented defence and settled themselves down as well as soon as it seemed effective enough. ... And happiness and a great order reigned on earth because the soul was missing. ... And all these animals lived happily without realizing they had lost the true life.]

The vigorous, the cunning, and the healthy survived and populated the earth as Darwin assured us they would, but in the process they lost 'la vita intensa, quella che segna il tempo' [the intense life that marks time (CA, 641)] and remained forever crystallized, since 'l'organo perfetto alla vita non può lasciarsi dirigere dall'anima' [the organ perfected for living can no longer be directed by the soul (CA, 642)].

One last creature, perhaps because it deferred choosing its mode of life far too long, ended up embodying the very essence of restlessness. While all the other animals gave in to the seduction of their perfected organs for life (claws, wings, fur), causing the naturalization of their being, this organism, because of its very imperfection and weakness, maintained the soul, and thereby delayed its adaptation to and determination by the environment.

> Imperfettissimo, non ebbe le ali e neppure quattro mani come i quadrumani, né quattro piedi come le fiere ma sempre due mani e due piedi soli, questi per portar lentamente quelle tuttavia male armate. (CA, 642)

> [Utterly imperfect, he did not have wings and not even four hands like the quadrumanes, nor four feet like the quadrupeds, but always only two hands and two feet, these to carry him slowly and those still badly armed.]

Out of the disappearance of the soul from the rest of the universe 'nacque il malcontento e torvo uomo' [the unsatisfied and sullen man was born (CA, 642)]. The gradual crystallization of the various organisms *uncovered* the 'birth' of man, whose specificity coincided not with his body, totally undetermined, but with his soul, 'malcontento,' in perpetual ferment.[4] Man constituted therefore the very essence of creation: the constant struggle for order and separation, for identity and difference. Because of a chance event this monstrous mutation survived, helpless and unsteady, equally ready to leap into the future or disappear unnoticed, a faint trace in a remote geological layer.

> Questo suo malcontento lo faceva andare e l'oggi doloroso s'illuminava della dimani incerta, imprecisabile ma luminosa di speranza. (CA, 642)

> [His discontent pushed him forward and the painful present was lit up by an uncertain tomorrow, indefinable but shining with hope.]

One should not be led astray by this tale's playful psychologization of scientific theory. Svevo's fable interprets and rewrites Darwin's theory by reintroducing the singularity of the human, whose primacy is not the result of divine grace but rather of a more or less willed process. Svevo anthropomorphizes Darwin's nature by reintroducing, self-consciously and parodically, human desire, the 'dissatisfaction of the soul,' in the place of Darwin's principle of the mutability of species; and the free will of all organisms to choose their own mutation and environment in the place of Darwin's impersonal principle of natural selection. But by doing so Svevo does not intend to return to either a deistic or humanistic view of nature. There is no longer a master plot, a distinguishable design. The restless man, born out of God's – but we can very well read nature's – indifference, becomes his own creator, he authors his own suspenseful narrative. Svevo's man evolved out of modernity, as it is epitomized in Jean-Paul Marat's plea: 'In the vast indifference I invent a meaning, I don't watch unmoved I intervene and I say that this and this are wrong, and I work to alter them and improve them. The important thing is to pull yourself up by your own hair, *to turn yourself inside out* and see the whole world with fresh eyes ' (Weiss 1984: 26–7; emphasis mine).

It is the restless man's resistance to the indifference of nature that creates humanity – no longer seen as a 'healthy' humanity, amazing mirror of a higher perfection, but rather a 'diseased,' unfinished humanity restlessly searching for its own idea of perfection. While telling this tale Svevo comes to expose Darwin's own denied anthropomorphism, as it can be detected in the unfolding of natural selection through a dialectic of weakness and strength and particularly in the use of a social concept of the struggle for existence to explain the activity of natural organisms.[5]

In the rhetorical organization of *The Origin of Species*, the struggle for existence provides the overall structuring metaphor and the prime mover of the history of the species.[6] 'I use the term Struggle for Existence in a large and metaphorical sense, including dependence of one being on another' (1985 [1859]: 116), announces Darwin. But, despite its protested inclusiveness, it tends to revert to its common-sensical connotations – competition rather than interdependence, adaptation or cooperation – ('as more individuals are produced than can possibly survive, there must in every case be a struggle for existence'; 1985: 117). After all, metaphors are narrative – they are little fables that tell a story – and their choice is motivated by the desire to tell one story instead of another. The metaphor chosen by Darwin as the theoretical cornerstone of *Origin*, is, as we know, the naturalization of an idea borrowed from the realm of political economy: 'A struggle for existence inevitably follows from the high rate at which all organic beings tend to increase' (Darwin 1985: 116). In *Twilight of the Idols*, Nietzsche warns us, in a section titled 'Anti-Darwin,' that 'one should not mistake Malthus for nature' and that 'wealth, luxury, even absurd prodigality' characterize life more than hunger and distress (Nietzsche 1975: 75). But although Nietzsche attacked 'the incomprehensibly one-sided doctrine of the "struggle for existence,"' arguing that 'the struggle for existence is only an *exception*, a temporary restriction of the will to life,' he too extolled the presence of a 'great and small struggle' that 'always revolves around superiority, around growth and expansion, around power.' Nietzsche's affirmative struggle might not 'smell,' as he accuses Darwin's of doing, 'like the distress and overcrowding of small people' (Nietzsche 1974: 292), but it is no less pervasive or necessary to his thought.[7]

Svevo, developing a critical stand towards both Darwin and Nietzsche, assigns to the struggle for existence a limited place and inverts its prime mover status by placing it at the end rather that at the beginning of a cycle of development. As the animals shed their souls, some 'crearono potenti organi d'offesa, zanne, artigli, e corna, altri per assaltare o per difendersi si fecero velocissimi e appresero anche a volare' [created powerful organs of offence, teeth, claws and horns, others to attack and defend themselves became very fast and learned to fly as well (CA, 641)]. With these perfected organs the adapted animals dived into their quotidian struggle.

Far from driving the process of change and adaptation, the struggle for existence becomes the static activity of the already fully adapted and crystallized organisms. On the other hand, what stands at the beginning of time for Svevo, spurring mutability and guaranteeing the possibility of evolving, is the *restlessness* of the soul, the *unhappiness* of all created beings. Rather than being a matter of blind obedience to the law of natural selection, evolution becomes the wilful product of desire, because, as Nietzsche observed: 'Improvements are invented only by *those who can feel* that something is not good' (Nietzsche 1974: 214; emphasis mine), the unhappy and dissatisfied men who maintain the 'intense life that marks time.'

By doing away with the organizing principle of the struggle for existence, the fable brings out in stark relief the opposition between the two existential economies of potentiality and success, an opposition that could be thought of as Darwin's opposition between mutability and adaptation, downplayed and smoothed over in *Origin*. For Svevo adaptation represents the atemporal, the synchronic, the apparently eternal blind present of nature, the loss of the real life, the one marked by time; for Darwin, adaptation is the successful outcome of selection *and* a marginalized stage of cooperation between species, organisms, and environments, an only temporary alternative to the war of all against all in search of survival and dominance. In their own ways both Darwin and Svevo favor mutability over adaptation. In Darwin's system, survival of the species as well as of individuals, and above all primacy, are guaranteed only by maintaining a hold on mutability, prompted by the struggle for life and sanctioned by natural selection. In Svevo's fable, dissatisfaction creates a temporal perspective otherwise unknown to the happy world of successful adaptation where the only movement is the circular and eternal recurrence of the struggle for existence. In the end, both for Svevo and Darwin, adaptation and mutability remain irreconcilable concepts. It is perhaps because of the consciousness of this tension – between being and becoming – that both authors look with a wary eye on the notion of progress: 'that vague but ill-defined *sentiment*,' in Darwin's words (1985: 343); 'un'ansiosa *speranza*,' [anxious hope] in Svevo's (1966: 860). For both, then, a feeling rather than an idea, an anxious hope rather than reason.

If the question of origins stands in the foreground of both Darwin's text and Svevo's fable, the question relative to the future of the species – the question of progress or lack thereof – keeps looming unaddressed on the horizon of both narratives. What, if not progress, will be the outcome of evolution? Who will be the inheritors of the future? In Darwin, as well as in Svevo, the question of the possibility and nature of progress is recurrently tied to a rhetoric opposing weakness and strength. Only by unravelling the relation between these two terms is it possible to understand Svevo's idea of humanity and the momentous implications that it raises for the relation of self and other.

It was only after writing *The Origin of Species* that Darwin fully adopted Herbert Spencer's reductionist ideas of progress, summarized in the expression 'survival of the fittest.' Nevertheless, already in *Origin*, despite some ambivalence – 'Natural selection will not necessarily produce absolute perfection' (Darwin 1985: 233); 'I believe in no law of necessary development' (348) – he chooses to close the book with a statement very near Spencer's position: 'And as natural selection works solely by and for the good of each being, all corporeal and mental endowments will tend to *progress* and *perfection*' (459). Even though the final goal of progress and perfection is here left open and unspecified, he previously linked 'the advancement of all organic beings' to one general law: 'multiply, vary, let the strongest live and weakest die' (263). Thus, to the extent it is possible to speak of progress, this is the prerogative of the strong, successfully adapted beings.

But while for Darwin the future is only a tension in his discourse (a movement unfolding through a remote past), for Svevo the future is the founding question of his restless man, virtuality being the very essence of his striving. It is this interest in the future that reveals the influence exerted by Nietzsche on Svevo's reflections, because it is in Nietzsche that one can find a challenging, though often contradictory and problematic reversal of Darwin's evolutionary argument.[8]

Again in 'Anti-Darwin' Nietzsche polemically critiques the outcome of the struggle for existence in these terms: 'Species do *not* grow more perfect: the weaker dominate the strong again and again – the reason being they are the great majority, and they are also *cleverer*. ... Darwin forgot the mind (– that is English!): *the weak possess more mind*. [...] He who possesses strength divests himself of mind' (1975: 76). Thus, Darwin is doubly wrong; nature does not move towards perfection, because the weak are the ones with the upperhand in the process of natural selection. Without seeing this evolution as degenerative, as Nietzsche seems to suggest, Svevo presents a similar view of the process when he observes that 'success is a great seducer,' and in nature as well as in society only the weakest can 'resist' its blandishments and thus prepare the future. In this sense, his position is much closer to the Nietzsche of *Human, All Too Human*, where, in the section titled 'Refinement through Degeneration,' he recognizes the positive function of weakness: 'Degenerate natures are of the highest significance wherever progress is to ensue. A partial weakening has to precede every large-scale advance. The strongest natures *maintain* the type; the weaker ones help to *develop it further*' (1995: 153–4).

Nevertheless, and despite his nuanced stand towards the theory of evolution, Nietzsche's positions of weak and strong are generally as fixed and recognizable as they were in Darwin. Where Svevo goes beyond both thinkers is in his consistently relativized deployment of the opposition of strength and weakness, because, as with other antinomies in his texts (old/young, healthy/sick), it is 'always relative, never absolute, rather discursive' (Saccone 1995: 83). Svevo perhaps owes more to a remark at the end of the passage entitled 'Benevolence' in *The Gay Science* where Nietzsche warns: 'It should be kept in mind that "strong" and "weak" are relative concepts' (1974: 176). Svevo's restless man is neither strong nor weak, he neither attacks nor defends himself. His imperfection, the inability to adapt, gives expression to a weakness outside any antonymic definition of the term: weakness explicitly is potential strength. In the end strength and weakness have no fixed definition except in relation to time and desire: the strongest, most successful individuals being such because they choose to live and 'dominate' the present; the weakest, unfinished, because of their allegiance to 'an uncertain tomorrow, indefinable but shining with hope.' The weaker do not dominate the strong, but they are, as long as they maintain their weakness, the future.

While Nietzsche's idiosyncratic relativization of weakness and strength would seem a closer point of departure for Svevo, Darwin too questioned this opposition. In the huge accumulation of examples on which the rhetorical organization of *Origin* rests, an analogy emerges that potentially reconfigures the theoretical thrust of his argument and offers the possibility of a very different story. While explaining the workings of natural selection on new species having arrived on an island, Darwin uses the following image: 'As with mariners shipwrecked near a coast, it would have been better for the good swimmers if they had been able to swim still further, whereas it would have been better for the bad swimmers if they had not been able to swim at all and had stuck to the wreck' (Darwin 1985: 177).

Here the terms *strength* and *weakness* are implicitly relativized and superseded by the context. At the same time, the struggle for existence is reconfigured, not as a simple contest but rather as the relative deployment of different strategies, different styles, in a rich and inventive 'arte d'arrangiarsi' (makeshift art). Nature does not favor mediocrity, it supports monsters. Independent of any idea of perfection, health, strength, or 'happiness,' to survive might have meant above all to capitalize on one's difference. Thus the general law that Darwin said dictated the survival of life forms on earth – 'vary, let the strongest live and the weakest die' (1985: 263) – would have to be rewritten: 'vary, and remember, strength and weakness are only reflexive products, the unpredictable outcome of a narrative.'

Svevo's man did not swim or fly or dig holes into the ground; he did not strike out, but stuck to the wreck left by God's disappearance from the world, and thus, diseased and unhappy as he was, became the embodiment of life-giving change. For Svevo it is the difference in man, the lack that marginalizes and threatens the weak individual with disappearance, that becomes his very strength. 'Il presente può avere il futuro in germe non in azione' [The present can have the future as potentiality but not as action (UT, 638)]. Only what resists what is, by remaining in a pure state of potentiality, can speak of and shape the future. The organisms that have successfully, that is *permanently*, adapted – in both Svevo's and Darwin's texts – are the strongest and happiest; but that which is present in any given context as the force and actualization of a form is, in fact, severed from the future. As soon as their strength and 'perfection' are achieved, they are doomed to be superseded by their offspring, the only future a successfully adapted animal can have.

The anthropologist Leroi-Gourhan observes that 'Our significant genetic trait is ... physical (and mental) *non*-adaptation,' (1993: 246) a condition achieved by 'placing outside ourselves what in the rest of the animal world is achieved inside by species adaptation' (235). Here we find the meaning of the act of 'turning himself inside out' praised by Marat and embraced by Svevo's restless man at the end of the fable, as his limbs 'invece che perfezionarsi quali ordigni divennero capaci di maneggiare quelli ch'essa creò' [instead of being perfected as tools, became able to use the ones that he created (CA, 642)], the infinite prosthesis of his body and ever-mutating materialization of his desire.[9] Because of his inability to adapt, man became, through the tool, the ultimate example of constant and uninterrupted adaptation to a changing environment. By divesting his future from his body – nature – on to the tool – technology – he became even more free to move from desire to desire, from tool to tool, from adaptation to adaptation, always changing and always remaining true to his desiring essence. Where will this solipsistic striving take 'l'uomo torvo e malcontento,' the surly, unhappy man? What will be the future of his unhappiness?

The Future of an Origin: The End of the Unfinished Man

[Man] is ... a 'travelling instance' a 'frontier instance.'
Charles Darwin, 'N Notebook'

Nur wer sich ändert ist mir verwandt. [Only he who changes remains akin to me.]
Friedrich Nietzsche, Beyond Good and Evil

E non doveva mai venire per l'uomo l'epoca in cui il tempo si fermi e i suoi ordigni opera della sua anima non piú si sviluppino?
[And won't the epoch ever come for man when time will stop and the devices, creation of his soul, will stop developing?]
Italo Svevo, 'La corruzione dell'anima'

The civilized future of the prehistoric lonely, restless man is another lonely, restless man. In the second section of the essay and allegorical fable 'L'uomo e la teoria darwiniana,' entitled 'Lo Sviluppo,' Svevo continues the reflection started in 'La corruzione dell'anima' and reveals human society to be another kind of natural environment. The majority of thinking animals, similar to those primitive organisms that disappeared in the mud as soon as they were created, develop qualities that, while they assure an immediate superiority in the struggle for life, lead to a premature crystallization (much like Jean-Paul Sartre's 'mineral life forms'). Success is only another way to speak of an arrested evolution.

> Nella maggioranza degli uomini lo sviluppo per loro fortuna e per fortuna dell'ambiente sociale, s'arresta. Lo sviluppo eccessivo di qualità inferiori, tutte quelle che immediatamente servono alla lotta per la vita, non sono altro che un arresto di sviluppo. (UT, 638)

> [In the majority of men, development, for their own fortune and the fortune of the social environment, stops. The excessive development of the inferior qualities, all those qualities that are immediately necessary to the struggle for life, are nothing else than an arresting of development.]

The inevitable crystallization, obsolescence, and decay of the perfect 'organs' – qualities, ideas, techniques – which further the needs and expectations of any given society, see the birth, again conceptualized as *resistance*, of 'the most human man that ever existed,' the ultimate essence of humanity.

> Io credo che l'animale piú capace ad evolversi sia quello in cui *una parte è in continua lotta con l'altra per la supremazia,* e l'animale, che ora o nelle generazioni future, abbia *conservata la possibilità di evolversi* da una parte o dall'altra in conformità a quanto gli sarà domandato dalla società di cui nessuno ora può prevedere i bisogni e le esigenze. (UT, 638; emphasis mine)

> [I believe that the animal most able to evolve is the one in which *a part is in continuous struggle with the other for supremacy,* and the one now or in future generations, which will *maintain the possibility of evolving* in one way or another in conformity to what a future society – whose needs and demands nobody can foresee – will require of him.]

The only true evolution, Svevo suggests here – thus setting his new man aside from the primitive technological man who externalized his evolution – is the one that takes place *inside* the human being, though not in the physiological body as with all the other animals, but rather in the mental space where ideas and desires compete with each other. Thus, in the context of a restless species, Svevo grants primacy to the human animal who has internalized the struggle for life and therefore has succeeded in maintaining 'the seed of the future,' an availability to the society to come, something that the other men lost – as the animals did before them – in the process of adaptation.

But who might this new animal be, this Nietzschean 'child of the future'? The narrating voice suddenly announces in a prophetic tone the birth of this new man, the first exemplar of a new species, transforming the text into a futuristic manifesto of a new humanity.

> Nella mia mancanza assoluta di uno sviluppo marcato in qualsivoglia senso *io sono quell'uomo.* Lo sento tanto bene che nella mia *solitudine* me ne glorio altamente e *sto aspettando* sapendo di non essere altro che un *abbozzo.* (UT, 638; emphasis mine)

> [Given my absolute lack of a definite development in whichever direction, *I am that man.* I feel it so clearly that in my *solitude* I take a great pride in it and *I am waiting* knowing that I am nothing else but an *unfinished man.*]

The weak man, who scientific theory left exposed on Mount Citherion, becomes the heir of the world. The voice saying 'I,' the narrator/writer, is this new man, 'l'uomo in abbozzo,' the unfinished man, the only one to fully embody the principle of mutability theorized by Darwin. The deviation from the law of natural selection coincides in the end with the writing subject; his potential actualization in a society yet to come finds its full expression in the eternally suspended present of language. In this willing suspension, the writer survives and lays his strong claim to the future.

If the primitive man distinguished himself from the rest of the animal kingdom by maintaining the soul, 'the intense life that marks time,' the 'uomo in abbozzo' sets himself apart by going one step further to intensify his life and put an even higher stake on the future: he suspends time. He does not just *resist* successful adaptation, he puts a brake on evolution by *waiting* in the belief that the deferred life is a more intense life, that delayed time is a richer time. All the odd idiosyncrasies of the Svevian character – the dreams, the intermittencies of consciousness, 'the last cigarette' – are everyday translations of this need for a rupture that signals the possibility of a more meaningful existence.

As many critics have pointed out, the 'uomo in abbozzo' is a direct descendant of Nietzsche's 'preparatory human beings' (Nietzsche 1974: 228). His homelessness, solitude, readiness for a still invisible future recall the silent and resolute 'children of the future' who cannot be at home in the present and 'far prefer to live on mountains, apart, untimely, in past or future centuries' (338–9). But, at the same time, the participation of the 'uomo in abbozzo' in the future does not express itself as a desire for action, a desire to overcome, but rather as an ironic desire to be still and remain unfinished, a mere *potentiality*. Thus, even if the internalization of the struggle for existence as restlessness seems to suggest a tension, a storing of energy that resembles Nietzsche's will to power, the 'uomo in abbozzo' does not plan a Dionysian squandering of energy but seeks the conservation of force as an end in itself: an unlimited life of latency substitutes for any foreseen performance of the will. If neither now nor then ... then when? Is this 'uomo in abbozzo' a superfluous man or will he eventually emerge from the wilderness and jump on the back of time? (228).

Another genealogy of Svevo's 'uomo in abbozzo' has been traced back through his early novelistic embodiment in *Una vita* as the 'inetto' – the misfit – to the figure of the Schopenhauerian contemplator, the individual that resists, by negating his desire and foregoing any fulfilment, the invisible will behind the world of phenomena. But the availability to the future of the 'uomo in abbozzo' shares nothing with the sterile and self-destructive defensiveness of a threatened subjectivity like that of Alfonso, the protagonist of *Una vita*. Rather, his resistance to the present and the actualization of desire is not a negation of desire but only a fuller commitment to its future. With the 'uomo in abbozzo,' Svevo chooses to ignore the overarching metaphysical forces of both Schopenhauer's all-encompassing will and Darwin's law of natural selection by reserving for himself the possibility of creating endless fictions of desire and delayed fulfilment.

In this way he sidesteps as well the Schopenhauerian critique of human desires that, as Clement Rosset observed in his study on the philosopher, are 'not only unsatisfiable, they are above all false in their very nature. For false I intend fictitious and unreal ... they are only figures.'[10] Svevo explicitly recognizes the fictional and constructed character of desire, and he accepts the constant displacement that it enacts as an unavoidable condition, but this does not make his fictions less real or necessary. The resistance to seeking fulfilment expressed by the constitutive act of waiting, the praise of potentiality and delay, is an attempt to step out of the endless chain of desire's strivings and illusions while simultaneously embracing the figures of desire. This willing suspension is the very essence of the desiring act rendered independent from any possible unfolding.[11] The representation of origin pursued in both fables is nothing other than the representation of the birth and survival of desire as the desire to desire, no longer an illusion, as Schopenhauer theorized, but an even more certain promise of fulfilment.

But again, at this point, a question becomes pressing: what is the future of this endlessly delayed desire? And, furthermore, how can such a suspension be ontologically and existentially sustainable? The 'uomo in abbozzo' seems to have forgotten, in his optimistic secular eschatology, that time is doomed to repeat itself and that the infinite possibilities projected, and we could say kept at a safe distance, in the future do uncannily resemble those of the past.

Already the two fables close with a pessimistic glimpse of unlimited development as the restless primitive man becomes a man, tired and bored, who 'spezza, uccide, tradisce' [breaks, kills, betrays (UT, 640)], blindly pushing forward in an insatiable yearning for progress. The Svevian epigraph to this section, taken from the end of 'La corruzione dell'anima,' suggests a critique of the achievements of man, who remains throughout his evolution and to the end of time 'il triste e malvagio animale guerresco' [the sad and wicked bellicose animal]. While the 'uomo in abbozzo,' by stepping out of temporality, seems to sidestep the predicament of the 'technological' man, he might simply be, as we will see, his most refined embodiment. In the very last pages of *La coscienza di Zeno* we find Svevo's final rewriting of the theory of evolution, used now to hypothesize not an origin but the reasons for an end.

In Zeno's closing reflection, we are introduced to the last descendant of the man who had projected evolution outside his body, the 'spectacled man,' a man who has become utterly cunning and weak. His ability to adapt to all changes and to be ready for anything to come, what first seemed to be the restless man's strength, is now recognized by Zeno as an original fault: human restlessness *is a sickness*, one that has 'polluted life to its roots.' The tool, the very emblem of human desire, becomes the embodiment of such a sickness – an ambivalence contained in the Italian word *ordigno*, which signifies a complex mechanism, simultaneously an innocent tool, and, more ominously, a bomb.

> Ed è l'ordigno che crea la malattia con l'abbandono della legge che fu su tutta la terra creatrice. La legge del piú forte sparí e perdemmo la selezione salutare. (CdZ, 895)

> [The tool creates disease because it denies what has been the law of creation throughout the ages. The law of the strongest disappeared, and we abandoned a healthy natural selection.]

At the end of *La coscienza di Zeno* Darwin's evolution loops back full circle. Against the horizon of the world's destruction by a final powerful 'ordigno' – the ultimate materialization of the desire for progress and the progress of desire – Zeno decides with an ironic reversal to embrace neo-Darwinian positions and chooses to be 'healthy' like the animal 'che conosce un solo progresso, quello del proprio organismo' [whose sole idea of progress lies in its own body (CdZ, 894)].

With this gesture the utopia of the 'uomo in abbozzo' runs up against the limits inscribed in its very conception. Restlessness and virtuality consume the future as much as they create it. Despite the unfinished man's efforts to put a brake on time, the world simply will not wait for his time to come, and if and when it will, his much cherished difference – virtuality, mutability, openness to the future – will turn out to be the constitutive sickness of the world as he discovers himself to be '[un] uomo fatto [...] come tutti gli altri, ma degli altri un po' piú ammalato' [a man made as all the others, only a little more sick than them (CdZ, 895)].

The history of modernity has been equated by many theorists to a history of increasing change and mutability. 'Come la modernità, l'uomo in abbozzo trae la sua forza dalla capacità di esistere per il futuro' [Similarly to modernity the 'uomo in abbozzo' finds its strength in the ability to exist for the future (Savelli 1998: 133)] concludes one recent study of Svevo, thus reinforcing an established view in Svevo's studies of the 'uomo in abbozzo' as the personification of modernity's project. But, while moving within this project, *Svevo's* 'modernism' articulates a critique of the broader tendency of modernity. In fact, while it upholds change and virtuality, it unfolds as an attempt to interrupt time: that is, it should not be forgotten that the 'man adapted to the future' is generated and sustained by a suspended present. It is into this present that Zeno, the last embodiment of the unfinished man, dives in a final attempt to escape the snares of a misconceived modernity. Like the Nietzsche of the *Genealogy of Morals*, Zeno articulates an ironic critique and subversion of the religion of the future as he rereads the history of modernity as a history of 'poisoning': 'La vita attuale è inquinata alle radici' [Our present life is poisoned to the root (CdZ, 894)].[12] Confronted with a personal and historical crisis, Zeno chooses to be finished, or 'healthy' – though healthy because he is now totally adapted to the 'poison.' From man of the future Zeno becomes the man of a 'poisoned' present, an affirmative strong animal crystallized in one single-minded pursuit – 'Come tutte le persone forti, io ebbi nella mia testa una sola idea e di quella vissi e fu la mia fortuna' [Like all strong individuals, I held in my head only one idea and for that I lived and made my fortune (CdZ, 893)], – the struggle to succeed in the world of business investment and wartime speculation. With Zeno as a ruthless speculator, adaptation becomes synonymous with parasitism. This act of adaptation, far from being simple conformism, is a final defiance, not only of Dr S. and his attempts at a 'cure' (the imposition of a conformist 'adaptation'), but of nature and society as well, in a last effort to transcend them. Zeno thus affirms once again his difference, his departure from the tensions and ambiguity of modernity's 'sickness' towards what we might see as the affirmative health of a postmodernity that 'loves its poison.'[13]

As the title of the first fable already suggested, the soul that brought forth change and a boundless yearning for the future carried within itself, like a dormant virus, the very limit of its own striving. At the end of *La coscienza di Zeno*, mutability turns out to be, by an ironic reversal, man's deadly adaptation, the principle of his own obsolescence. From this perspective even Zeno's last-ditch attempt at a fictional health is dismissed in his final musings, where only the disappearance of man and all his possible fictions will bring about 'true' health:

> Forse traverso una catastrofe inaudita prodotta dagli ordigni ritorneremo alla salute. [...] un uomo fatto come tutti gli altri, nel segreto di una stanza di questo mondo, inventerà un esplosivo incomparabile [...]. Ed un altro uomo fatto anche lui come tutti gli altri, ma degli altri un po' piú ammalato, ruberà tale esplosivo e s'arrampicherà al centro della terra per porlo nel punto ove il suo effetto potrà essere il massimo. Ci sarà un'esplosione enorme che nessuno udrà e la terra ritornata alla forma di nebulosa errerà nei cieli priva di parassiti e di malattie. (CdZ, 895)

> [Perhaps some incredible disaster produced by machines will lead us back to health. ... a man, made like all other men, will in the quiet of his room invent a dreadful explosive ... And another man, made as well like all other men, but a little sicker than them, will steal that explosive and crawl to the centre of the earth with it, and place it just where it would have the maximum effect. There will be a tremendous explosion, but no one will hear it and the earth will return to its nebulous state and go wandering through the sky, free at last from parasites and disease.]

As an explosion seals man's unfinished narrative, it becomes clear how the tools, the restless man's proud progeny, the ticking bombs that could put a stop to man's time, are in fact the true inheritors of the future.

If Svevo's insight has become commonplace in our cybernetic fin de siècle, drowned as it is in both lamentations about the marginalization of the human by technology and complementary celebrations of the outstripping of materiality through technological advancement, what has not lost urgency is his call to invent and reinvent the meaning and value of what is human, the need for an ongoing search for creative narratives of the human animal.

One such narrative lies back at the origin of the 'unfinished man.' In 'La corruzione dell'anima' Svevo left open and unexplained the mechanics of the restless man's evolution:

> E progredì *per un caso*, un caso che sarebbe inesplicabile se non si dovesse pensare che sia stato tentato piú volte. (CA, 642; emphasis mine)

> [And he evolved because of a *chance occurrence*, an occurrence that would be inexplicable unless we thought it had been attempted many times.]

What was this chance event that granted man's survival and evolution? How could the primitive man resist the immediacy of adaptation? This originary resistance survives unexplained, even after Zeno's ironic rapprochement with Darwinism at the conclusion of *La coscienza di Zeno*. If the future is nowhere to be found in the present, it might very well be forgotten in the past, *perhaps in somebody else's past*. To return to that chance occurrence – less an action than a *pause* – means to look through the incessant flow of becoming and disappearing to find something that has been left behind: the articulation of a different origin, an *other's* origin to the human story.

In the Shadow of the Mammoth: Symbiosis and the Birth of Subjectivity

Animals as critics. – *I fear that the animals consider man as a being like themselves that has lost in a most dangerous way its sound animal common sense; they consider him the insane animal, the laughing animal, the weeping animal, the miserable animal.*

Friedrich Nietzsche, *The Gay Science*

The curse of battle and toil leads back to the boar ... Old books are wrong. The world was made on a Sunday.

Vladimir Nabokov, *Speak Memory*

Can new origins be created for humans, other than those which are canonically handed down to those children of the future who patiently seafare their way to a land that is far away from fatherlands and Oedipal Complexes?

Keith Ansell Pearson, *Viroid Life*

'L'uomo e la teoria darwiniana' opens with the conference held by the famous entomologist Erich Wasmann in 1907 in Berlin on the symbiotic behaviour of parasites and hosts in different ant families.[14] On this occasion, the Jesuit scientist stressed the importance of cooperation, or 'amicable selection,' while downplaying the role of natural selection in the evolution of the species. This controversial contribution to the Darwinian debate sparks in the mind of the narrator the sense of a discovery and thus prompts the writing of the fable. But to the reader's surprise, the section to follow, the manifesto of the solipsistic, post-Darwinian man, 'l'uomo in abbozzo,' has very little to do with symbiosis. It is only in the last section, 'L'evoluzione,' that Wasmann's semi-

Between Darwinian Origins and Modernist Ends 35

nal insight is addressed allegorically with the fable of the man and the Mammoth. Because of this unevenness in tone and intent, Svevian criticism has approached this text in an overly partial way, widely quoting the theoretical formulation of the unfinished man, which so clearly sheds light on the nature of Svevo's male protagonists, while leaving in obscurity the final fable. But it is the fable that both gives unity and an underlying rationale to the piece by staging the encounter of man with his other. The choice of narrative one exhumes from a reading of the 'essay' is fraught with consequences for the overall interpretation of Svevo's work: Is it the story, by now canonical, of the solipsistic and ironic hero of modernism?[15] or is it rather the story of the emergence of modernism and its 'hero' through the association with the other?

The question of how the weakest of all animals could have survived and evolved – the question that in 'La corruzione dell'anima' was answered with a paradoxical reversal: How could the world have evolved at all without the weak man? – affords once again the point of departure for the last section, 'L'evoluzione':

> Una superbia inspiegabile in un animale fatto tanto male lo teneva eretto e visibile. I quadrupedi lo raggiungevano facilmente e lo azzannavano e i quadrumani lo coglievano in ogni rifugio. Perciò invano l'uomo moderno investiga le zolle per trovare le orme dei suoi immediati predecessori. Non furono molti e devono essere stati riprodotti piú volte perché come apparivano venivano distrutti. (UT, 638)

> [An unexplainable haughtiness in an animal made so badly kept him erect and visible. The quadrupeds could easily reach him and eat him, the quadrumanes could catch him in any refuge. In vain modern man investigates the earth to find the steps of his immediate predecessors. They were few and they must have reproduced very often because as soon as they appeared they were destroyed.]

This ridiculously erect animal who refused to adapt to one environment or climate, who did not want to sacrifice any part of life by migrating, hiding, or limiting in any way his freedom of movement, eventually, 'deve essersi conquistato *l'intervallo di pace* di cui abbisognava per poter prepararsi a vivere nella rude natura' [must have conquered the *interval of peace* that he needed to prepare himself to live in raw nature (UT, 639; emphasis mine)] in order to survive.

The encounter with another animal provided such a moment of

reprieve. The passage from the solipsistic world of restless striving to the society with an 'other' is the chance event that puts the human clock in motion by momentarily stopping it. The pause is at the same time the condition for a leap forward in evolution,[16] and a move towards adaptation, the other being the only 'environment' to which man finally adapted.

> L'uomo fatto cosí non poté salvarsi che quando visse all'ombra di un animale piú forte di lui. [...] Fu allora che avvenne la società piú strana che fosse rischiarata dal sole. Il piccolo uomo si mise al servizio dell'animale piú grande il Mammut la cui grossa pancia gli faceva da scudo. (UT, 639)

> [A man made in this way could save himself only when he lived in the shadow of a stronger animal. ... Then arose the strangest society that ever appeared under the sun. The small man put himself in the service of the bigger animal, the Mammoth, whose great belly became his shield.]

Man made himself useful to the Mammoth by scratching his back with his supple hands and freeing him of insects. The good-natured Mammoth, on its part, willingly accepted the services offered by the improvised servant and in exchange protected him from surrounding nature. The Mammoth, 'finished' in his body and soul, adapted to man as to a new environment:

> Dal Mammut il servizio del piccolo uomo divenne tanto importante ch'egli sentiva il bisogno della sua presenza come degli alberi di cui viveva, dei prati su cui si moveva, persino dell'aria che respirava. Cosí è fatto l'animale privo d'anima. Non è lui che si evolve perché già perfetto rinunziò alla vera vita. (UT, 640)

> [For the Mammoth the service of the small man became so important that he felt the need of his presence as much as the trees on which he lived, the fields on which he moved, even the air that he breathed. So it is made, the animal without a soul. It is not the one to evolve because, already 'finished,' it has renounced the true life.]

For his part, the small cunning animal with a restless soul soon took for granted the presence of the big Mammoth as he thrived in the safe space of its shadow: 'A quell'ombra egli si mise a costruire i suoi ordigni [...] inventò una nuova evoluzione fuori del proprio organismo' [In that shadow he started to build his tools ... and invented a new evolution outside his organism (UT, 639)]. And so man and Mammoth lived, or better, could have lived happily thereafter, joined in a perfect association.

'Ma l'uomo avendo l'anima non s'accontentava di nessuna sicurezza' [But man, having the soul, was not satisfied with any certainty (UT, 639 (UT, 640)] and as soon as he developed tools that could replace the Mammoth, he promptly moved on.

> Se l'uomo non avesse avuto l'anima inquieta egli sarebbe ancora il pacifico servo del Mammut e molti malanni sarebbero risparmiati alla nostra terra, i magnifici boschi vergini sarebbero tuttavia intatti, ricetto di animali forti, sani e bizzarri. Ma l'uomo fece la sua prima rivoluzione senz'affatto vedere le orrende conseguenze del suo agire. Cosí procedette anche in seguito. Quand'è stanco o seccato, la sua anima lo trascina a spezzare i contratti, a dimenticare i benefici, a odiare quello che ieri amò. (UT, 640)

[If man did not have a restless soul he would still be the servant of the peaceful Mammoth and many calamities would have been spared to our earth; the magnificent virgin woods would be still intact, home of strong, healthy, and bizarre animals. But man made his first revolution without seeing the horrible consequences of his actions. In this way he proceeded even later. When he is tired and bored, his soul pushes him to break contracts, to forget benefits, and to hate those who just yesterday he loved.]

Thus, self-interest, disloyalty, and indifference to the other, first experienced in this primal scene of man breaking his association with the Mammoth, became the rule of all human progress to follow. The fable ends with the image of the Mammoth's final obsolescence as man invented dwellings on water in which to live safely. But just before this abrupt ending, the narrator adds a few words that force the reader to go back to the association and to reflect on its meaning:

> Questa prima rivoluzione fu d'importanza enorme per l'uomo e per il Mammut. Nessun'altra l'eguaglia. (UT, 640)

[This first revolution was of momentous importance for the man and the Mammoth. No other equals it.]

In what does its momentous importance lie? The narrator has already stressed how man's obvious gain, a mastery of the future freed from the burdensome other, is an ambiguous one, as it brings misfortune on the rest of the planet. Now, by saying that the revolution was so momentous for *both* actors, he openly admits the perspective of the animal participant, the other left behind. From this point of view, man's revolution becomes momentous not because of what was gained but rather because of what was unconsciously lost. In the end, the reader is left with the suspicion that through his 'revolutionary' gesture man might have left his future behind.[17]

The question raised in the previous sections of whether becoming and development truly has, as Darwin, Nietzsche, and apparently, Svevo, seem to believe, a deeper meaning and a greater value than *what is* constitutes the dramatic core of the fable. On the one hand, there is the Mammoth who lives in a boundless present, mindless of the effect that the environment has on his life – 'Intorno a lui la natura si modifica ed egli non se ne accorge neppure se tali mutamenti implicano per lui la morte' [Around him nature changes and he does not even realize if such changes bring forth his own death (UT, 640)] – and on the other, the man who forges 'consciously' the course of his future, a boundless future of both achievement and destruction. Despite the radical difference in the experience of time and thus in consciousness, the stories of these two actors have overlapping endings. In fact, if the Mammoth cannot foresee the environment bringing forth his own death, man moves forward 'without seeing the tremendous consequences of his actions,' the destruction he brings upon the environment and eventually on himself. Both bodily adaptation *and* mental evolution unfold in blindness, both meet the same deadly outcome. It becomes rather arduous at this point to see how the push towards change – movement and restlessness – is more life-giving than that towards adaptation and fixity. As the opposition between being and becoming and its implied hierarchy of value is put into question, the narrator redirects the reader's attention to an in-between space, what could be defined, oxymoronically, as a dynamic space of being. The space of the association, which was glossed over in the telling of the fable by man's overarching teleology, is ambiguously recuperated at its end as an unexplored utopian moment that outstrips man's understanding, a moment charged with as yet unrecognized and unfulfilled promise.

The recognition of man's blindness and the sense of loss that pervades the end of the essay introduce a suspension in the narrative of man's futurity, thus forcing the reader to turn critically upon a cherished myth of emancipation. Similarly, the abrupt ending of the fable, by denying the reader a sense of closure, sends him back to the mysterious opening lines of the piece to look for a thread he might have lost in the process of reading.

> Ora io ho il senso di avere scoperto qualche cosa, ma non ne sono sicuro e per assicurarmene feci questo monologo ... (UT, 637)

> [Now I have the sense of having discovered something, but I am not quite certain of it, and to find assurance I wrote this monologue ...]

The fable is the way to ascertain a discovery, the narrative experiment to test a hypothesis. This discovery, announced in the first paragraph and never mentioned again, is the one inspired by Erich Wasmann's reflections on parasites and hosts in different species of ants:

> A me almeno che non sono della materia parve una scoperta l'evoluzione constatata nell'ospite a seconda della grandezza e natura del padrone di casa ... (UT, 637)

> [To me, a neophyte in the field, the evolution observed in the guest according to the dimensions and nature of the host or home-owner seemed a discovery ...]

In light of this discovery, man's evolution is not only made possible, but is mysteriously molded, by the Mammoth's 'dimensions and nature.' Man's blindness coincides with the failure to recognize this debt, a misrecognition that becomes a loss. By betraying the Mammoth, man betrays a part of himself. From this perspective, the fable of the man and the Mammoth, far from being the tale of the 'unfinished' man who 'turns himself inside out' to embrace the promise of mastery – a tale of evolution as externalization – becomes an allegory of symbiosis, that is, of interdependency, and, most importantly, *internalization of the other*.[18]

Donna Haraway points out the following stage directions implicit in the construction of traditional fictions of origins: 'In the major Western narrative for generating self and other, one is always too few and two are always too many. In that dialectic lies the fiction made into reality of the escalation and repressive sublimation of combat as the motor of the personal and collective history' (Haraway 1990: 143). By featuring, so to speak, one and one-half characters – the weak animal whose soul enjoys an unbounded evolution beyond his bodily limitation, and a strong animal whose soul is buried in a crystallized body – Svevo's fable of origin subverts through parody the structure underlying major myths of origin, namely the enlightment myths of subjectivity and society exemplified in the writings of Rousseau and Hegel, and in so doing suggests an alternative narrative for the human story. As Haraway's statement suggests, the staging, present in both Rousseau and Hegel, of the encounter of two equals at the origin of society leads inevitably to a narrative of combat: the struggle of life and death, and the enslavement of one to the other. In Svevo, on the other hand, difference – a qualitative difference – between the two actors *precedes* struggle and slavery with unexpected consequences for the ensuing narrative of personal and societal origins.

By staging the encounter of the man with the giant yet benevolent Mammoth, Svevo reverses Rousseau's myth, presented in the 'Discours,' of the primitive man's encounter with his fellow man: first defined as a 'giant' and only in a second moment as a 'man.' Paul de Man's reading of the myth stresses how this change of designation is a conscious operation meant to disguise the original fear of the other, to disguise 'the ontic difference under an illusion of identity.'[19] By mixing man and animals in his fable, Svevo explicitly makes difference the founding element of the encounter: humanity emerges from the confrontation with an incommensurable rather than an identical other. Thus, Svevo's fiction of origin is from the start an allegory of the fundamental inequality and incommensurability inscribed in human relations. Rather than condemning, as Rousseau does, this originary pact based on slavery as one that must be overthrown and superceded by a social contract based *on equality,* Svevo's – *because it is based on the recognition of difference* – is the inauguration of the only social contract we can ever know, one that is a forever developing experiment in association and community. It is precisely Svevo's skepticism about original freedom and equality that makes his fable an alternative, and potentially more emancipatory, path to the future: Whatever the risk of living together, one cannot forget that living alone amounts to extinction.

It could be argued at this point that the association between the man and the Mammoth – a superior and an inferior species – is a simple matter of 'manipulation.' Svevo's cunning man single-handedly creates the conditions of his own evolution through a 'trick of unlikely success': the institution of slavery by the slave himself in order to gain his freedom.

> Egli deve essersi conquistato l'*intervallo di pace* di cui abbisognava per poter prepararsi a vivere nella rude natura e non era possibile per lui che un solo mezzo: *La schiavitù.* (UT, 639; emphasis mine)

[(Man) must have won the *interval of peace* he needed to be able to prepare himself to live in raw nature, and he had only one means available to do so: *slavery*.]

This Machiavellian move on the part of the weak man bypasses first the moment of combat (slavery is in fact a way to escape a struggle he could not possibly win) and then that of reciprocal recognition, as man uses the strong animal as a shield and then simply moves onward, while the Mammoth lags behind, like an obsolete, discarded tool. The first tool to be invented is an idea of the other as a prosthetic device that leads to all the other infinite prostheses man creates for his 'unfinished' body. Nevertheless, despite the declared instrumentality this imprints on the association, the Mammoth is not – as the calculating man would like it to be – a mere step in his ascent (or descent). The openness to the future of the unfinished man is predicated on the 'finished' other, thus it is relational rather than self-willed and autonomous. Even if in the fable man seems to 'emerge' from nature as a self-contained, self-conscious individual – 'un uomo dall'anima completa, malcontenta, torva, traditrice e furbesca' [a man with a soul that was complete, unhappy, grim, treacherous and cunning (UT, 638)] – he is nonetheless *lacking*: he cannot be without the other. Furthermore, and contrary to all appearances and to his own belief, he might himself be nothing else than an impression left by the other, as the structure underlying the symbiotic relation comes to suggest.

Symbiosis, from the Greek 'cohabitation,' implies a long-lasting relationship with reciprocal advantage between quite distant species. As Darwin first observed, a symbiotic relation presupposes a radical difference: 'The dependency of one organic being on another, as of a parasite on his host, lies generally between beings remote in the scale of nature' (1985: 126). But besides this difference, and perhaps because of it, there is a close interconnectedness between the two actors of the cohabitation, as Darwin again stresses: 'The structure of every organic being is related, in the most essential yet often hidden manner, to that of all other organic beings with which it comes into competition for food or residence, or from which it has to escape, or on which it preys. This is obvious in the structure of the teeth and talons of the tiger; and in that of the legs and claws of the parasite which clings to the hair on the tiger's body' (127). By living together, working for each other, man and Mammoth, the two unlikely, incommensurable actors, end up being 'related in a most essential yet hidden manner.' Notwithstanding his indifference and desire to control and manipulate the other, man, the 'guest,' owes his particular structure to the nature of the Mammoth. Although the fable does not represent this moment, the implication is that man was changed by the Mammoth and in turn, we have to assume, the Mammoth by man: the relation with the stronger animal should be recognized as an *internal* one, constitutive of the subject's self and of intersubjectivity.

It is striking how this moment, even though enacted at the 'lower' level of the body, is comparable to the Hegelian act of reflection and recognition involved in the apprehension of the world and the other. Judith Butler's reading of Hegel's *Phenomenology* helps pinpoint the similar implications linking the act of reflection with the physical symbiotic connection: 'reflection always presupposes ontological relatedness. In being reflected in and by that piece of world, the subject learns that *it shares a common structure with that piece of world*, that a prior and constituting relation conditions the possibility of reflection, and that the object of reflection is nothing other than that relation itself' (Butler 1987: 8). What is noteworthy in this context is the retracing of 'ontological relatedness,' not to a common essentialized identity but rather to the 'sharing of a common structure.' The symbiotic relationship suggests that in spite of the radical difference between the actors there can be reflection and recognition, and, differently than in Hegel, that this recognition is achieved not through a struggle for self-affirmation but through proximity, collaboration, and reciprocal altruism.

Thus the relationship between man and Mammoth, which the author defined as slavery, presents, under closer examination, an extremely complicated instance in which no clear hierarchy is defined. As in Hegel's encounter of like-minded (and shaped) selves, categories such as self and other, guest and host, might end up intermixed to the point of dissolution. Keith Ansell Pearson has stressed how symbiosis is characterized by 'the impossibility to declare with any ontological certainty who is the host and who is the parasite' (139). But not only: current biological theories define symbiosis as 'a challenge to the boundaries of the organism' (Pearson 1997: 132).[20] Roles are not just reversed; through the relationship both actors are permanently changed. The symbiotic relation is an intersubjective space for the invention of self and other, for reciprocal contamination and penetration, recalling Deleuze's image of the wasp and the orchid.

Man's trick of making himself a slave of the other disguises the nature of his dependency by overstating it. In this economy of forces, otherness, far from being expendable or only a necessary surplus for the actualization of the subject's desire, sets the very condition of his self-reproduction. Thus, in the very moment the desire of the unfinished man to go beyond himself is represented it meets a radical critique, so that to go 'beyond himself' would mean partaking of the Mammoth's destiny, of its world of adaptation, of its bodily limitation, of its 'perfected' finitude, of its acknowledged desire and need for the other. As a critique of the temporality of Darwinian evolutionism – and of the Hegelian dialectic – Deleuze and Guattari have defined this instance of change through symbiosis as '*creative involution*,' understood, as Pearson has noted, not in the sense of a Freudian regression but rather as a 'block of becoming that represents the "transversal communication" between heterogeneous populations' (Pearson 1997: 130). In this view, temporal becoming and the individual are fused into a 'rhizome,' namely an outspreading of possibilities, exchanges, connections, and contaminations that, to use Deleuze's vocabulary again, 'deterritorialize' the sovereignty of the self as it reflects, becomes, mingles with, and takes the place of the other (Deleuze and Guattari 1987: 238–9).

Vladimir Nabokov claimed that *Homo poeticus* – born in 'a voluptuous pause in the growth of the rest of nature' – was the necessary precondition for the evolution of *Homo sapiens*. He thus stressed how man, before engaging in the world of 'techné,' had to experience 'poiesis,' the act of self-invention through a narrative. In Svevo's fables of the primitive man the act of self-invention through technology puts an end to and supersedes the narrative act. Thus, the human animal escapes a natural world that knows one possible plot of struggle, evolution, and adaptation only to create an equally compulsive narrative that, by imposing its own inevitable logic, excludes the unfolding of any other story in favor of a teleology of progress, technological advancement, and, finally, – as represented in the 'last' man, Zeno the speculator – capitalist accumulation. In neither the natural nor the technological environment is there any apparent place for *poiesis*. As Svevo/Schmitz – the writer who put poetry aside to enter the world of commerce – once observed: 'La storia termina quando si fa ciò che si deve senz'esitazioni e proteste' [The story ends when one does what one must without hesitations and protests (Pds, 845)]. This observation suggests how the 'human' story is neither a story of origins, progress, or ends, but rather always and only a story of hesitations and protests, delays, detours, or, otherwise said, of contaminations.[21] The 'interval of peace,' equated in the opening lines with 'the shadow of another,' sets the stage for the first act of *poiesis*, an unfulfilled act of promise and potentiality. Outside the association neither the man nor the Mammoth have a story, only a common destiny of blindness and death; it is only within their odd society, in the shadow it creates, that a story can unfold. But, what *is* the story of the man and the Mammoth? It is the fictional staging of the birth of subjectivity *as* a shadow across history, the 'altruistic' interconnection with the other.

In this allegory of origin the status of the other, and therefore of woman, in Svevo's narrative is already implicitly inscribed though mysteriously unfulfilled. How do man and Mammoth 'share a common structure'? What is the extent of their reciprocal contamination? How do they play out their symbiont nature? These questions, only hypothetical in the context of the fable, find a textual answer once this allegory is transposed to the stories narrating the association of men and women in Svevo's work. The symbiotic nature of the association, by enacting an inevitable contamination between self and other, the guest and the host, opens unexpected horizons for Svevian man where worn-out concepts of progress, future, individuality, and male and female can be reinvented. It is in these unresolved tensions, within an ambiguous space that is not appropriated, but rather appropriates the possibility of a redefinition of subjectivity, that the figure of the woman has to be read in her relation to male subjectivity.

Thus this reading of the Svevian 'Urszene' between man and a Mammoth 'buried' in its body suggests the concealed ontologization of woman taking place, although in different forms, throughout Svevo's narrative. The Mammoth, as the woman, is the naturalized other who openly plays a double function: on the one hand, it constitutes a surplus, playing a complementary role for the weak but cunning slave; on the other hand, as the very instance that allows desire to unfold, it suggests a critique of the boundlessness of the unfinished man. The woman, like the Mammoth, is limited within herself; 'with a body that betrays [her] individuality,' she constitutes the basis of 'man's fantastic self-reproductive projects' (Haraway 1990: 143). Yet this 'woman as lack' really covers up a lack in man whose nature has still to be assessed, a lack that, for the moment, could be jokingly described as a sort of 'womb-envy,'[22] what Derrida defines as 'the anterior default of a presence,'[23] a lack that allows man to glimpse another, enviable economy of forces. The relation between man and woman as subject and object of desire, the artist and his muse, the pedagogue and the pupil, constitute various materializations of the first pact struck between the man and the Mammoth. But as we now know, the symbiotic association unfolds in ways that have far-reaching consequences: namely the reversibility of roles, and, more profoundly, the inevitable contamination of both actors. If the allegory of origin openly stages an appropriation, it does not take into account the fact that the unfinished man might become the one appropriated, might become a Mammoth for the other. Svevo's allegory of symbiosis inaugurates a redefinition of subjectivity in terms of a 'problematic investment in non-self.'[24] What started as the story of the boundless self-reproductive dream of the primitive man – a Nietzschean reflection on the transhuman condition – has become the story of dependency and contamination – the creation of an intersubjective space that potentially can stage a move across gender boundaries.

In his lack of a critical vocabulary, Svevo will write of this condition 'come la fine del secolo [glie]lo permetterà e non altrimenti' [as the end of the century will allow [him] and not otherwise ('Diario per la fidanzata,' 1968: 784)], that is, in the only way poets write about the unknown and the untold, by telling stories about this passage, this unexpected contamination, the disguised love of the other's poison.

chapter two

Of Artists, Women, and Jews: Svevo and the Modernist Contamination

If 'creative destruction' was an essential condition of modernity, then perhaps the artist as individual had a heroic *role to play (emphasis mine).*

David Harvey, *The Condition of Postmodernity*

On the problem of the actor. –
Falseness with a good conscience; the delight in simulation exploding as a power that pushes aside one's so called 'character,' flooding it and at times extinguishing it; the inner craving for a role and mask, for appearance; an excess of the capacity for all kinds of adaptations that can no longer be satisfied in the service of the most immediate and narrowest utility – all of this is perhaps not only peculiar to the actor? ... What good actor is not – a Jew? ... Finally, women. *Reflect on the whole history of women: do they not have to be first of all and above all else actresses?*

Friedrich Nietzsche, *The Gay Science*

With the aphorism quoted above, Nietzsche, who so consistently celebrated the Dionysian artist, ever-changing and illusory, pays an idiosyncratic tribute to the commonplaces and typologies of his time, which were to ripen fully only in the following century. Against a subtext – unspoken because unspeakable – of truth, 'character' (only utterable in Nietzsche's text in quotation marks), integrity, singularity, and identity parade the whole epistemological paraphrenalia of the actor: compulsive falseness, simulation, inner craving for the domain of the other, the life of the surface, and a pathological capacity for adaptation. The mimicry, symbiosis, and parasitism embodied in the abstract persona of the actor are denounced as a threat of dissolution, as the impending future of a slowly degrading civilization. If Nietzsche eventually decided to embrace this age of crisis as a time of promise and change, others chose to overcome it by an act of self-purification, by encapsulating the sea of otherness in well-defined and physiognomically identifiable forms. Modernism's ambiguous pull between the dissolution of a once monolithic subject and the contemporaneous exaltation of that subject on the way to dissolution is already foreshadowed in Nietzsche's 'problem of the actor.'

But in modernity the problem of the actor is nothing but the answer to another problem. 'Life itself has become a *problem*,' Nietzsche writes in *The Gay Science*, 'Yet one should not jump to the conclusion that this necessarily makes one gloomy. Even love of life is still possible, only one loves differently' (1974: 36). Modernism can be seen as the unfolding of this different way of loving, a love expressed by an art that aspires to be 'mocking, fleeting, divinely untroubled, divinely artificial ... above all, an art for artists, for artists only!' Redefined through the categories of simulation, mimicry, and appearance, art consciously posits itself as an act of construction. The modernist artist, possessed by what Walter Benjamin defined in Proust as 'the mimicry of a man of curiosity' (Benjamin 1969: 208), emerges as a playful and problematic symbiont. And, nonetheless, alongside this unstable agent modernism cherishes a more established ideal: the romantic image of the artist as a hero, cleansed and reborn through the fire of the futurist call to raze the museums. Through an act of 'creative destruction' the heroic artist affirms his individuality amid the ashes of a world rendered obsolete by his creation. In a replay of the contradictory impulses in the Darwinian fable, mimicry and symbiosis merge and ambiguously coexist with a rhetoric of struggle and self-affirmation in the figure of the modernist artist.[1]

How is the heroic subjectivism of the modernist artist to be read in the context of what has been critically defined as the feminization of modernism, namely the crisis of the classical subject and its master narratives brought on by modernist textualism? If truth 'has become woman' by foregoing its status as essence in favor of movement, performance, and the very unfolding of writing, the artist seems to have remained male, his status still tied to romantic ideals of mastery, property, and self-identity. This tension finds a literary form in what Alice Jardine has termed 'Gynesis,' the modernist putting into discourse of woman. This figure 'at work in the male text,' Jardine concludes, 'is rooted in male paranoia' (1985: 263). In his *Concept of Modernism*, Astradur Eysteinsson notes how the representation of male impotence – 'a prominent feature in modernist literature; we need only think of Kafka or Beckett' – even as it creates 'space for "other" discourses, a space inhabited, among other things, by a ghostly female subject,' facilitates as well a 'masculine recuperation of the feminine' (1990: 98).[2] By occupying a feminine speaking position, the male writer is able to reaffirm the identity of the artist above the fray of disruptive discourses of sexual, racial, and national difference. 'Creative destruction' becomes a fitting oxymoron for the 'heroic' undermining of male power pursued by the modernist artist. The figure of the artist as hero and/or actor bespeaks the contrasting desire of the male author to embrace and yet subordinate, in relation to himself, the dissolution of male images and traditional linguistic forms of power enacted in the modernist text.

Following Harvey's observation, artists like Proust, Joyce, and Eliot would be the true *heroes of modernity*, while Italo Svevo would appear to have missed the agonistic call. Even though Svevo's aesthetic is undoubtedly inspired by a modernist sensibility for the ephemeral, the random occurrence, the spacialization of time, his flat, arid, and 'clerk-like' prose fails to destroy and remold a new world in and through language. For Svevo the aesthetic experience does not constitute a safe haven where universality is redeemed from the chaos and fragmentation of modern times. If the heroic gesture accomplished by modernist artists could be described as a paradoxical monument to an ephemeral subject, Svevo, rather than creating such a monument, takes a particular pleasure in experiencing his own dissolution in the act of writing. And so the failed-artist protagonists of his novels, described with the value-laden term *inetti*, far from being heroes, are parodies of any gesture of control. For Svevo, chronic 'weakness' offers an occasion to stage the unheroic, unredeemed materiality of life, or, in Zeno's words, the 'illness' that remains incurable because it *coincides* with life itself, and specifically a life lived in the body, marked by the unmomentous time of everyday life. Pushing aside a prevailing binary logic that opposes truth and falseness, character and mask, strength and weakness, the protagonists of Svevo's novels embrace mimicry, compulsive adaptation, and symbiosis to investigate, against the social and cultural grain, the nature of their difference. Thus Svevo writes, as an Austrian subject and assimilated Jew, from a constructed and idealized Italian national identity, as a Triestine and German-speaking author, within a constructed Italian language, and, as a male author, through an ongoing confrontation with the unfathomable position of the other, be it the position of the strong assertive man, or, even more significatively, that of the woman, the ultimate repository of modernism's 'ansiosa speranza' [anxious hope (Svevo 1966: 860)].

Giacomo Debenedetti and the Mystery of Svevo's Modernism

> E' di ieri, 1925, l'invito dell'amico triestino molto *à la page*, che ci insinuava tra le mani *La coscienza di Zeno* con una complicità da 'fratello' framassone, tenebrosa, confidenziale ed evasiva.

> [It was only yesterday, in 1925, that a Triestine friend, very *à la page*, insinuated into our hands *La Coscienza di Zeno* with a dark, confidential, and evasive sense of complicity worthy of a Masonic 'brother.'] [3]

With these words Giacomo Debenedetti recollects the first appearance of Italo Svevo, the Triestine author who had been writing in semi-obscurity for more than thirty years, on the Italian literary scene. The '*affaire* Svevo,' in the critic's recollection, started as a somewhat shady and illicit transaction, the subterranean effort to grant citizenship to an artist *sans papiers*.[4] '– Leggi' – intimated the anonymous friend – 'naturalmente, ci vuole un poco di pazienza: bisogna sopportare il peso del *fatras* e dello zibaldone. Ma Joyce, che per caso ha conosciuto Svevo qui a Trieste, lo ammira.' [Read; naturally, it requires a little patience: you have to put up with the weight of the *fatras* and the hodgepodge. But Joyce, who met Svevo by chance here in Trieste, admires him (SeS, 27)]. Through the authority of Joyce, Svevo was successfully smuggled into Italy, but it was only 'with a certain effort at getting accustomed,' or, in Svevo's own words, 'come un pezzo d'aglio nella cucina di gente che non ne vogliono sapere' [like a piece of garlic in the kitchen of people that cannot stand it (Svevo 1966: 874)], that the Italian critics eventually welcomed the Triestine author. Reading Svevo's work involved coming to terms with a vague and nonetheless nagging resistance. Like the novelistic genre within the Italian tradition as a whole, Svevo appeared as 'una flora precaria e d'acclimatazione, paradossale e irripetibile' [a precarious and imported flora, paradoxical and unique (SeS, 29)]. What was it that made Svevo and his world disturbingly different?

Following Ettore Schmitz's sudden death in 1928, his literary alterego, Italo Svevo, openly became a candidate for inclusion in the pantheon of great Italian authors. Giacomo Debenedetti's essay 'Svevo e Schmitz,' the centerpiece of the monographical issue that the journal *Il convegno* dedicated to the departed writer in 1929, was the first comprehensive analysis and serious appraisal of Svevo and his contribution. Svevo's originality and importance in the meager landscape of the Italian novel are stated by Debenedetti in the following terms:

> il modo di osservazione psicologica e l'andatura narrativa di Svevo, pur nati sotto i segni del romanzo naturalista, parevano auspicare e rinfrancare le piú ambite conquiste della narrativa novecentesca. Questi due aspetti dei romanzi sveviani: la loro classicità (nel senso dei grandi modelli ottocenteschi) e la loro *sconcertante attualità*, riassumono i motivi seri e validi del 'caso' Svevo ... (SeS, 31; emphasis mine)

> [Svevo's psychological observation and his narrative rhythm, although born under the sign of the naturalist novel, seemed to foreshadow and support the more ambitious conquests of twentieth-century narrative. These two aspects of the Svevian novels: their classical quality (in the tradition of the great nineteenth-century models) and their *disconcerting timeliness*, summarize the serious and valid reasons supporting Svevo's 'case' ...]

Nevertheless, doubt pervades Debenedetti's appraisal. After an initial assessment of Svevo's masterful and original appropriation of the realist and naturalist models, Debenedetti devotes the major part of his essay to defining the limits of Svevo's artistic achievements in light of his unpopularity – 'Perché allora Svevo non fu [...] popolare, e non lo è nemmeno oggi?' [Why then was Svevo not popular, as he is still not today? (SeS, 38)].[5] To the reader's surprise, the crucial issue of Svevo's 'disconcerting timeliness' is pushed aside by this somewhat spurious question, and remains totally unaddressed. Neither is any contemporary literary movement or author mentioned by Debenedetti – the same critic who introduced the work of Proust to Italy – to help place Svevo in his time. Separated by the originality of his narrative choices from the naturalist and realist traditions, Svevo is left alone on the threshhold of modernism, just a step away from gaining full citizenship among his contemporaries. And, nonetheless, Debenedetti's opening statement did clearly articulate a tension that held the promise of defining Svevo's art. For it is exactly in that elusive gap between tradition and the new, a no-man's-land that Debenedetti declines to explore, that the meaning of Svevo's contribution, his 'disconcerting timeliness,' is to be found.

Instead, Debenedetti, setting out to define the 'limit' that 'disturbs'

Svevo's novels, chooses to analyse another boundary, the more treacherous terrain that spans between the novelistic world and autobiography.

> Per colui che potè parere dapprima un narratore per eccellenza si pone essenziale, chi voglia andare in fondo *d'un certo disagio*, il problema del rapporto tra romanzo e autobiografia. (SeS, 38–9; emphasis mine)
>
> [If one wants to get to the bottom of *a certain uneasiness*, the problem of the relation between novel and autobiography emerges as essential for the man who at first appeared to be a novelist par excellence.]

For Debenedetti such 'uneasiness' concerns a question of citizenship, and more precisely a problem with his identity papers: 'il rapporto tra il pseudonimo dell'artista Svevo e il nome vero dell'uomo, Schmitz' [the relationship between the pseudonym of the artist Svevo and the real name of the man, Schmitz (SeS, 39)] betrays a silence that impinges on Svevo's artistic achievements. According to Debenedetti's famous thesis, Svevo does not quite reach the stature of a great novelist because he left his Jewish origins in the shadows.[6] In a letter to the director of the literary journal *Solaria*, Alberto Carocci, later included in *Saggi critici*, Debenedetti defends his much criticized reading, and observes: 'Non è detto' – he concedes – 'anzi non è quasi mai vero, che la biografia dell'uomo illumini utilmente l'opera dell'artista: ma qualche volta può incuorarci in una definizione malagevole' [It is not necessarily the case, rather it is almost never true, that the biography of the man can fruitfully illuminate the work of the artist; but it can sometimes encourage us towards an arduous definition (1945: 79)]. What is the source of this difficulty, bordering on uneasiness, that the critic alludes to? More than to Svevo's reticence about his cumbersome otherness, it should be traced to the critic's own discomfort before Svevo's 'disconcerting timeliness,' a modernism still fluidly escaping critical understanding and canonization. And, nonetheless, Debenedetti's point is well taken insofar as the question of Svevo's Jewishness 'encourages' us towards the question of modernism – the question, in fact, of otherness and its representation. The flaw in Debenedetti's reading lies in its ultimate attempt to contain in an external type, the figure of the Jew, that which hides itself in the very process of inspiring all figuration: the otherness that inhabits the self.

Debenedetti's critique, as well as his occasional faint praise, is based on a nineteenth-century aesthetic of symbolic unity. Svevo's secondary characters 'ai quali sono stati largiti liberamente da natura i piú felici istinti di vivere, di possedere la vita, di accaparrarsene i doni' [whom nature showered liberally with the happiest instincts for living, for possessing life, for hoarding its gifts (SeS, 45)] satisfy such requirements. Before these characters the Svevian protagonist, for whom 'la vita rimane sempre [...] un indecifrabile e caotico enigma' [life remains forever ... an undecipherable and chaotic enigma (SeS, 62)], stands, according to Debenedetti, 'con nostalgia desolata e lamentosa' [with a mournful and desolate nostalgia (SeS, 45)]. If the heroes of the great realist novels attest to the healthy unity between inner life and action, Svevo's characters, by breaking the natural link between consciousness and the outside world, are 'inetti consapevoli' [conscious misfits (SeS, 56)] for whom '[le] certezze cerebrali non diventano mai esperienza' [cerebral certainties never become experience (SeS, 62)]. Stendhal, Tolstoy, and Balzac are in Debenedetti's analysis the normative models of 'savoir vivre'; Svevo, on the other hand, 'mette deliberatamente in gioco la possibilità di stare al mondo' [deliberately puts in question the possibility of existing in the world (SeS, 50)]. By an ironic reversal, it is the critic whose perception is shaped by nostalgia. We see it at work in Debenedetti's longing for a once orderly novelistic world in which the author held a privileged vantage point, knowing 'il punto di chiusura del circolo' [the closure of the circle (SeS, 73)]; the character thought and acted according to a coherent script; and life could be fully represented as a 'mistero in piena luce' [mystery in full light (SeS, 76)].

Debenedetti's reading of Svevo rests on a fundamental epistemological assertion against which Svevo and his characters are measured. His critical perspective is much like the one Georg Lukács used to critique modernism in general. Both critics retain a belief in the interrelated existence of a knowable objective reality and a healthy subject whose 'decisioni scattano lineari, precise ed efficaci: che son così perché son così, volute da un sano istinto, prima che vagliate dalla ragione' [decisions spring up direct, precise, and effective: they are the way they are because willed by a healthy instinct, rather then analysed by reason (SeS, 62)]. Debenedetti's comparison mistakes the search for the *not yet* with the failure to accept *what is*, and shares with his fellow skeptic about modernism the aesthetic dictum that 'only human praxis can concretely show the essence of men.'[7] He sees the Svevian characters, by contrast, as defined only by their limitations and failures: the *menschliche Gestalt* is deformed and irretrievable in Svevo's text. It is now up to the critic, through an act of interpretive will, to recuperate the lost synthesis, even if only in a somewhat negative and degraded form.

The problem of the Svevian character is the absence of character. Immaturity and the inability to act in the world are, according to Debenedetti, the first 'limiti naturali e irreparabili del personaggio sveviano' [natural and irreparable limits of the Svevian character (SeS, 62)]. But the truly irreparable structural flaw, at the same time a 'sin' and a 'hereditary defect,' that undermines him is 'l'impossibilità di diventare, di fronte all'esistenza quotidiana, *come* gli altri' [the impossibility of becoming before everyday experience *like* the others (SeS, 63)]. Difference stands at the core of his failure, not in the sense that he cannot be like others, but rather, as Debenedetti soon specifies, that he is compulsively like all others – strong, weak, masculine, feminine – with whom he comes in contact:

> una eccessiva impressionabilità lo spinge a cristallizzare intorno ai piú svariati nuclei che gli vengano offerti dall'esterno, anzichè ad imporre la sua forma e le sue preferenze. [...] come un ciottolo fluitato da un torrente, prende via via la forma che il singolo momento gli dà. (SeS, 66)
>
> [an excessive impressionability pushes him to crystallize around the most various nuclei offered to him from the outside, rather than impose his own shape and preferences. ... Like a pebble carried by the stream, he takes at every turn the shape that the singular moment bestows on him.]

Impressionability, what Nietzsche called 'an excess of the capacity for all kinds of adaptations,' and the willingness to lose one's contours in the surrounding world are for Debenedetti the defining characteristics of the Svevian protagonist. Although expressed in negative terms, Debenedetti here arrives at articulating the symbiotic-parasitical relation of Svevo's character to the world. Debenedetti's reading – an illuminating case of the blindness of an analysis rich in critical insights – recognizes the intersubjective space of the Svevian narrative and the pervasiveness of a 'parasitical' economy of which Svevo is not, as Debenedetti thought, a passive and resigned portrayer but an acute and conscious investigator.

The vicarious-reflexive relationship with the world and the other, disparaged by Debenedetti, finds a self-conscious and fully articulated expression in a short unfinished piece by Svevo entitled 'Diario di bordo.' There, symbiosis explicitly becomes the plot in a narrative project of exploring interiority through the relation with the other. The first-person narrator of the piece is a young doctor who has decided to participate in an expedition to the North Pole. Against the backdrop of this outwardly daring adventure, the doctor pursues his own exploratory mission, namely the study of why anybody, in this case the adventurous captain and crew, might strive for such a fantastic aim. The writing of the 'personal' diary coincides with a travelogue of the captain's intentions:

> Parla del polo come sua meta ma io, che conosco meglio di lui l'animo suo dirò questo che annoto per vedere, se ne avrò il tempo, di confrontarlo con l'esito [...]. Come e perché due nature tanto dissimili come la mia e la sua si trovino unite è facile dire: Io mi legai a lui per vedere se vivere una vita come è la sua sia piú divertente che vegetare la mia. ('Diario,' 1968: 481)

> [He talks of the pole as his aim, but I, who know his soul better than he does, will be taking notes to compare them, if I will have the time, with the results. ... How and why two natures so different as mine and his are tied together is easily said: I bound myself to him to see if living a life like his were more fun than vegetating in mine.]

The Svevian author, like the young doctor, expresses a frustrated yet openly dramatized desire to understand himself by living in the shadow of the other. The constant confrontation with other realities is not, as Debenedetti would have it, a strategy to escape life, but rather a way to experience it more fully; it is an ongoing experiment in adaptations, symbiosis, and contamination by other existential economies.

Svevo's entire oeuvre can be read in light of this search. From the initial defeat in *Una vita*, where the man of mimicry, because of his immaturity, is simply condemned as inept, Svevo's subject progressively affirms, from *Senilità* to *La coscienza di Zeno*, his will to becoming, the 'uomo in abbozzo' being the ultimate theorization of a character without character. Debenedetti's elaboration of a critical paradigm based largely on the first more naturalistic and pessimistic novel *Una vita* prevents him from following the maturation of Svevo's reflection and thus from recognizing his contribution.[8]

What Debenedetti instead wants is for Svevo to be the captain adventurously striving to conquer the North Pole, or, to put it differently, to hunt and capture the prey for the reader, be it language, literary form, or meaning. But Svevo's text is itself a seductive and deceptive North Pole, one which on closer inspection is revealed to be what it always was, a deserted wasteland from which meaning has vanished to another, still imperceptible horizon. Not unlike the young doctor, reader and critic are uneasy hosts of a parasitical text, one that marginalizes the heroic plot in order to dramatize its own symbiotic pursuit.

In Debenedetti's reading, passivity, characterlessness, symbiosis become symptoms of an infectious and therefore worrisome disease that spreads to all levels of the narrative. If the Svevian 'hero' is defined in his shapes and colors by the outside world, the novelist Italo Svevo seems to be equally unable to appropriate any style or literary model without falling prey to it and becoming passively absorbed by its language: 'Svevo muta tranquillamente maniera, senza che si possano avvertire cambiamenti sostanziali dell'ispirazione' [Svevo changes style with nonchalance without us being able to observe any substantial mutation in inspiration (SeS, 70)]. But this is not all; the openness to mutability and otherness infects the materiality of Svevo's novels to such an extent that they seem to be generated 'per una continua corrosione analitica del tessuto narrativo' [by a constant analytical corrosion of the narrative texture ('Lettera a Carocci' 1945: 83)]. The text passively yields to the reader – 'i romanzi di Svevo rimangono deformabili per opera di chi li ripensa' [Svevo's novels can be deformed by the person who rethinks them ('Lettera' 1945: 83)] – and this feminine compliance to interpretive violation arouses the critic's suspicion and moral condemnation. Debenedetti's reading attempts to compensate for this lack of autonomy in the Svevian narrative by molding Svevo's text into a human, and, more precisely, a male figure.

That Debenedetti and the readers of his time would try to take critical distance from such 'grey' and 'unheroic' stories and shun indulging in the seduction offered by the 'weak' text finds an explanation in the political and cultural atmosphere of a nation under Fascism. Italian culture had been dominated, from the erotic and vitalistic novels of Gabriele d'Annunzio through the Futurist Manifestos celebrating action and destruction, by an intellectual cult of the *Übermensch*. Now in the seventh year of Mussolini's rule, the academic and literary institutions, after pushing aside d'Annunzio and the Futurists' antics, translated this cult into an artistic norm that Debenedetti himself, thirty years later in his 1964 lectures at the University of Rome, would sketch with the irony of hindsight:

> un'arte sana, tonica, costruttiva e come taluno anche diceva, un'arte virile, sul modello ideale di quel *vir* per eccellenza che si era impossessato delle sorti del nostro paese. (1971: 527)

> [a healthy, invigorating, constructive art and, as one even used to say, a vir-

ile art, on the ideal model of that exemplary *vir* who imposed himself on the destinies of our country.]

Clearly Alfonso Nitti, Emilio Brentani, and Zeno Cosini, Svevo's weak, deformable characters, could hardly find citizenship within this ideal pantheon. From this perspective, the resistance to Svevo on the part of the Italian readership becomes part and parcel of a general refusal of modernist art, and the weakness, sickness, and chaos it represented. But Debenedetti's 1964 analysis of the reception of modernism in Fascist Italy goes actually one step further.

> Il lettore reagiva, proiettando l'insicurezza da lui provata, su quei romanzi che gliela provocavano: li accusava di essere loro gli insicuri, cioè difettosi esteticamente, informi, difformi, anomali, privi di quella solida ed evidente struttura, per cui il romanzo sarebbe o dovrebbe essere, anche se non se l'è mai dichiarato, il legittimo erede del discorso [...]. Li accusava inoltre di essere oscuri, quanto quella poesia che da un pezzo lui, il lettore borghese, aveva accantonata come indecifrabile. (1971: 530)

[The reader reacted by projecting the insecurity he experienced back on to the novels that induced it in him: he accused them of being the ones that were insecure, that is aesthetically defective, amorphous, different, anomalous, devoid of that sturdy and evident structure by which the novel could or should be made, even though it was never declared as such, the legitimate heir of discourse ... Furthermore, he accused them of being obscure, much like that poetry that for some time he, the bourgeois reader, had set aside as indecipherable.]

The dismissal of Svevo's art is revealed, in this analysis, to be an act of self-defence against that which threatened not only political but engrained artistic and moral convictions. Here Debenedetti performs a cultural analysis of the Fascist literary establishment, which, if projected back on to his 1929 essay on Svevo, becomes a masterful, though indirect, act of self-criticism.

But in 1929, confronted with the need in this difficult context to attain 'una definizione malagevole' [an arduous definition (SeS, 79)] of Svevo's work, Debenedetti borrows from a longstanding popular tradition, the nineteenth-century pseudoscience of physiognomy, an image that is the necessary negative corollary to the Fascist ideology of power.

Dietro il ritratto morale del personaggio di Svevo [...] par che occhieggi un'impresionante somiglianza. [...] Ci sembra di veder vagare attraverso i tratti di questo personaggio delle sembianze conosciute. Ritroviamo, accennati, i segni fisionomici di quell'astratto individuo psicologico, [...] delineato da Otto Weininger in *Sesso e carattere*, sotto il nome di 'ebreo.' (SeS, 66)

[Behind the moral portrait of the Svevian character ... an impressive likeness seems to emerge. ... In the traits of this character a familiar resemblance seems to be visible. We find, hinted, the physiognomical signs of that abstract psychological type ... sketched by Otto Weininger in *Sex and Character*, under the name of the 'Jew.']

Thus for Debenedetti, himself Jewish, the yielding, submissive, and characterless quality, which unites the author, his style, and his characters, finds Lukács's 'aesthetic effigy of ... reality, one that is appropriate in content, formally homogeneous and closed' (Eysteinsson 1990: 188), in the figure of the Jew. The latter is at the same time the hermeneutic key for resolving Svevo's mystery and a fitting antidote to the contamination and dissolution emanating from the Svevian text.

The discourse of race substitutes for a confrontation with Svevo's modernist aesthetic: the 'disconcerting timeliness' that threatens to envelop all becomes a 'reassuring otherness' that can be easily contained. With the familiar image of the Jew, Debenedetti sutures the tear in Svevo's text between the world of interiority and the world of (in)action. Jewishness explains as well what Debenedetti calls the 'abbraccio mostruoso' [monstrous embrace (SeS, 67)] between the character and his author, an author that displays towards his protagonist – mostly in *Una vita* – 'l'appassionata reazione del corresponsabile. [...] quell'affetto morboso, che giudica continuamente e condanna' [the passionate reaction of the accomplice. ... a morbid love, that continually judges and condemns (SeS, 48)]. This shared atavistic guilt, which according to Debenedetti unites author and character, erases the recognition of a particular characteristic of Svevo's modernist fiction: namely the progressive loss, from *Una vita* to *La coscienza di Zeno*, of a privileged vantage point from which to search for a new centre of consciousness in the world, a loss expressed by the progressive collapsing of the positions of narrator and protagonist.[9] The opening up of the abyss of consciousness in the smooth surface of the realist novel, a disorienting act of freedom, is translated in Debenedetti's analysis into a descent into a terrifying underworld – 'il fondo delle proprie origini ebraiche' [the bottom of his Jewish origins (SeS, 66)] – where an ancestral will denies freedom, character, and, finally, the possibility of any story being told.

But the dangers of modernism contained by the discourse of race are fully embodied in another otherness that, although present in Debenedetti's discourse, cannot be openly figured there. It is in the outlining of the Weiningerian typology of the Jew that this otherness appears on the scene:

> l'ebreo sarebbe dunque diseredato di ogni felice istinto del vivere e privo di abbandono, a paragone col tipo antitetico dell'ariano; inoltre una instabile molteplicità del fondo morale lo renderebbe plastico, disponibile e deformabile a tutti gli urti: *femminilmente* passivo, come dice il Weininger, che alla donna nega, come si sa, immaginazione, intelligenza creatrice e moralità. (SeS, 67)

> [In comparison with the antithetical type of the Aryan, the Jew, then, would be disinherited of any happy life instinct and lacking in abandonment. Furthermore, an unstable multiplicity of his morality would render him plastic, available to and deformed by all pressures: *femininely* passive, as Weininger says, who denies to the woman, as we know, imagination, creative intelligence and morality.]

To reach a complete figuration, the discourse of race has to rely on the discourse of gender; the racial characteristics are in the end, and perhaps they have always been, sexual ones. The traits of Svevo's *inetto* – passivity and plasticity – foreshadow the Jewish type, and, in a descending order on the biological chain, the Weiningerian woman. Svevo's character is a Jew, the Jew is like the woman, ergo Svevo's character is like a woman. Femininity, used by Debenedetti as an explanatory digression to illustrate the mark of race, is in reality at the core of what makes Svevo's character other. Once again, this time buried in the negative language of sexual inferiority, another crucial insight of Debenedetti's reading emerges: the intimate and ambiguous alliance between the figure of the *inetto* and the woman, what Debenedetti will reproachfully define as a 'torbida reciprocità' [turbid reciprocity (SeS, 59)].

This parallelism is supported by Debenedetti with a quote from the Svevian text, a passage from *Senilità* that describes the relationship between the weak protagonist – Emilio Brentani – and his strong friend – Stefano Balli – who, 'quando si trovava accanto il Brentani, poteva avere la sensazione d'essere accompagnato da una delle tante femmine a lui soggette' [when in the company of Brentani, could have the feeling of being in the company of one of the many females subjected to him (S, 1993: 336)]. Debenedetti comments on the passage by saying that 'par quasi che Svevo precorra Weininger, riconducendo sotto i segni della femminilità le disposizioni del suo protagonista' [by bringing the dispositions of his protagonist under the sign of femininity, Svevo almost seems to anticipate Weininger (SeS, 68)]. First Weininger explains Svevo, then Svevo foreshadows Weininger, forming an interpretative circle that securely contains any excess that might spill over into more disquieting questions of narrative representation.

The discourse of race therefore plays in Debenedetti's essay a double role. On the one hand, it is substituted for an explicit discussion of Svevo's disquieting modernist aesthetic, and on the other it provides a more comforting construct than the unstable mark of gender, which, according to Mary Jacobus, signifies 'the ambiguity of subjectivity itself [returning] to wreak havoc on consciousness, on hierarchy, and on unitary schemes designed to repress the otherness of femininity' (Jacobus 1986: 5). Speaking of Svevo's modernism is tantamount to discussing the gendered contaminations of his symbiotic and ever-becoming subject, a subject already constructed from its very first appearance by that pseudonym that so much fuelled the critic's suspicion, and that to this day surrounds Svevo with an ambiguous halo. Talking of Svevo's choice of pseudonym, Marina Beer wrote in 1979:

> nel mondo moderno, nel quale gli unici soggetti che cambiano il proprio nome dopo la nascita sono le donne e i figli naturali, darsi uno pseudonimo significa a volte situarsi in un punto di parola femminile e lievemente illegale ... (13).

> [in the modern world, where the only subjects who change their name after their birth are women and natural children, to take a pseudonym means at times to place oneself in a speaking position that is feminine and slightly illegal ...]

This link between illegality and femininity reiterates all that is improper, contaminated, and constructed in the identity of the Triestine author. But Debenedetti's interpretation has been fundamentally altered: now the Woman and not the Jew is the mystery smuggled into Svevo's text.

The Weiningerian Connection

The citation of Weininger, a necessary point of reference for much of the Italian intelligentsia in the 1910s and 1920s, plays a crucial role in Debenedetti's argument, and, beyond the borrowing of a fashionable legitimacy, affords an answer to Debenedetti's interpretive anxieties. But what is the actual import of the connection between Svevo and Weininger? This question cannot be avoided, particularly because Weininger afforded an explanatory approach to Svevo's representation of women for the latter's early critics, an approach that has continued even to the present. Fifty years after 'Svevo e Schmitz,' Marina Beer faithfully retraces the path opened by Debenedetti:

> Svevo anticipa Otto Weininger nella sua concezione della donna in *Una vita* e *Senilità*, e anche nella *Coscienza* – il femminino sveviano è piú spesso weiningeriano o bachofeniano che freudiano. ... Le analogie con Svevo (secondo la nota analisi debenedettiana) senz'altro esistenti e profonde, vanno ricercate forse di piú nella coincidenza dei temi che in quella delle soluzioni. (Beer 1979: 19)

> [Svevo anticipates Otto Weininger in his conception of the woman in *Una vita* and *Senilità*, and even in the *Coscienza* – the Svevian feminine is more often indebted to Weininger or Bachofen than Freud. ... The analogies with Svevo (according to the well-known analysis of Debenedetti) are without a doubt present and profound, but they are to be found more in the coincidence of themes than that of solutions.]

Even though Beer limits their connection to one of shared themes, to even speak of the 'femminino sveviano' as Weiningerian amounts to both a misreading of Svevo and a misunderstanding of Weininger's metaphysics of gender.

With the 1903 publication of *Geschlecht und Charakter* – a monumental defence of a besieged Cartesian subject – Otto Weininger became the champion of a paranoid discourse on otherness, expanding extravagantly on Nietzsche's elusive remarks on the problem of the actor. It is in the work of this young Austrian Jew, who committed suicide in 1905, that the deceptive oppositions of strength and weakness, character and characterlessness, activity and parasitism are brought to their extreme consequences, creating what one reviewer of the time called a 'metaphysical Darwinism,' namely a metaphysics of race and gender.

Otto Weininger's *Geschlecht und Charakter*, even at the time of its appearance in 1903, seemed thoroughly anachronistic in a cultural scene where the theory of the unconscious and a radical critique of language had put all traditional philosophical categories into question. Notwithstanding, and perhaps precisely because of this intellectual anachronism, Weininger's work had an astounding public success: between 1903 and 1927, twenty-six editions were printed just in German. In Italy the work of Weininger, first introduced by the Florentine magazine *La voce*, was widely popular, even to the extent that *Geschlecht und Charakter* became the more acceptable substitute for a Freudian psychoanalysis censured by both the Catholic and Fascist intelligentsia.[10] Translated into Italian in 1912, *Geschlecht und Charakter* was known in multilingual Trieste as early as 1905 and was reviewed in the local newspaper, *L'Indipendente*, by Svevo's cousin Steno Tedeschi. Although the enthusiasm aroused by *Geschlecht und Charakter* is disquieting in light of the open anti-Semitism and misogyny that pervade it, many intellectuals of the time hailed it as innovative and a work of genius – the modernists Gertrude Stein, Karl Kraus, and James Joyce among them. Freud, who read the book still in its manuscript form, is said to have been 'one of [his] most avid readers' (Gilman 1986: 250); and Ludwig Wittgenstein commented mysteriously that the book needed only to be negated to reveal a great truth.[11] If the book's solution to the contemporary malaise seems risible in its romantic literalness – the ascetic ideal of the genius – the fear and anxiety it expressed were real and timely. It was the representation of this fear more than its answers that account for the unqualified success of Weininger's work.

The motivating force in Weininger's reflections is the reaction to a modernity seen in terms of a degraded and degrading otherness.

> Judaism is the spirit of modern life. [...] Our age is not only the most Jewish but the most feminine. [...] the time of a superficial anarchy [...] a time of communistic ethics [...]. The decision must be made between Judaism and Christianity, between business and culture, between male and female, between the race and the individual [...]. Mankind has the choice to make. There are only two poles, and there is no middle way. (1906: 329–30)

The defence system that Weininger devises against the forces of anarchy is a Manichean one in which the stark oppositions between Aryan and Jew, male and female, and spirit and body take on the religious overtones of an exclusionary theology. In order to isolate and save the purity of the genius vis-à-vis the two main contaminating agents – the Woman and the Jew – Weininger proceeds to a grotesque essentialization of sexual and racial difference.

Freud's theorization of sexual difference, already controversial enough, at least eschewed an essentialist rhetoric in favour of one open to constructivist reevaluation:

> In conformity with its peculiar nature, psychoanalysis does not try to describe what a woman is – that would be a task it could scarcely perform – but sets about enquiring how she comes into being. (Freud 1955a: 116)

Weininger, by contrast, seeks to describe unequivocally what a woman is, in a series of biological and philosophical 'proofs' of woman's inferiority. Thus, in *Geschlecht und Charakter*, woman is posited as pure sexuality, either mother or whore. She is incapable of memory, intelligence, and logic. Woman is empiricity, all the differences of the world that cannot be assimilated into a unified consciousness. While the man-monad is sharply defined against the world – 'man has limits, and accepts them and desires them' (1906: 287) – the woman is 'always living in a condition of fusion with all the human beings she knows' (1906: 198). She shares this shapelessness, parasitism, and contamination with the world with that other agent of the world of matter, the Jew. Of the 'womanly' Jews, the 'match-makers,' Weininger stresses a similar lack of individuality and 'an extreme adaptability':

> [The Jew] adapts himself to every circumstance and every race, becoming, like the parasite, a new creature in every different host, although remaining essentially the same. (1906: 320)

The Woman and the Jew are the two unsettling representatives of the anxiety of modernism that finds a figuration in the unresolved, contradictory, and finally repressed tension between a dream of cleanliness, unity, and propriety and the threat of materiality, multiplicity, and parasitism. But even a rigid essentialism, in order to attract followers, needs its opening to transcendence, its path to grace. As the example of the author of *Geschlecht und Charakter* himself demonstrates, a radical difference separates the Jew and the Woman, and on this difference is built Weininger's greatest ambition: his *imitatio*.

In *Geschlecht und Charakter*, as in the *Divine Comedy*, the descent into the world of otherness and corruption is the walk of redemption for the

Jew, Weininger. Focusing on the figure of the first fully 'Aryanized' Jew, the great example in self-purification, namely Jesus Christ, Weininger theorizes a dream of self-cleansing, of rejection of the otherness contained in one's self, the expulsion of the feminine and the Jew in order to become one and undivided, a pure ascetic genius. Only men, and more precisely Jewish men, could achieve such a transcendence. Women, Jewish or gentile, are and remain essentially other: materiality beyond the scope of any redemption. Despite Gertrude Stein's admiration and enthusiasm for Weininger's reflections, the woman, differently from the male Jew, has no chance of self-purification, because, if race – in Weininger's analysis a metaphysical and psychological disposition – can be overcome, sex is an indelible mark of impurity and difference. The true mark of otherness is, in the end, not a racial but a sexual one.

Weininger's redemptive project offers Debenedetti a strategy for explaining Svevo's writing. Just as Weininger threw away 'questo personaggio che lo infestava [...] dentro l'involucro di una tesi antisemita' [this character who infested him ... wrapped in an anti-Semitic thesis (SeS, 68)], Svevo, according to the critic, freed himself of such a character in a novelistic figure (e.g., Alfonso in *Una vita*) 'con una implacabilità, un gusto della ritorsione, che ricordano l'appassionata ferocia dell'antisemitismo semita' [with an implacability, a desire for reprisal, that recalls the passionate ferocity of Jewish anti-Semitism (SeS, 68)]. But what Debenedetti reads as a similarity is really a point of radical difference between Svevo and Weininger. As it has been rightly observed, the only affinity between the two authors 'can perhaps be noted in precisely what Weininger repressed in himself. *Svevo represents everything Weininger wrote against.*'[12] While Weininger indulges in a dream of self-healing and purification, of becoming whole – a simultaneous transcendence of his Jewishness, femininity, and modernity – Svevo revels in a life posited as an unredeemable 'sickness,' difference and contamination. He is parasitic to the core; his passivity goes beyond that of Weininger's Jew into the territory of the sexually unredeemable.

'Non si capisce la lettura di Debenedetti,' Lavagetto acutely observes, 'se anche dietro di lui non riconosciamo Weininger, e se anche nelle sue parole non si coglie "l'appassionata ferocia dell'antisemitismo semita"' [We cannot understand Debenedetti's reading, if we fail to recognize Weininger behind it, and if we fail to grasp the presence of 'the passionate ferocity of Jewish anti-Semitism' in his words (1989: 243)]. By projecting on to Svevo his own Jewish self-hatred, Debenedetti reads Svevo's act of affirmation as an act of fear.[13] Here lies the great misunderstanding between critic and author. By repeating the gesture at the root of the Weiningerian project, Debenedetti's reading unfolds as an act of resistance to an 'actuality' that remains disconcerting and troubling, that 'timeliness' of Svevo's writing.

The accusation that Svevo had hidden his origins is not Debenedetti's main concern; behind it lurks the real cause of uneasiness: the 'feminine' character of Svevo's style, language, speaking position, and finally of his 'hero.' The feminization of the modern keeps the threat of Debenedetti's similarity to Svevo, their shared and embattled status of Jew-as-outsider, at a distance. With this act of feminization, therefore, Debenedetti's critical discourse first 'emasculates' Svevo's accomplishment as a writer, and, second, negates his presence as a dangerous double of the critic by displacing him into a sphere of absolute otherness, the feminine. Debenedetti's critical judgment is tainted with the desire to distance itself from the 'illness,' the difference through which Svevo decided to live and write. 'Io conobbi un gobbo' writes Svevo in 'Orazio Cima,' 'che aveva tanto bene attrezzato il proprio spirito intorno alla protuberanza che aveva nella schiena che sarebbe stato un uomo perduto se avesse potuto curarla. Era il gobbo piú spiritoso di Trieste ... Ma qui egli proprio non c'entra. ...' [I knew a hunchback who organized his spirit so well around the hump on his back that he would have been a lost man if he could have been cured of it. He was the funniest hunchback in Trieste ... But here he is truly out of place (1968: 266)].

Woman as the disquieting locus of absolute otherness looms large in the discourse of modernity: we see it powerfully at work in both Weininger's defence of the unassailable wholeness and purity of the genius and Freud's rummaging in the flotsam of a sunken consciousness. Against this intellectual background what Debenedetti defined initially as Svevo's 'disconcerting timeliness' begins to emerge. The work of the Triestine author is timely in enacting the textual dissolution of the classical subject, and, at the same time, disconcerting because the figure of the woman is the ground on which his subject experiences this dissolution, his critical becoming, his contamination. The figure of the woman is the locus of the modernist gap – at the same time a point of suture and tear – that separates tradition and the new, the no-man's-land that Weininger and Debenedetti are afraid to explore, and in which Svevo will lose himself charting a new territory by writing between self and other, and, hopefully if anxiously, beyond.

But even Weininger, the monolithic defender of a crumbling male identity, knows better than many of his readers would allow. Once one chooses to focus on the contradictory nature of his text, a nature that may account for the breadth of its popularity, one is struck by a text profoundly self-embattled, disturbingly conscious of its own madness. In the bombastic celebration of the endangered species of the male genius, Weininger repeatedly surprises the reader with insights that are damning to the overall conception of his argument – insights that keep one interested in his shameless manifesto.

A metaphysics of difference that celebrates the expulsion of otherness and the affirmation of a self-contained genius coexists in the same text with a lengthy opening section that proclaims and 'scientifically' demonstrates the inherent bisexuality – therefore contamination – of all human beings. The obsessive pounding of a rhetoric of hatred and discrimination is often contradicted by a discourse that cannot keep qualities that pertain to the genius categorically separated from the qualities of his two eternal muddlers. In the final analysis, what differentiates the goal of the artistic genius 'to live in all men, to lose himself in all men, to revel himself in multitudes' (Weininger 1906: 106) from the state of fusion and multiplicity ascribed to the woman and the Jew? Even those monads that supposedly 'have no windows, but, instead, have the universe in themselves' (287) have a constitutional need for the other; in fact:

> no one can understand himself were he to think of nothing else all his life, but he can understand another to whom he is partly alike, and from whom he is also partly quite different. (Weininger, 1906: 110)

For the embattled self of Otto Weininger, intersubjectivity and bisexuality are at the same time despised historical threats and necessary existential and biological conditions.

But the most unexpected insight of Weininger's project is his final admission of the necessary economy at the heart of his speculative system and of the oppression – hence violence – on which the existence of the male genius is predicated:

> If women ever become masculine by becoming logical and ethical, they would no longer be such good material for man's projection; but that is not a sufficient reason for the present method of tying woman down ... (1906: 340)

So, at the end of the book, the destiny of the pure, absolute genius, rather than soaring in solitude, seems inextricably tied to that of the woman, the feared double, the ensemble of all the worst qualities of the Ego. By drawing this connection, Weininger may have been the first to give expression to a fundamental modernist and feminist insight: the presence at the heart of all male discourse of the drama of sexual difference.

Barbara Johnson, using the visual metaphor of negative and positive space, has defined the dream of psychoanalysis as a dream of 'symmetry,' the dream of representing 'sexual difference as a recursive figure, in which both figure and ground, male and female are recognizable, complementary forms' (Johnson 1998: 19). But often, against the will of their painter, figure and ground disfigure and reconfigure one another. If Weininger's dream is one of a monumental male figure that negates all background, be it sex, body, or matter, Svevo's text dramatizes in dreamlike fashion this fluid relation of figure to ground, expressing the deep and overwhelming realization that the world could be, and will be, articulated differently. In this sense, Svevo's texts, rather than being projected on the ghostly shadow of a negated other, are told *in the shadow of the other*: they are the dialogic story of that asymmetrical, uneven, and, above all, unpredictable relation of figure to ground.

In contradistinction to any dream of purity or symmetry, the story of symbiosis is a story that sidesteps narratives of castration and recognizes, with both fear and desire, the merging of the figure into the ground and the becoming figure of the ground, that is, the contamination that presides over all stories and that makes of identity, sexual, racial, and national, an ongoing creative and transformative project.

Svevo in the Woman's Cage

He was, he dreaded this castrated woman. He was, he dreaded this castrating woman. He was, he loved this affirming woman. At once, simultaneously or successively, depending on the position of his body and the situation of his story, Nietzsche was all these.

Jacques Derrida, *Spurs: Nietzsche's Styles*

Svevo did read Weininger. 'Svevo fruì di *Sesso e carattere* in modo frammentario e casuale' [Svevo used *Sex and Character* in a fragmentary and casual way (1982: 206)], writes Cavaglion in *Otto Weininger in Italia*. After stressing their radical differences, Cavaglion lingers over some common traits linking Svevo and Weininger: a profound dislike for England and *a hatred for women*. Before Weininger ever appeared on the scene, misogyny in Trieste was in Cavaglion's words 'un requisito fondamentale del "crogiuolo'" [a fundamental requirement of the 'melting pot' (1982: 208)].[14] Because of this cultural background, the representation of woman in Svevo has been automatically read by critics – Beer, Cavaglion, and Scandiani, among others – as Weiningerian *avant-la-lettre*. But how can Svevo be all that Weininger is not and still share that misogynist ideology that is the mainstay of the Weiningerian discourse? Although Cavaglion usefully retraces Svevo's references to the Austrian philosopher, he recognizes as well their profound divergence when, comparing Weininger's idea of total memory to Svevo's dramatization of memory as forgetting, he writes:

> In Svevo la memoria tende addirittura a sconfinare nel regno profano (e direbbe Weininger, tipicamente 'femminile') della menzogna, dell'inganno, della 'bugia.'(Cavaglion 1982: 205)

> [In Svevo memory tends even to trespass on the profane – and Weininger would say, typically 'feminine' – realm of untruth, deceit, and the 'lie.']

Strangely, and in language that reminds us of Debenedetti, Cavaglion describes Svevo's difference as a transgression, a going beyond, that is again 'typically feminine.' First for Debenedetti, then for Cavaglion, Weininger plays the highly useful role of impressing on Svevo the mark of gender, in a manoeuvre that marginalizes Svevo's, and we could even argue Weininger's, critical philosophical insights.

Confronted with Svevo's embarrassing submission to the profoundly unethical sphere of the feminine, the critics seem to argue that Svevo hates women exactly because he recognizes in them his own weakness, a sexual corollary to Jewish self-hatred. But Svevo knows better than to equate the modernist experience of time with weakness. Thus, it could be argued instead that Svevo hates women because he envies their strength. Or it could be that he loves them because they are what he is or what he wants to be. His texts, with their complex ambiguity, offer the only answer that is possible to these questions. Thus, in *La coscienza di Zeno*, the same Zeno who denigrates women *à la* Weininger because 'ogni giorno che sorge porta loro una nuova interpretazione del passato' [every day brings them a new interpretation of the past (CdZ, 712)] had himself inaugurated the writing of his memories with an implicit call for constant and open-ended interpretation, proclaiming: 'Ricordo tutto, ma non intendo niente' [I remember everything, but I understand nothing (CdZ, 535)].

In fact, it is through *La coscienza di Zeno*, the only point in Svevo's work where Weininger is explicitly mentioned, that we can best grasp what is at stake in Svevo's 'use' of Weininger, and therefore begin to understand, finally beyond Weininger, Svevo's representation of woman, 'una problematica splendidamente ambigua e complessa' – Giuseppe Scandiani acutely observes – 'di fronte alla quale ai nostri occhi impallidisce il credo di Weininger, ingenuo, univoco, unilaterale' [a splendidly ambiguous and complex problematic that makes Weininger's ingenuous, univocal, and one-sided creed grow pale and fade before our eyes (1983: 554)].[15]

After proposing to one of the Malfenti sisters, the homely Augusta, Zeno takes a night walk through the city with his rival Guido, who has already won the love of the beautiful Ada, the sister initially courted and loved by Zeno. It is during this fateful walk, as a sparkling and ebulient Guido pulls a humiliated and resentful Zeno to his side, that Weininger makes his first appearance:

> di punto in bianco, egli si mise a dir male delle donne. [...] Era ben dotto, e ad onta della mia stanchezza stetti a sentirlo con ammirazione. Molto tempo dopo scopersi ch'egli aveva fatte sue le geniali teorie del giovine suicida Weininger. [...] Mi venne persino il dubbio ch'egli volesse curarmi. Perché altrimenti avrebbe voluto convincermi che la donna non sa essere né geniale né buona? A me parve che la cura non riuscí perché somministrata da Guido. Ma conservai quelle teorie e le perfezionai con la lettura del Weininger. Non guariscono però mai, ma sono una comoda compagnia quando si corre dietro alle donne. (CdZ, 634–5)

> [Then suddenly, out of the blue, he began speaking against women. ... He seemed to know a great deal, and tired as I was I listened to him with admiration. It was not till long afterwards that I discovered he had adopted the brilliant theories of the young suicide Weininger. ... I almost wondered whether he was trying to cure me of my love. Otherwise why was he so anxious to convince me that women were incapable either of genius or goodness? I think the cure might have been efficacious if it had been administered by anyone but Guido. But I remembered his theories and supplemented them later by reading Weininger. They never do cure one, but it is well to keep them in mind when one is running after women.]

Zeno appropriates Weininger with a self-irony that recognizes the usefulness of Weininger as a tool, a reassuring crutch, for supporting men in the pursuit of sexual exploits.

But criticism has missed the more significant, and more implicit, presence of Weininger in the conversation that preceded this one. There, Weininger is not greeted as a potential ally of Zeno's light pursuits, but rather as a spirit hostile to Zeno's ironic consciousness. To Guido's announcement of his engagment with Ada, Zeno reacts by criticizing Guido's breathtaking violin performance in the Malfenti home by saying: 'Adesso capisco perché ad Ada piacque tanto quel Bach svisato a quel modo!' [Now I understand why Ada liked your travesty of Bach so much! (CdZ, 634)]. In order to defend his musical genius, Guido launches on a tirade against all women, their lack of fantasy, imagination, and ethics, and therefore their inability to judge or understand a genius, namely himself, Guido Speier. Weininger is used by Guido to attack all women, Ada in particular, and above all to attack Zeno, who, with his disparaging remark, revealed a similar 'feminine' lack of appreciation.

Weininger, music, and genius reappear together in another episode of *La coscienza di Zeno*, this time in a radically different scenario. Copler, an old friend of Zeno, introduces him to a young and needy singer, Carla Gerco, who will eventually become his lover. In a first philanthropic visit to the young woman, Zeno witnesses a test of her musical talent:

> Cantò 'La mia bandiera.' Dal mio soffice sofà io seguivo il suo canto. Avevo un ardente desiderio di poterla ammirare. Come sarebbe stato bello di vederla rivestita di genialità! (CdZ, 665)

> [She sang 'La mia bandiera.' I sat on my soft sofa listening to her, and wishing with all my heart to be able to admire her. How wonderful it would be to discover she was a genius!]

It is not at all accurate to say, as Cavaglion does, that Svevo in this way 'si tradisce e fa ripetere a Zeno il concetto che poco prima aveva messo in bocca a Guido Speier' [betrays himself by having Zeno repeat the concept that a little earlier he had put in Guido Speier's mouth (1982: 209)]. On the contrary, what Svevo consciously does here is express the desire of his character to see the theories of 'the brilliant Austrian philosopher' refuted. In the very moment that Zeno has the opportunity to act on these theories that 'never heal but are good company when one runs after women,' that is, in the seduction of Carla, he desires instead to see them challenged by the existence of a female genius. In Svevo's hands, Weininger becomes his vehicle to represent ironically, and thus distance, the misogyny permeating a whole society.

Confronted with Guido's unambiguous misogyny, Zeno's misogyny not only fades, but, as the episode with Carla shows, becomes something altogether different. Already the discussion that Guido and Zeno have about the image of the woman in the moon strongly reveals their differences:

> una grande luna s'avanzava nel cielo intensamente azzurro dov'era ancora limpido, una di quelle lune dalle guancie gonfie che lo stesso popolo crede capaci di mangiare le nubi. Era infatti evidente che là dov'essa toccava, scioglieva e nettava.
>
> Volli interrompere il chiaccherio di Guido [...] e gli descrissi il bacio nella luna scoperto dal poeta Zamboni: com'era dolce quel bacio nel centro delle nostre notti in confronto all'ingiustizia che Guido accanto a me commetteva! [...] Guido dovette adattarsi di lasciare per un momento in pace le donne e guardare in alto. Ma per poco! Scoperta, in seguito alle mie indicazioni, la pallida immagine di donna nella luna, ritornò al suo argomento con uno scherzo di cui rise fortemente, ma solo lui, nella via deserta: – Vede tante cose quella donna! Peccato ch'essendo donna non sa ricordarle. (CdZ, 635)

[a great moon was climbing into the sky, intensely blue where it was still clear; one of those full-cheeked moons which, according to popular belief, are able to devour the clouds. In fact one could see that its touch was clarifying and cleansing.

I tried to interrupt Guido's continual chatter ... by telling him about the kiss that the poet Zamboni thought he had seen in the moon; how sweet that kiss seemed in the moon of our dark nights when compared with the injustice done me by Guido ... Guido was obliged to leave women alone for a while and look up at the sky. But not for long! Directly he discovered with my help the pale woman's face in the moon, he resumed his argument with a witticism at which he alone laughed loudly, in the deserted street: 'What a lot of things that woman sees! It's a pity that being a woman she can't remember them.']

The image of the woman in the moon appears in Zeno's defence against the injustice of Guido, an injustice that, while unspecified, is understood as perpetrated at one and the same time against him and women. The woman derived by Guido from Weininger is congealed in the form of an edifying illustration, a closed and complete idea for ready usage. Before this type, literature ceases to be. Zeno, therefore, escapes both his own and Guido's misogyny in an elusive image. Only in the detour of literature, in its correction of life, only in the design of the moon, as it were, might Zeno reach some consoling truth. If both men in different ways strive to keep the woman at sidereal distances, only Guido will be successful in freezing her in a degraded cliché; Zeno, if somewhat ironically, will be willing to sit with Carla and listen to the still uncertain and amateurish voice of the other.

Once we recognize misogyny as a conscious object of Svevo's representation, rather than an implicit element of his ideology, the Svevian character is open to a new reading. His desire for the other, a desire for symbiosis, escapes the logic of gender, and invests equally, although differently, both men and women. In the fragmentary story 'Orazio Cima,' the timid narrator befriends a strong assertive man and his lover. As in 'Diario di bordo,' the relationship that ties the weak narrator to each member of the couple is profoundly symbiotic, but of a rather different nature. Towards Orazio Cima, a fearless and brutal hunter, the artist almost has the attitude of a scientist observing an anterior stage of consciousness, anxious to understand how it is possible to live like an animal striving only towards one goal. On the other hand, Antonia, Orazio's lover, offers the narrator an unexpected and disquieting mirror image.

> Devo anche dire che io vivevo ambedue quegli individui. Lui così attivo e giovine come io non sono mai stato e lei che con tanta brutalità difendeva la dolcezza ch'è il mio destino, e che io non sapevo difendere perché me ne vergognavo come di un'inferiorità. (1968: 265)

> [I have to say that I lived in both those individuals. He so active and young as I have never been and she who with such brutality was defending the sweetness that is my destiny, that which I did not know how to defend because I was ashamed of it as an inferiority.]

The woman occupies a space of 'dolcezza' that belongs to both her and the narrator and defines both of them, with the difference that she is able thereby to affirm and therefore invert the sign of her 'inferiority.'[16]

In his study of Otto Weininger's critique of Jewish masculinity, John Hoberman has tied what he calls 'the exceptional status of the Jewish male' to 'his exclusion from a European ideology of adventure' (Hoberman 1995: 145). The 'risk-taking as an end in itself' and 'martial athleticism' that characterize the ethos of self-assertion of the knightly and then bourgeois adventurer are the measure of the failure of Svevo's character to live, rather than vegetate – i.e., write – and, at the same time, the measure of his success in articulating an alternative existential economy, one that along the way deconstructs gender boundaries. This economy of 'sweetness' and 'inferiority' is inscribed in a little fable written by Ettore Schmitz for his daughter Letizia:

> La porticina della gabbia era rimasta aperta. L'uccellino con lieve balzo fu sull'uscio e da lì guardò il vasto mondo prima con un occhio e poi con l'altro. Passò per il suo corpicino il fremito del desiderio dei vasti spazii per cui le sue ali erano fatte. Ma poi pensò: Se esco potrebbero chiudere la gabbia ed io resterei fuori prigioniero. La bestiola rientrò e poco dopo, con soddisfazione, vide richiudersi la porticina che suggellava la sua libertà (Pds, 860).

> [The door of the cage had been left open. The little bird with a light jump was on the threshold and from there it looked at the wide world first with one eye then with the other. Through its little body went a thrill of desire for the vast spaces for which its wings had been made. But then it thought: if I go out they could close the cage and I would remain a prisoner outside. The little bird went back inside and after a while it saw with satisfaction the door of the cage being closed, sealing its freedom.][17]

Svevo's bird has, like Macario's seagulls in *Una vita*, real wings to fly with, but it chooses desire over instinct, the willingness to inhabit its difference, to live as strength what could be simply read as a limitation, an inferiority, a weakness. This fable, which can be read as an epigrammatic plot outline of Svevo's novels, allegorizes what Adorno and Horkheimer defined, in *The Dialectic of Enlightment*, as the 'utopia of happiness without power' (cited in Le Rider 1993: 174).[18] The subjects who embodied such a utopia were for the Frankfurt School thinkers precisely the Jews and Women who troubled Svevo's contemporaries, 'human beings according to nature, whose existence is a kind of challenge to the instrumental rationality of modernity derived from the enlightment' (Le Rider 1993: 175). The cage is Svevo's representation of this problematic utopia. It is within such a cage outside of time, a place of desire and of freedom, that Svevo's subject encounters the woman. The cage could be likened to the shadow of the mammoth, the space of intersubjectivity that the primitive man chose by making himself slave of the other. Symbiosis is the desire for such a cage, the ethic of 'tutela,' the connection with the other or perhaps just its shadow.

chapter three

Between Darwinism and Dreams: The Stories of Alfonso and Annetta in *Una Vita*

Stracciate anche voi le vostre carte oh! formiche letterarie. [Do shred your papers oh! you literary ants.]

[Le nuvole] correvano così da credere che scappassero o inseguissero. E' vero che qualcuno imperversava su se stesso. S'arrotolava in modo che quella ch'era apparsa una bocca andava a figgersi sull'addome che subito si sformava. [(Clouds) were running as if they were in flight or in pursuit. It is true that somebody was raving against himself. He was rolling up so that what seemed to be a mouth held a grip on the abdomen that immediately lost its shape.]

Italo Svevo, 'Pagine di diario e sparse'

If literature could truly say what the relations between the sexes are we would doubtless not need much of it.

Barbara Johnson, *A World of Difference*

Feeling compelled to correct the critical opinion of the poet and critic Eugenio Montale, who described *Una vita* as 'un grosso romanzo dominato e percorso da parecchi temi fondamentali dei quali nessuno sembra avere il predominio' [a big novel dominated and intersected by many fundamental themes, none of which seems to predominate (cited in Svevo 1968: 802)], Svevo wrote in his 'Profilo Autobiografico' of 1928:

> Certo per l'autore la relazione di Alfonso e Annetta, la ricca figliuola del banchiere Maller, è la parte più importante del romanzo che dapprima portava il titolo *Un inetto*. (1968: 802)

[Certainly for the author the relationship between Alfonso and Annetta, the rich daughter of the banker Maller, is the most important part of the novel that initially bore the title *Un inetto*.]

Although authors are not necessarily the best judges of their work, it is tempting, given a long critical tradition since Montale that has focused so much on charting the multi-layered life of Alfonso, to follow Svevo's suggestion and read *Una vita* through Alfonso's relationship with Annetta.[1]

In the search for a comprehensive interpretation of the novel's complex structure, Svevian criticism has treated the character of Annetta as an indispensable if marginal accessory to Alfonso's idyll. The literary collaboration with Annetta, only one of many events in Alfonso's grey life story, has thus tended to acquire its position and significance only in relation to other apparently overarching interpretative structures. Nonetheless, the crisis of the petit-bourgeois intellectual, the historical and existential meaning of his '*inettitudine*,' the failure of the romantic vision of the world, and, at a formal level, the obsessive mirroring of the main plot in the secondary stories – in short, all the great themes of Svevian criticism of *Una vita* – come to a head precisely in that collaboration. It is in their literary and sentimental relations that 'la vecchia storia che non si racconta piú' (the old story that nobody tells anymore) of which Mazzacurati speaks – namely, the impossibility of writing and living a Bildungsroman – is consumed and from its ashes rises 'una nuova storia di quelle che non si raccontano ancora' [a new story that nobody has yet been able to tell (1974: 238)] – the story of a *Bildung* that resides in intersubjectivity and its uncertain beyond.

This symbiosis with the other in the form of literary collaboration is by no means an isolated occurrence within the Svevian imaginary. Biographically, Alfonso and Annetta's literary relationship has an important antecedent in the collaboration between Ettore Schmitz, alias Italo Svevo, and Elio Schmitz, reader, critic, and humble historian of the more talented brother. Textually, this collaboration will return in one of Svevo's later short stories, 'Una burla riuscita,' in the symbiosis between the old Samigli brothers. Furthermore, symbiosis as collaborative dreaming will be at the core of Emilio's relations with Angiolina in *Senilità*, without mentioning the endless examples of pedagogical symbiosis – see chapter 5 – of which Alfonso's lessons to Lucia are an important example in *Una vita*.

In rejecting the tragic interpretation of Alfonso's story as the solitary struggle of a fallen hero with the world, Eduardo Saccone observes that 'il monologo [di Alfonso] è un falso monologo: è un dialogo' [Alfonso's monologue is a false monologue: it is a dialogue (1977: 157)], a frustrated search for the Hegelian *Anerkennung*, the recognition of the other that guarantees the satisfaction of desire. In *Una vita*, this dream of recognition and reciprocity, of symbiotic connection with the other, designated as a *dream of sweetness*, is the site of a still timid and often contradicted alternative to what Lavagetto defines as 'le leggi che governano il mondo costruito da Svevo sulla base di Darwin e Schopenhauer' [the laws governing the world that Svevo builds on the basis of Darwin and Schopenhauer (1993: xxx)]. This essay will dwell in the gap intervening between 'the world built by Svevo' in *Una vita* that condemns the dream of reciprocity and intersubjectivity as weakness and solipsistic indulgence and the world *of* Svevo built on the pursuit of that dream. The poetics of contamination and potentiality later theorized in the figure of the 'uomo in abbozzo,' and poetically affirmed in the character of Zeno, is contained in *Una vita* only as a negative moment. 'Inettitudine' has long been the name for this moment. But, as Giuseppe Langella pointedly observes, this term should be put to rest as 'inadequato allo scopo di definire efficacemente in maniera non riduttiva, l'intima natura del protagonista' (inadequate to offer an effective and non-reductive definition of the intimate nature of the protagonist).[2] Alfonso's refusal to perform as a coherent, self-contained, organic subject, his fictional and existential 'weakness,' his unappeasable desire for self-definition, are all unmistakable forebodings of modernism. The woman, namely Annetta in this novel, occupies the site of this poetic and anthropological mutation.

The Letter to the Mother, a Palimpsest of Alfonso's Dream

In *Una vita*, well before the novel-writing with Annetta, Alfonso is engaged in an important act of collaborative dreaming with the other: the letter to the mother. The letter opens with an insistant attempt to reconstruct, down to the materiality of the paper, the dialogic instance inside which Alfonso's dream can exist. Much more than a simple 'occhio convivente' (cohabiting eye) in front of which Alfonso 'ridisegna ... la propria biografia ideale' [redraws ... his ideal biography (Mazzacurati 1974: 223)], the figure of the mother is anxiously evoked as one that can guarantee recognition.

> Iersera appena ricevetti la tua buona e bella lettera. Non dubitarne, per me

il tuo grande carattere non ha segreti; anche quando non so decifrare una parola, comprendo o mi pare di comprendere ciò che tu volesti facendo camminare a quel modo la penna. Rileggo molte volte le tue lettere; tanto semplici, tanto buone, somigliano a te; sono tue fotografie. Amo la carta persino sulla quale tu scrivi! La riconosco ...³

[Only last night I received your dear and beautiful letter. Do not doubt it, for me your great character has no secrets; even when I cannot decipher a word, I understand or I seem to understand what you meant by letting your pen run on in such a way. I reread your letters many times; so simple, so good, they resemble you; they are photographs of you. I even love the paper on which you write! I recognize it ...]

Ironically, the mother undergoes a process of objectification because of this descriptive effort, becoming one thing with her letters. Like a photograph, she is frozen into a cliché, the silver plate that replicates a model, a fetishized object that offers itself silently to the narrative of the observer. Alfonso's first interlocutor is a silent other who is co-opted into his dream, a protective deity of that realm of authenticity to which he desires to return. It will be the task first of the narrator, 'che ad ogni passo smentisce le belle teorie, i nobili programmi' [who at every step belies the beautiful theories, the noble programs (Saccone 1977: 148)], and then of Annetta, a much more active interlocutor, to challenge Alfonso's dream.

A palimpsest of romantic and realist models, Alfonso's letter to the mother has been rightly interpreted as a *mise en abîme* that, with apparent ingenuousness, mercilessly reveals the character's attempt 'di atteggiarsi ad eroe "positivo"' [to pose as a 'positive' hero (Mazzacurati 1974: 224)]:⁴ the young man who, exiled in the arid city environment – Maller's bank – where he is treated with haughtiness and indifference, dreams of escape to the countryside where 'all'ombra delle quercie, respirando [...] [la] buona aria incorrotta' [in the shade of the old oaks, breathing ... the good uncorrupted air (UV, 4)] he can read his beloved poetry. But the import of the letter cannot be exhausted in a negative, parodic moment. In fact, if the content of the letter and its overblown style are highly conventional and as such are made an object of scorn by the author, the letter's *anxious interrogation of the other* is the genuine expression of Alfonso's search for a dialogue. Exactly because of this search, Alfonso is something more than a predictable or contemptible epigone of an inauthentic romantic dream.

To better understand the excessive and therefore innovative nature of Alfonso's desire for a dialogue it is instructive to compare *Una vita* with its most immediate literary model, Balzac's *Louis Lambert*, a book that Svevo, not without a touch of sadism, has Macario, Annetta's cousin, recommend to the unknowing Alfonso. The ideal biography sketched by Alfonso in the letter to the mother is a wishful copy of Balzac's 1835 semi-autobiographical novel: the story of an *enfant prodige* who, taken away from the idyllic peace of the countryside, suffers in the degrading and shabby atmosphere of a rigid college.[5] 'Les douleurs d'un pauvre enfant aspirant après la splendeur du soleil, la rosée des vallons et la liberté' [the sorrows of a poor boy who pines after the radiance of the sun, the dew of the valleys and freedom (Balzac 1927: 76)] ironically echo the longings of Alfonso. Lambert, who will eventually become, in his biographer's description, 'the man who dedicated his whole life to thought,' is a parodic model for Alfonso, ironically presented by his narrator as the future innovator of Italian philosophy. History appears to be repeating itself, or at least Alfonso would like it to be; but as we know, if the first time it is tragedy, the second, filtered through the perspective of a disenchanted narrator, will be farce.

But it is Alfonso's critical reaction to the book and not the thematic parallelisms that are of interest here. Remaining oddly indifferent to the plot, Alfonso focuses his attention on the ideas presented in *Louis Lambert* and the relationship between the author and his character.

> ... egli non ammirò tanto i pregi artistici dell'opera, quanto l'originalità di tutto un sistema filosofico esposto alla breve ma intero, con tutte le sue parti indicate, e regalato dall'autore al suo protagonista con la splendidezza di gran signore. (UV, 80)
>
> [... he did not admire the artistic qualities of the work, as much as the originality of a whole philosophical system briefly explained but complete, with all its parts sketched out, and offered by the author to his protagonist with the munificence of a great gentleman.]

Alfonso's reflection unconsciously creates a surprising commentary on the text. If the direct citation of Balzac's novel gives the author of *Una vita* the chance to reveal his character's historical belatedness, it also unexpectedly offers Alfonso a chance to point to the origin of his malaise: an ironic, disillusioned narrator who mercilessly debunks his character's undertakings. Alfonso might be a poor imitator of worn out romantic models, but his intellectual as well as his existential 'poverty' derives in direct proportion from the 'stinginess' of a narrator who, himself left penniless by centuries of intellectual squandering, bequeathed him only a fragmented 'Idea morale nel mondo moderno' ('Moral Idea in the Modern World'). The narrator of *Una vita* has nothing to give; he only takes away what he himself has long lost. *Una vita* results from an operation of subtraction: all the poetic and intellectual models – naturalism, Schopenhauerian existentialism, Darwinism – have been consumed before being represented. As a consequence, the only intellectual gifts to the character are internal to the story; old, recycled gifts that Alfonso will make the mistake of assuming to be normative – that is authorial – descriptions of reality. Within the fiction, Macario is the main bearer of such tainted gifts.

There is a touch of envy in Alfonso's critical reflection on *Louis Lambert* that lends to Alfonso's desire for a dialogue a meta-narrative dimension: the unspoken desire for a loving author. Within the narrative structure of *Una vita*, Alfonso cannot but submit to the ironic recognition of the third person narrator – arguably the first failed dialogue, the original sin at the root of his story. But within the story he will actively search for a loving biographer, thus trying again to fulfil the destiny of Louis Lambert, who found, in an admiring disciple, the narrator who faithfully recorded his story. Already the letter to the mother reads as an invocation to that loving and perceptive listener who will be able to understand, and to register in his heart and eventually on paper the story of a life, though it will be Annetta who discovers a 'character' in Alfonso and undertakes the drafting of his biography. But as Alfonso is no Louis Lambert, Annetta is far from being a humble disciple.[6]

The Dialogue with Annetta

After the first unhappy visit to the Mallers' home, where the dreamy young clerk experiences Annetta's indifference and arrogance, Alfonso joins the literary circle started by Annetta, the so-called Wednesday group. Now the young woman, herself an aspiring writer, seeks out with interest the company of the timid would-be philosopher and *literato*. One Wednesday, by a series of fortunate coincidences, Alfonso is left alone with her. In the parlor fallen into twilight, Alfonso has the opportunity to talk about his life, and, this time, in an unhoped-for fulfilment of his dream, it is exactly the cold and haughty Annetta who becomes the attentive and sympathetic listener.

Sorridendo Annetta gli aveva chiesto: – E la sua nostalgia? Me ne hanno parlato molto! – Non esiste piú!- rispose Alfonso. [...] Gli chiese di spiegargli che cosa fosse la nostalgia. – E' difficile! – cominciò Alfonso – ma qualche cosa credo di poterne dire – . Raccontò che prima di tutto era una malattia organica perché soffrivano i polmoni per la differenza dell'aria, lo stomaco per la differenza dei cibi, i piedi per la differenza del selciato. Quello che però rinunziava a descrivere era l'intensità del desiderio di rivedere i luoghi che si aveva abbandonato, [...] l'aborrimento per il palazzo in cui si abitava, alludeva a quello della banca, la via grande, spaziosa, e persino il mare: [...] – E me odiava molto? – Odiarla no! ma avrei voluto essere molto lontano da lei ... (UV, 105–6)

[With a smile Annetta asked him: – And your nostalgia? I heard a lot about it! – It does not exist anymore! – answered Alfonso. ... She asked him to explain in what nostalgia consisted. – It is difficult! – started Alfonso – but I believe that I can say something about it – . He told her that first of all it was an organic sickness because the lungs suffered for the different air, the stomach for the different food, the feet for the different pavement. What he avoided describing was the intense desire to see again the places that one abandoned ... the abhorrence for the building where one lived – he meant Maller's bank –, for the big spacious street, and even for the sea ... And did you hate me a lot? – I did not hate you! but I wanted to be very far from you ...]

Disguised as a theoretical disquisition on the nature of nostalgia, which allows him to take distance from his 'malcontento' by projecting it into the past, the letter to the mother returns point by point in all its motifs: the physical discomfort, the radical opposition between city and countryside, the hatred for colleagues and city people in general – a hatred mitigated by his respect for Maller's daughter – and finally the desire for flight. In the crescendo of feelings, the poetic nostalgia from which the disquisition took its point of departure opens the space for a true grief: the desire to be treated as an equal, the refusal of a subaltern position to which he feels condemned: 'gli piaceva la libertà, e anche quelli che non erano pari suoi voleva poter trattare come tali' [he liked freedom, and even those that were not his equals he wanted to be able to treat as such (UV, 106)].

After so often swallowing his thoughts as if they were humiliations, Alfonso finds an admiring listener in Annetta, and melts in a dialogue as sweet as a monologue. To talk about himself as if talking to himself, in the reassuring presence of the other, wipes away any sense of subordination:

> Ah! era cosí bello parlare da pari a pari con Annetta. Sentiva la *dolcezza* di confidarsi a lei con libertà *come se monologasse* e questa *dolcezza* diede colore alla sua parola che, per quanto impacciata, fino ad allora era stata da letterato, ricercata e fredda. (UV, 106; emphasis mine)

> [Ah! it was wonderful to speak with Annetta as his equal. He felt the *sweetness* to freely confide in her *as if delivering a monologue* and this *sweetness* gave color to his words which, although awkward, had been up to that moment affected and cold, the words of a man of letters.]

It is a magical moment for Alfonso, who, after having pursued megalomaniacal fantasies during the grey hours spent in the office, lives to the full his dream of 'sweetness,' a dream of equality and recognition, that erases a world of struggle where the only choice is to be strong or weak.

But if the atmosphere of intimacy recalls that of the letter, Annetta is not the mother. If the mother can provide a faithful, silent shadow in which Alfonso can pursue his dreams – like the primitive man his evolution in the shadow of the mammoth – Annetta's shadow is a disquieting one. As soon as the gas lamps unexpectedly light up the room, Annetta, the other, is revealed directly before Alfonso, and stops short his outpourings that were on the verge of becoming a declaration. Alfonso realizes with disappointment that Annetta is far from being contained by his dream:

> fu nello stesso tempo abbacinato dalla luce e messo in istato di misurare quanto falso fosse il passo ch'egli stava per fare. *Annetta era sempre la stessa*; dava seccamente degli ordini a Santo ... (UV, 107; emphasis mine)

> [he was at the same time blinded by the light and suddenly able to measure how false was the step he was on the verge of taking. *Annetta was still the same*, she was curtly giving orders to Santo ...]

The sweetness of the initial conversation will not be recreated: Annetta will always be beyond his dream, irreducible to it. Assertive and self-contained, not a faithful mammoth in whose shadow to dream, but a strong woman pursuing her own dreams, dreams that do not differ much from those of the 'malcontento uomo.' This excess is described paradoxically as 'sameness,' a way simultaneously to acknowledge *and* devalue Annetta's difference, her ambiguous and therefore equal subjectivity. But who and how unchanging is this Annetta?

The Idea of Annetta

A long string of clichés envelops the character of Annetta in *Una vita*. Macario, the smart talker, the brilliant popularizer of ready-made knowledge, is responsible for explaining away her personality to Alfonso and to us. His sermons ranging from scientific and philosophic topics to strategies of seduction will deeply influence Alfonso's perceptions of bodies of knowledge as well as women's bodies and specifically the 'body' of Annetta.

Upon his first encounter with Alfonso, as they leave Maller's house where the young clerk was humiliated by Annetta, Macario creates, with the passion of a rejected suitor, a biography/photograph of his cousin which will indelibly mold Alfonso's future impressions:

> Che vanerella eh! [...] una cara donna però, bella, dotta troppo, tanto che di spesso appare di non essere educata. [...] Però artista non sarà giammai ... forse in qualche istante di forte ebollizione del sangue ... [...] Annetta ha la memoria ferrea, le qualità matematiche pronunziatissime, lo spirito pronto per cose concrete, solide, come suo padre. Non capiscono caratteri, non sentono musica, non distinguono il quadro originale dalla mala copia. (UV, 34–5)

> [What a vain girl, eh! ... a dear woman though, beautiful, too learned, so much so that often she does not seem educated. ... But an artist she will never be ... perhaps in some moment of intense turmoil ... Annetta has a tenacious memory, pronounced mathematical qualities, a responsive mind for concrete, solid things, like her father. They do not understand characters, they have no ear for music, they cannot distinguish an original painting from a lousy copy.]

Annetta summarizes in her persona all those qualities that Alfonso already discovered in the city dwellers: vanity, indifference, philistinism. But Macario's patronizing sermon does not stop there. His outpouring takes on mysogynistic overtones as he tells Franco Sacchetti's story of the friar who makes a vow to marry a woman cruel to her husband only to punish her wickedness. Thus he comments: 'Per Annetta verrebbe voglia di fare dei voti simili, solo allo scopo di annientare quella superbia che secca, che offende' [With Annetta one would desire to make similar vows, if only to destroy that haughtiness that annoys and offends (UV, 36)]. And finally he crudely concludes his tirade with words that betray the anxiety underlying his rhetoric:

> Quando m'imbatto in queste donne tanto attive e tanto aggressive, tanto *inquietanti* insomma, mi vien fatto di pensare a quell'inglese che ad una troppo focosa rammentava che pagava per baciare e non per venir baciato! (UV, 36–7; emphasis mine)

> [When I come across such active and aggressive women, in short so *disquieting*, I am reminded of that Englishman who warned an excessively fiery woman by saying that he was paying to kiss and not to be kissed!]

The Annetta that Alfonso 'conoscerà' – but it would be more appropriate to say 'riconoscerà' – during the courting is contained entirely in Macario's descriptions: a literary person who, though well-educated, is utterly lacking in artistic sensibility; the wife that one would marry only in order to tame her (an image that will find an echo in the motif of the 'orso domato,' protagonist of the novel written by Alfonso and Annetta); an aggressive lover, a lover that Alfonso will escape for fear of being ensnared. Through the deforming lens provided by Macario, Alfonso, and much of Svevian criticism with him, will understand and misunderstand Annetta as a 'seduttrice vanitosa [...] fredda trionfatrice del desiderio altrui' [vain seductress ... cold master of the desire of the other (Fava Guzzetta 93)], (Moloney 1986: 92). Unrecognized, she remains *always the same*: the cliché impressed by the frustrated desire of a rejected man. To this image Alfonso will constantly return to justify his diffidence, suspicions, rancor, sudden hatred, and final refusal of the woman: 'Era proprio quale Macario l'aveva descritta! Fredda e vana, ed anzitutto vana' [She was exactly as Macario described her! Cold, vain, first of all vain (UV, 134)]; 'La durezza e la vanità di Annetta che gli sembrava di avere scoperte allora allora non avrebbe mai saputo dimenticare' [The harshness and vanity of Annetta he thought he discovered in that instant, he could have never forgotten (UV, 135)]; 'egli aveva sofferto al ritrovarla quale Macario l'aveva descritta' [he suffered to recognize her in Macario's description (UV, 143)].

'Il secolo è vecchio,' Svevo wrote, 'ed il concetto ha avuto il tempo di conquistarsi nel cervello un posticino proprio, dal quale lui, figliulo snaturato delle cose, le impedisce e le falsa' [The century is old ... and the concept has had time to conquer its little place in the brain from which it, the perverted son of things, thwarts and falsifies them ('Per un critico' 1968: 609)]. *Una vita* is the dramatization of the inauthenticity of a life dominated by concepts and quotable maxims.[7] More than anything else the image of the woman is hindered and falsified by such concepts. In the stereotype that envelops the character of Annetta, the decrepitude of the ideological world of *Una vita* becomes fully palpable. *Woman* for Alfonso is the product of a theory, a goddess made 'piuttosto per essere adorata che abbracciata' [for being adored rather than embraced (UV, 57)]. Under the sway of his conception Alfonso will fail to know Annetta and his own desire. If he pays dearly for this self-deception, Annetta is still paying for it in Svevian criticism, where she remains enveloped in Macario's idea of her.

Annetta Writing Alfonso, or The Perils of Collaborative Dreaming

As Macario predicted, and Alfonso hoped and feared, the 'woman so disquieting,' instead of remaining enticed by the sweetness of the first dialogue – like the mother before her, a shadow within which the dream can unfold – arms herself with pen and ink and takes hold of Alfonso's confession with the idea of writing a biography: 'Quel caratterino che le si rivelava con tale ingenuità le sembrò meritevole di venir descritto [...] "Racconteremo la sua vita."' [That little character that revealed itself to her with such ingenuity seemed worthy to be described ... 'We will narrate your life' (UV, 107)]. Flattered at this point in his self-esteem and elated by the unhoped for intimacy, Alfonso enthusiastically greets Annetta's idea of a common writing project. Suddenly his anonymous existence is projected onto a stage larger than his life, a novel/biography, where the sweetness of the monologue turned into a dialogue will be recreated over and over with every new reading. Alfonso seems to be sharing Louis Lambert's destiny: even he has found a loving biographer. This utopian moment will soon vanish as Annetta will reveal more and more the imperious traits of Madame de Staël, who discovered and confined Louis in the college, rather than those of Louis's young schoolmate and chronicler. But for the time being, the only time in the novel, Alfonso lives his dream.

While recalling Alfonso's past timidity – 'Non era poi mio ufficio di farla parlare –' [After all it was not my task to make you speak (UV, 107)], Annetta exposes with an unfailing writerly instinct the core of

Alfonso's story. What looms on the horizon is not really Lambert's 'histoire de cet homme qui transporta toute son action dans sa pensée' (Balzac 1927: 51), but rather, more modestly, the story of 'quell'uomo che attendeva di venir fatto parlare' [that man who was waiting for leave to speak (UV, 107)]. 'Furono queste le prime idee che diedero ad Annetta l'intenzione di fare un romanzo insième' [These first ideas gave rise to Annetta's intention of writing a novel together (UV, 107)]. Though described by Macario and Alfonso as a bad psychologist and writer, Annetta retraces with her initial inspiration the steps of the author of *Una vita* himself. Alfonso, who entered the narrative scene asking his mother for her permission ('Non ti pare, mamma, che sarebbe meglio che io ritorni? [...] Dopo scritta questa lettera sono piú tranquillo; mi pare quasi di avere già ottenuto il permesso di partire' [Don't you think, mother, that it would be better if I came back? ... After this letter I am more tranquil; I have the impression of having already obtained permission to leave (UV, 4–5)], who, after the seduction of Annetta, will abandon the city after receiving her leave to do so – 'poiché ella glielo imponeva, sarebbe partito' [since she ordered him to, he would leave (UV, 202)] – and who again will wait at his mother's deathbed for the world of the city to come and kneel at his feet, is fully contained in the figure of the man waiting for leave to speak, and, by extension, to act. This insightful formulation of Alfonso's 'weakness' foreshadows the future 'uomo in abbozzo,' the man who will define himself in the pause provided by the shadow of the mammoth.[8]

But Annetta, who earlier on admonished Alfonso – 'quando si desiderava qualche cosa nella vita bisognava sapersela conquistare' [when one desired something in life, one should know how to get it (UV, 106)] – cannot be the poet of the man who dwells in the pause and for whom the contemplation of a goal is a goal in itself, beyond any final attainment. 'Io non sono buono di conquistare nulla,' writes Ettore Schmitz to Livia in 'Diario per la fidanzata,' 'Io non voglio conquistare nulla. Io voglio avere e tenere senza sforzo. [...] Se non posso avere e tenere senza sforzo, io volentieri rinunzio, senza esitazione rinunzio' [I am not able to conquer anything. I do not want to conquer anything. I want to have and keep without effort. ... If I cannot have and keep without effort, I gladly give up, without hesitations I give up (Svevo 1968: 776)]. It is in this radical refusal of the logic of struggle that Alfonso's existential predicament is understood. As the switch of verbs from 'I am not able' to 'I do not want' suggests, the refusal to 'conquer' is not a matter of intrinsic inability, 'inettitudine' (as the conquest of Annetta later in the novel will prove), but rather a choice that affirms difference. But unlike Ettore, Alfonso is unable to accept his difference. The novel that Alfonso and Annetta write is the damning evidence of this failed recognition.

With the usual self-assurance that Alfonso deeply envies, Annetta takes hold of Alfonso's confession and gives a first synopsis of his story: 'un giovinetto che venne da un villaggio in una città e il quale s'era fatto delle idee ben strane sui costumi della città. Trovandoli in fatti differenti da quanto aveva ideato si rammaricò' [a youth who moved from a village to a city and who held very strange ideas concerning city customs. Finding them in reality quite different from what he had imagined, he felt regret (UV, 107)]. After her initial insight, Annetta perpetrates the first act of critical misapprehension and corrects Alfonso's life: 'Naturalmente invece che impiegato la faremo ricco e nobile, anzi soltanto nobile. La ricchezza serbiamo per la chiusa del romanzo' [Naturally instead of a clerk we will make you rich and noble, or rather only noble. Wealth will keep for the ending of the novel (UV, 107)]. By introducing a tangible goal in a discouragingly uneventful life, Alfonso's 'grey epic' is definitely abandoned.

But while they betray Alfonso's life story, Annetta's changes unexpectedly approach Alfonso's dream, a fantasy that he pursued at the beginning of the novel during the grey hours in the office:

Centro dei suoi sogni era lui stesso, padrone di sé, ricco, felice. Aveva delle ambizioni di cui consapevole a pieno non era che quando sognava. Non gli bastava fare di sé una persona sovranamente intelligente e ricca. Mutava il padre, non facendolo risuscitare, in un nobile e ricco che per amore aveva sposato la madre, la quale anche nel sogno lasciava quale era, tanto le voleva bene. [...] Con questo sangue nelle vene e con quelle ricchezze si imbatteva in Maller, in Sanneo, in Cellani; [...]. Ma egli li trattava con dolcezza, davvero nobilmente, non come essi trattavano lui. (UV, 13)

[His very self was at the centre of his dreams, in full control, rich and happy. He had ambitions of which he was fully conscious only in his dreams. He was not satisfied to make himself a highly intelligent and rich person. He did not resurrect his father; instead he changed him into a rich nobleman who married his mother for love, who remained even in the dream as she was, that much he loved her. ... With this blood in his veins and with all that wealth he ran into Maller, Sanneo, Cellani ... . But he treated them with sweetness, like a real nobleman, not at all like they treated him.]

Annetta's faithful *mise en abîme* of Alfonso's dream has the startling effect of sanctioning the possibility of its realization. At this point Alfonso's and Annetta's desires proceed hand in hand, their relationship seeming to actualize a common dream of grandeur concealing a longing for equality.

Arriving home after the conversation with Annetta, Alfonso undertakes the writing enthusiastically. Dazzled by finding himself in the words of the other, Alfonso confuses the composition of the novel with the satisfaction of his desire for a dialogue, the possibility of a collaborative dream.

> 'Un giovane nobile impoverito viene a cercare fortuna in città ... perseguitato dal principale e dai compagni ... amato da costoro perché con atto intelligente salva la casa da grossa perdita ... sposa la figlia del principale.' (UV, 109)

> ['A young impoverished nobleman came to the city in search of fortune ... persecuted by his chief and colleagues ... loved by them because with an intelligent act he saves the firm from a great loss ... he marries the chief's daughter.']

Confronted with this summary, however, which reveals the banality of the plot and the embarrassing allusions to his own situation, the enthusiasm of the inexperienced novelist somewhat wanes. Removed from the ennobling and unreachable realm of fantasy and exposed on paper, the dream loses the heroic aura with which an exalted imagination endowed it. If initially pleasing, the *mise en abîme* of the dream in the collaborative novel will from now on fill Alfonso with disgust and pain.

Svevo observed that to name the conduct of an individual is tantamount to a revelation: he will see himself. But for Alfonso the naming of his dream will occasion only a brief glimmer of the truth, not a true self-consciousness. With a metonymical shift, like the *Verschiebung* that Freud would describe in a few years time as central to the *Traumarbeit*, Alfonso shelters himself from this knowledge by transferring the cheap fantasy of success and its authorship from himself to the other. As soon as Annetta, carried away by her desire, appropriates Alfonso's 'novel' for her own: 'il romanzo di una giovine nobile che per essere stata tradita da un duca, nella prima ira, acconsente di sposare un ricco industriale' [the story of a noble young woman who, because betrayed by a duke, in her first anger consents to marry a rich industrialist (UV, 115)],

Alfonso, who 'scorgeva con facilità il lato ridicolo o falso nelle opere altrui' [often noticed the ridiculous and false in the work of others (UV, 100)], promptly recognizes in Annetta's novel a vulgar feuilleton that offends his sensibility: '[l'] abbozzo di una commedia, la commedia di ogni sera' [(the) sketch of a comedy, the comedy of every evening (UV, 116)]. Stepping into a disinterested intellectual persona, Alfonso transforms a painful act of self-criticism into an objective act of literary criticism and tears apart his own melodramatic dream heard from the lips of the other. In the process, shame will invest only the other and leave dream and dreamer unscathed, while subverting the possibility of sharing that dream.[9]

But, we might ask, what is the difference between the dreams of Annetta and Alfonso? Both have as protagonists impoverished nobles who heroically conquer happiness and wealth, and both lend themselves as perfect material for a fashionable feuilleton. What sets them apart, once put on paper, is their narrative style. While Annetta's work, according to Alfonso, is hopelessly, if honestly, dressed in 'panni [...] melodramatici e chiassosi' [loud, melodramatic clothing (UV, 173)], Alfonso's novel, in Annetta's judgment, exhibits, like *Una vita*, a grey and unadorned style that strives to 'ennoble' the banal melodrama. Although it can be tempting to fix the poetical allegiances of the two inexperienced novelists – Annetta, a follower of late romantic popular literature *à la* Dumas, and Alfonso, an epigone of French naturalism – any such attempt would run into contradictions. What is important for the author of *Una vita* is the fact that, whether 'gaudy' or 'grey,' the words of both dreamers/writers are following a manner, they are literature hollowed by convention (Fava Guzetta 1991).

Alfonso's literary and sentimental relationship with Annetta will be a tormented one not because of Annetta's coldness, the vulgarity of her literary taste, or her petty aspiration to succeed, but rather because she herself is a dreamer and a writer. Far from providing any protective shadow for Alfonso's imaginary pursuit (like the mother did), she amplifies, through a mirroring gesture, Alfonso's half-conscious dreams. To know her amounts to knowing himself and 'lo faceva soffrire il conoscersi' [to know himself made him suffer (UV, 124)].

Reflections through a Dream

The feuilleton is the pure, unsublimated form of the dream. 'Non amo il letterato che rappresenta in tale modo il mondo' writes Svevo in the second appendix to 'Corto viaggio sentimentale,' 'ma adoro il pubblico che lo applaude' [I do not love the writer who represents the world in such a way, but I adore the public that applauds him (Svevo 1968: 499)]. This observation about the reception of an entire genre by the author returns in *Una vita* as a reception of the specific content of that genre by the character. When Annetta proposes to Alfonso that they fashion their writing on the saleable plot of the 'orso domato,' Alfonso replies that 'gli era già accaduto di commoversi su lavori siffatti, commozione però che mai non aveva diminuito il suo disprezzo per il lavoro e per l'autore' [occasionally he was moved by such works, an emotion though that never diminished his contempt for the work and its author (UV, 115)]. The ambiguous coexistence of emotion and contempt – participation and distance – that characterizes Alfonso and Svevo's reception of the feuilleton, is symptomatic of an internal split between the dreamer who is moved by the melodramatic story and the critical reader and author, who can write only by observing and despising the tears of others. In *Una vita*, this internal splitting finds a parallel dramatization: within the story in the *dédoublement* of Alfonso and Annetta, and then within the *discourse* in the relationship between Alfonso and his narrator.

Already, in 1929, Giacomo Debenedetti pinpointed this ambiguous mixture of distance and participation expressed by the Svevian narrator who persecutes his character as a judge, 'ma un giudice istruttore che sia anche un po' complice del reo' [but a judge who is an accomplice of the offender (1945: 62)]. Complicity implicates a repressed mirroring in the discourse and dreams of the other. Although insistently negated by the narrator's relentless irony, participation is nonetheless visible in the text in what Mazzacurati defined as 'lo slittamento interno della scrittura' [the internal sliding of writing (1974: 254)] between the point of view of the narrator and that of the character. With the narrator of *Una vita* we are far from the naturalist posture of impersonality. If the naturalist narrator has been likened to 'una divinità assente dal creato' [a divinity absent from creation (Lavagetto 1993: xvii)], Svevo's narrator inhabits a world long abandoned by the divinity, remaining like a fallen angel, a demonic presence who through Alfonso loves and despises his past, though not quite abandoned, illusions.

Giving vent to the same 'irritata voglia di correggere' [annoyed desire to correct (Debenedetti 1945: 51)] that the narrator expresses towards him, Alfonso stigmatizes Annetta's shortcomings (her coldness, her calculating character, the vanity of her literary ambition, her sensuality) with gestures that on more than one occasion perfectly parallel those of

Between Darwinism and Dreams 89

the narrator. Thus, Alfonso's scorn towards Annetta's artistic pretensions – 'quella donnetta che si era sentita nascere improvvisamente una vocatione avera destato la sua ilarità' [that silly woman who suddenly felt the rising of a vocation aroused his hilarity (UV, 100)] – echoes the narrator's earlier ridiculing of Alfonso, the aspiring writer who 'gettava in carta qualche concettino' [threw on paper some little concepts (UV, 56)]:

> Di notevole in queste espansioni si era che il giovinetto sembrava soffrisse di certo male mondiale [...]. Teneva questi scritti in conto di annotazioni rudimentali di cui voleva servirsi in un lontano avvenire per opere maggiori, drammi, romanzi e peggio. (UV, 56)

> [Those effusions were noteworthy because the youth seemed to suffer from a certain universal malaise ... He regarded these writings as rudimentary notes he would have used in a far future for bigger works, dramas, novels and worse.]

But if the narrator attains an ironic self-consciousness through the description of the self-deceptions of his character, the character's criticism of Annetta only furthers the false consciousness of a failed recognition.

Though mocked, Annetta too has the dual nature of the feuilleton: embarrassing, yet capable of being quite moving. Thus the 'silly woman' is described soon afterwards as 'testa dell'intelligenza' [the head of intelligence (UV, 98)], and immediately again a few pages later as 'la faccia bianca con i tratti marcati dell'intelligenza e dell'attività' [the white face with the marked traits of intelligence and activity (UV, 105)]. This ambivalence, the 'commozione e disprezzo' [emotion and contempt] that Annetta inspires suggests that the woman in fact remains somewhere else, out of reach or sight of Alfonso and the reader. Occasionally rippled by this textual oscillation, the text most often closes over Annetta's subjectivity 'senza che si potesse indovinare l'ordine delle sue idee' [without being able to divine the flow of her thoughts (UV, 180)]. Although Alfonso treats Annetta as an unchanging, unconscious mammoth in whose shadow, albeit uncomfortably, he can dream, change, and project a future, Annetta too, though more opaquely, dreams, changes, and projects a future. Alfonso's story is contained in Annetta's, with all its weaknesses and potentialities. In fact, by remaining in the parallel shadows of Alfonso and the narrator, Annetta reveals both the limit of Alfonso's story and his narrator's ability to tell it, and, in the process, suggests, if only negatively, a critical point of view beyond theirs ... and the novel itself.

Nowhere is the mirroring that ties Alfonso to Annetta more evident, or ironic, than in Alfonso's ongoing protestations of their difference. The most extreme rejection of the undesirable mirror comes after the seduction, when Annetta reflects the image of Alfonso's own guilt, her 'fall' metonymically replacing his responsibility as seducer.

> La sua ripugnanza per Annetta, egli andava dicendosi, era spiegabile, anzi naturale. *Non v'era nulla di comune fra lui e quella donnetta ch'egli aveva potuto conoscere tanto esattamente* come se gli fosse stato dato di saperne ogni azione, ogni parola, ogni pensiero da lei avuto *dacché era nata.* Quando ella parlava dimostrava piú che altro il desiderio di piacere, quando scriveva era vana, e vana e sensuale quando amava. (UV, 216; emphasis mine)
>
> [His repugnance for Annetta, he kept saying to himself, was understandable, indeed natural. *Nothing united him to that silly woman who he had a chance to know so accurately* as if he had been able to know every action, word, every thought she had *since she was born.* When she spoke she revealed above all the desire to please, when she wrote she was vain, and vain and sensual when she loved.]

At this point Alfonso's ignorance of Annetta equals the ignorance of his own self. Alfonso forgets that *he* was the one who complained of not possessing a subtle enough language for seduction; he forgets that he constantly used the vacuous and pathetic tones of the melodrama in his writing – 'Amata sposa [...] Partirò!' [Beloved bride (...) I'll leave! (UV, 202)] is the opening of his farewell letter to Annetta – and he forgets that he loved according to the capriciousness of a sensuality that he himself, returning to Trieste, will compare to that of a 'ragazzo malaticcio' [sickly boy (UV, 246)]. In the final estimate, all his gestures towards Annetta appear to have been inspired by the feuilleton that he so despised. If the narrator of *Una vita* learns to accept his shortcomings by maintaining an ironic distance, Alfonso, being unable to achieve this reconciliation, simply alienates to the other that part of himself he refuses to recognize. The refusal of Annetta is nothing other than, once again, a refusal of himself.

In contrast to these protestations of difference, Alfonso and Annetta's common vocation as writers, a vocation that preceded the collaborative project, offers the crucial instance of reciprocal recognition. The common will to represent their dreams simultaneously unites and divides them. During the fatal afternoon that marks the beginning of their literary collaboration, they describe to one another their work. Each description constitutes the plot of an ideal biography, one that foreshadows a destiny whose unfolding will mock the aspiring authors. Annetta's project, which will eventually take over the collaborative novel, is

> la biografia di una donna unita a un uomo non degno di lei. Si trattava di un'anima d'artista che col tempo faceva sí che il carattere del marito mutasse. (UV, 108)
>
> [the biography of a woman joined to a man not worthy of her. She had the soul of an artist who with time succeeded in changing the husband's character.]

The story's happy ending ironically heralds the rather unhappy destiny of Annetta as wife of the cold and 'ragionatore' Macario, cruel debunker of her artistic aspirations. Alfonso, on his side, confides to Annetta his philosophical project, a distillation of his novel of the noble and rich young man:

> – Se in una società fondata sulle nostre idee morali [...] si trovasse un individuo avente l'energia di porsi al disopra di tutte queste idee, starebbe meglio di tutti ... (UV, 108)
>
> [– If in a society founded on our moral ideas ... an individual existed having the energy to set himself above all these ideas, he would be better off than anybody ...]

Although it is presented in a grey and stern style, his narration also has a happy ending, one that will find its paradoxical fulfilment in the suicide that closes the novel. Both these works, equally ridiculed by the narrator, are, despite differences of genre and gender, dreams of control and emancipation, dreams that each character has hastily fashioned into a literary plot.

The two plots offer enlightening examples of the different materials from which men and women could draw in order to build their identities in turn-of-the-century society. Thus, following the fashion of the time, Annetta tries to force back the suffocating limits of the house by cultivating her artistic soul and redeeming a fictional husband in the process as well; the man, with a dizzying jump, projects his existence into a space of unlimited freedom, beyond every spatial and temporal determination. Both these fantasies seem initially to find a common ground in the feuilleton Alfonso and Annetta dreamt together. If in the feuilleton Annetta 'receives confirmation, and, eventually, affirmation that love really is what motivates and justifies a woman's life' (Robinson 1978: 222) – let us remember the confession that she makes to Alfonso: 'La vita era quella che le dava lui quando la baciava; il resto non valeva niente' [Life was what he gave her when he kissed her; the rest was worth nothing (UV, 180)] – Alfonso as dreamer/reader will find in the feuilleton a confirmation of his fantasies of success, a confirmation immediately denied by Alfonso qua philosopher, who, despising both readers, will state his absolute detachment from the triviality of any plot. Thus, even though both sexes will dream, read and act out the feuilleton Annetta alone will have the dishonor – and the honesty – of putting her signature to it.

For these two characters the warning pronounced by Svevo rings true: 'Il nostro destino sarà di studiare la vita e di non comprenderla perché non avremo saputo viverla' [Our destiny will be to study life without understanding it, because we would not have known how to live it (Pds, 814)]. Alfonso and Annetta confuse life and literature, and thus fail to recognize that a writer's allegiance is not to the future and its fulfilments, but to the past and its disappointments, or, at best, as Zeno will teach, to a present and its 'corrections.' If writing allows the narrator to define the behaviour of a character and the sickness of his age, it represents for the characters an incurable illness that attacks their vital faculties, their ability to live and know themselves. As Svevo wrote, only when literature, 'che fa purtroppo tanta intima parte del nostro animo' [which unfortunately pertains so much to the intimate part of our soul] will die, 'ci vedremo tutti fino in fondo' [will we be able to see each other to the bottom], a prospect at the same time liberating – 'Ci daremo subito del "tu" e c'irrideremo a vicenda come meritiamo' [We will treat each other intimately and will mock each other as we deserve (Pds, 829)] – and deeply unsettling, in Svevo's own words 'macabre.'

On the eve of the aesthetic revolution of modernism – *Una vita* was written in 1892 – Svevo narrates the impossibility of writing a novel according to nineteenth-century models. He openly and self-reflexively expresses this crisis of representation as a crisis of sexual difference. As Barbara Johnson observed: 'It is not the life of sexuality that literature cannot capture; it is literature that inhabits the very heart of what makes sexuality problematic for us speaking animals. Literature is not only a thwarted investigator but also an incorrigible perpetrator of the problem of sexuality' (Johnson 1989: 40). Literature's double and ambiguous pursuit of the problem of sexuality finds an insightful representation in *Una vita* in the *mise en abîme* of Alfonso's and Annetta's story in the feuilleton.

Although from a stylistic point of view *Una vita* goes beyond the naturalistic tradition, it fails nonetheless to inaugurate a new style. Similarly, while the literary and sentimental relationship between Annetta and Alfonso suggests a challenge to hierarchies of class and gender, it fails to articulate a new intersubjectivity. The protagonist of this Bildungsroman is transformed from a man who is author of his own destiny into the man who waits. Through this pause, this shadow, Annetta, the strong other, intrudes into the story, demanding her own *Bildung*. Nevertheless, as Alfonso and Annetta fail to constitute a shared subjectivity in a new story, the status quo has a free hand to reassert its harsh order in the emptiness opened between the I and the other, an emptiness expressed sardonically by the product of their labor, the hackneyed feuilleton.

The Darwinian Plot

The plot of the feuilleton, even if it petrifies Alfonso and Annetta's dreams into clichéd tableaux, is still not responsible for the outcome of their story. The Social Darwinist ideology of struggle, a plot based on the confrontation of strong and weak according to the unmovable laws of nature is the truly domineering master narrative against which Alfonso and Annetta unknowingly rebel and with which they ambiguously comply.

Although radically opposed to the one of the feuilleton, the popularized version of the Darwinian narrative appearing in *Una vita* is oddly complementary to it. Svevo gives a helpful framework to compare the two competing discourses in the appendix to 'Corto viaggio sentimentale,' where he articulates the morality underpinning the popular novel:

> L'egoismo, l'odio e l'indifferenza per il proprio simile sono abominati e non occupano che un posticino misero, celato: cioè occupano intiero il piccolo cuore di ognuno. Il grande cuore, quello che scuote tutta la terra gravata da tanta umanità, è veramente grande e generoso. (Svevo 1968: 499–500)

[Egoism, hatred and indifference for other human beings are abhorred and they occupy but a miserable, hidden space: that is they occupy in full everybody's little heart. The huge heart, the one that shakes the whole earth full of humanity, is truly great and generous.]

The Darwinian narrative accomplishes an exact inversion of this scenario by giving the instincts of self-preservation centre stage. Egoism, objectified as natural selection, one's allegiance to the individual and species' survival, becomes the big pulsating law of life; goodness and altruism, on the other hand, left even without a heart to inhabit, become superfluous literary by-products, the 'voli poetici' [poetic flights] that Macario benevolently concedes to the weak Alfonso. At most, they are troublesome symptoms of a bad conscience. Svevo's irony inhabits the space between these two extremes – the affirmative culture of the feuilleton and the Machiavellian optimism of popular Darwinism – the only space that could account for the displaced position of the human actor, the beast endowed with a 'heart.'

The contrapuntal interplay between the dream world of the feuilleton and the 'real' world of Darwinian instincts creates the sustained tension in the novel. It is between these two ideological narratives that the story of Alfonso and Annetta is imprisoned, though not without having had the possibility of unfolding when the spell of the feuilleton is broken.

'Che cosa vuole quest'imbecille?' ['What does this idiot want?' (UV, 138)], Alfonso cries aloud during one of the writing sessions with Annetta, finally exasperated by their hero's absurd behaviour. And, as if in jest, he kneels in front of Annetta, and unexpectedly kisses her. The story of Alfonso and Annetta could have begun on an independent basis at this point. But Alfonso, left to his own devices, cannot find within himself the gestures and words to express it. Unable to author his own story, he reaches for another narrative to dictate his behaviour. In Macario's disquisition on the art of seduction, Alfonso will find the most expedient tool to further his story with Annetta, and, within the conceptual world of the novel, the point of transition to the reason of reality: to the Darwinian ethic of struggle. By embracing Macario's advice for once in the novel, Alfonso will *act*, like a beast of prey – a 'healthy' novelistic character in Debenedetti's sense – and swiftly and successfully seduce Annetta.

As if retracing Svevo's own cultural encounter with Darwinism, certainly mediated by the reading of Francesco De Sanctis's essay 'Il darwinismo nell'arte,' Darwinist theory makes its way in *Una vita* filtered through a discourse on art. Macario's extemporaneous lecture to Alfonso in the public library on the poetics of naturalism is the first articulation of what will turn out to be a cohesive body of knowledge, sharing a common language and ideas. Macario's speeches are important theoretical as well as structural moments in the novel: through them Svevo narratively explores the implications of poetics, ideologies, and ethical choices, dramatically testing their effects on his character. So Alfonso reports Macario's ideas:

> Parlava di creazione fatta dall'uomo, la quale, per i risultati, non aveva niente da invidiare a quella biblica. Nel metodo differivano alquanto, ma ambidue le creazioni finivano coll'arrivare alla produzione di organismi che vivevano a sé e che non portavano alcuna traccia di essere stati creati. (UV, 77)

> [He was speaking of a man-made creation, one that for its results, had nothing to envy in the biblical one. As far as method they differed somewhat, but both creations produced organisms that lived on their own and did not reveal any trace of having been created.]

As Alfonso himself notices, Macario's language reflects the standard hybrid rhetoric of naturalist manifestos ('alcune idee erano cosí belle che parevano rubate' [some ideas were so beautiful that they seemed stolen]). Fictional characters are 'organisms,' a direct spawn of the self-contained beings of biology ('vivono a sé' and 'non portano alcuna traccia di essere creati'). It is this organic conception of subjectivity that Svevo challenges in *Una vita*, at both a poetic and a theoretical level.

Showing the resilience of the naturalist aesthetic and a certain critical anxiety in approaching a character without character, Alfonso is still today interpreted against this rhetoric of unity and coherence. But it is exactly within the 'traccia imprecisa e contradditoria' [an imprecise and contradictory trace (Lavagetto 1993: xix)] left behind by Alfonso, a trace that contradicts the seamless naturalist creation and 'che impedisce di ricostruire una fisionomia univoca e di configurarle un destino' [that prevents the reconstruction of a univocal physiognomy and the configuration of a destiny], that Svevo unravels and reconstructs his character's subjectivity on new foundations. The 'man who waits' – a first tentative and contradictory sketch of the 'uomo in abbozzo' – constitutes the moment of disembodiment of the nineteenth-century 'organism,' the opening up, to use Renato Barilli's words, 'di altri modi antropologici di vivere' [of other anthropological ways of living (1972: 61); (Fava Guzzetta 152)], and, we should add, of making literature. Far from 'living within himself,' free of any trace of creation, he is involved in an ongoing and therefore contradictory process of self-construction and dissolution, imitation and contamination with the outside world.

If Macario's first lecture could be read as a meta-narrative attack on Alfonso qua fictional character, the second one, taking place during a memorable sea outing, is a direct attack on Alfonso's moral character, the existential economy of the future 'uomo in abbozzo.' Inspired by the marvellous 'fitness' to life of the daring seagulls, Macario illustrates the Social Darwinist doctrine for a seasick Alfonso. 'Solitarii, ognuno volando per conto proprio' [Lonely, each flying on his own], the seagulls are perfect examples of finished and self-contained organisms: driven by an undivided instinct for hunting, built to pursue that instinct, unfettered by excessive intelligence. Coming ironically at a time in which Alfonso was in pursuit of a 'solida salute' [solid health (UV, 81)] that would help him adapt to the hard city life, this memorable lesson is perfectly tailored to his 'weak' persona.

> E lei che studia, che passa ore intere a tavolino a nutrire un essere inutile! Chi non ha ali necessarie quando nasce non gli crescono mai piú. Chi non sa per natura piombare a tempo debito sulla preda non lo *imparerà* giammai e inutilmente *starà a guardare come fanno gli altri, non li saprà imitare.* (UV, 84; emphasis mine)

> [And you who study, who spend whole hours at a table to feed a useless body! Who does not have the necessary wings when he is born, they will never grow on him. Who does not know by nature when to plunge on the prey, he will never *learn* it and *he will uselessly watch how the others do it, without being able to imitate them.*]

Macario's deterministic lesson negates adaptability to celebrate the fixity of a natural system composed of organisms fit for a life of struggle. In this ecosystem, there is no space for the man waiting for leave, the man who lives in the shadow of other, 'stronger' organisms in order to learn ('non imparerà giammai'), the man who, instead of 'appetites,' has dreams. Macario's brilliantly accurate debunking of Alfonso pretensions to 'strength' paradoxically achieves an articulation of the still unconscious existential economy of the Svevian character, the particular nature of his dream that, far from having the form of desire, as Lavagetto rightly observed, is rather a diaphragm that safeguards 'la possibilità di travestimento,' that is, the possibility of imitating the other and thus of becoming something other, what later will be theorized as the virtuality of the 'uomo in abbozzo.'

Profoundly conscious of his difference, and at the same time proud and humiliated by it, Alfonso anxiously asks: ' – Ed io ho le ali?' to which Macario replies:' – Per fare dei voli poetici sí!' [' – And do I have wings?'' – For poetic flights yes!' (UV, 84)]. But as Svevo well knows since his first story 'Una lotta' – staging the struggle between a poet and a gymnast over the favours of a woman – the Darwinian world of struggle permeates the poetic sphere as much as any other. Alfonso's relationship with Macario is a clear demonstration in point, a veiled confrontation that 'si gioca fin dall'inizio, per buona parte, sul terreno della capacità di parlare' [that is played out since the beginning, for the most part, on the terrain of one's ability to speak (Fava Guzzetta 30)]. The word in *Una vita*, as Fava acutely observed, is the site of struggle, and nowhere does it become more clear than in Annetta's literary circle. But it is in the relationship with the woman/dreamer/writer that the Darwinian plot is complicated and potentially subverted.

The strong and wilful Annetta, who scares Alfonso out of his dreams, made her first appearance as an emancipated woman whose determination makes her irreducibly other during the meetings of the Wednesday club.

> Avendola dinanzi agli occhi dimenticava i suoi sogni. Ella era tutta intenta alla formazione della sua società letteraria e la sua naturale freddezza, che nel ricordo poteva pigliare l'aspetto di qualità secondaria, là invece era imponente e dava il colore a tutte le altre qualità sue. *Non era una donna quando parlava di letteratura. Era un uomo nella lotta per la vita, moralmente un essere muscoloso.* (UV, 99; emphasis mine)

> [As she stood under his eyes he forgot his dreams. She was totally concentrated in the formation of her literary society and her natural coldness, that in [Alfonso's] memory could appear to be a secondary quality, there was instead imposing and gave color to all her other qualities. *When discussing literature, she was not a woman. She was a man in the fight for life, morally a muscular human being.*]

The grotesque depiction of the 'muscular woman' is the perfect representation of those women 'so active and aggressive, in short so disquieting' described earlier by Macario. Their uncanny character lies in the fact that they are an aberration from the norm, that Darwinian law that dictates and powerfully naturalizes social relations: a weak specimen who proudly sports around the scandal of her strength.

As the narrator points out, this type 'non poteva piacere a un sentimentale' [could not please a sentimental man] like Alfonso. Nonetheless, the dreamer who although 'alto e robusto [...] sembrava debole e incerto' [tall and robust ... seemed weak and uncertain (UV, 6)] and the woman, by definition weak, yet strong and aggressive – both oddly enclosed within the same descriptive oxymoron – do share a similar existential economy.

Annetta and Alfonso, with the exception of an initial encounter in Maller's office and a final one in the streets of Trieste, spend their narrative existence sequestered in the library of the Mallers' house. They inhabit the library as a cage, which, like the bird of Svevo's fable, they stepped into with the unconscious ambition to rewrite reality according to their dreams. Even if this first symbiosis unfolds as a struggle, in this utopian gesture lies the profound affinity between the Svevian dreamer and the affirmative woman, 'lei che con tanta brutalità – as the narrator in 'Orazio Cima' states – 'difendeva la dolcezza ch'è il mio destino, e che io non sapevo difendere perché me ne vergognavo come di un'inferiorità' [she who with such brutality defended the sweetness that is my destiny, and which I could not defend because I was ashamed of it as if of an inferiority (1968: 107)]. Sweetness is the name of their common destiny; the choice is to defend it against the levelling norm or deny it to court acceptance in the world. Betraying both himself and Annetta, Alfonso will choose eventually, even only for a brief moment, to gain citizenship in the world of struggle.

'Non dovremmo mai accettare il linguaggio dei nostri nemici' [We should never accept the language of our enemies], warns Pasolini in *Petrolio* (1992: 88). But Alfonso, in his desire to prove himself 'fit,' will unquestioningly accept the language of the Social Darwinist Macario and mold his actions and judge his inaction according to the Darwinian ethos. Alfonso seduces Annetta and proves how Macario was mistaken on his account, namely, by judging him 'incapace di lottare e di afferrare la preda' [unable to fight and catch the prey (UV, 183)]. And, more importantly, he implicitly proves Macario's doctrine to be wrong: the weak can successfully imitate the stronger. But at what price he makes his point! Alfonso betrays Annetta and himself, her and his sweetness. To add a further bitter twist to this debacle, it is at the moment of his betrayal that Annetta pronounces for the first time a 'we' that explicitly joins their stories: 'Che cosa abbiamo fatto!' [What have we done! (UV, 179)]. But Annetta's recognition comes too late for Alfonso. The betrayal of an economy of 'weakness' and 'sweetness' short-circuits his story. While Alfonso will fumble blindly through his existential contradiction, Annetta will unfailingly point to it in the letter she writes to him after they become lovers, thus displaying once again a greater insight into their story: 'tu però non volesti sempre la stessa cosa' [you, though, did not always want the same things (UV, 185)].

Seen within the perspective of the man who waits, Alfonso's refusal to win – to marry Annetta – far from being baffling or a sign of a 'coscienza forse non del tutto matura, sia del personaggio che del narratore' [yet immature consciousness whether of the character or of the narrator (Saccone 1977: 151); (Langella 1992: 184–5)] is a gesture coherent with a character who, like Ettore in the 'Diario per la fidanzata,' does not want to conquer anything because no conquest gives possession. Only what is given freely – here, recognition from the other – is worth conquering.

Alfonso, and in a measure his narrator, does not yet know this. But he does know that this gesture existentially defines him, and in the last pages of the novel he keeps returning to it in reiterated attempts at self-understanding.

> Ora sapeva perché aveva rinunziato ad Annetta. Non aveva nulla da rimproverarsi perché aveva agito *secondo la propria natura* ch'egli non ancora aveva conosciuto. (UV, 284; emphasis mine)

> [Now he knew why he renounced Annetta. He did not have any reason to blame himself since he acted *according to his nature* which he had not yet known.]

But his newly discovered detachment, that superior nature of the Schopenhauerian contemplator before life, immediately crumbles as Alfonso recognizes that all life, his nature included, is the stage of Darwinian struggle. No alternative is possible. Confronted with the unaccountable discrepancy introduced by his desire, Alfonso concludes that 'si sentiva incapace alla vita' [he felt unfit for life (UV, 321)], thus sealing not only his worldy destiny but his critical afterlife as well.

Literalizing what Barilli defined as 'la pedagogia immanente a tutta l'opera di Svevo ... un invito continuo a spegnere in noi l'istinto di dominio e proprietà, cui invece l'*ethos* borghese assicurava una fondazione "naturale"' [the immanent pedagogy of Svevo's *ouevre* ... a constant invitation to extinguish in us the power and property instinct, for which the bourgeois ethos assured on the other hand a 'natural' foundation (1972: 49)], Alfonso resolves to kill himself or rather to kill that organism that knows no dream beyond conquest:

> Bisognava distruggere quell'organismo che non conosceva la pace; vivo avrebbe continuato a trascinarlo nella lotta perché era fatto a quello scopo. (UV, 321)

> [That organism that did not know any peace had to be destroyed; alive it would have kept on dragging him into the struggle because that was what it was made for.]

Alfonso's defeat is but the external manifestation of the impasse faced by the young Svevo. Being unable to narrate beyond the 'organism,' the indivisible, founding unit of both Darwinian theory and the poetics of naturalism, the author of *Una vita* simply supresses it in Alfonso, through his suicide.

And nonetheless the dream, the alternative, is present to the very end; in fact it precipitates it. Beautiful, queenly, and dignified, Annetta glides by the marginalized and despised Alfonso in the streets and rekindles in him a by now absurd but irrepressible hope: to reopen the dialogue. 'Non gl'importava piú neppure dello scopo per cui chiedeva quel colloquio; il suo desiderio principale era di riabilitarsi agli occhi di [Annetta]' [He did not care anymore about the purpose behind that talk (to regain his position in the bank), his main desire was to rehabilitate himself in Annetta's eyes (UV, 315)]. Alfonso will not meet Annetta, however. In her place, her brother Federico will come and challenge him to a duel. At this point for Alfonso

> Unica soddisfazione che potesse avere era di convincere Annetta ch'ella sul suo conto s'ingannava. Le avrebbe scritto una lettera, un addio da moribondo. (UV, 320)

> [The only satisfaction that he could attain was to convince Annetta that she was wrong on his account. He would write a letter to her, the farewell of a moribund.]

To the end, self-knowledge is confused with a rhetorical act to be played out in the presence of the other. The letter, an exteme attempt to project a fictional image of himself, is never written. In the place of the failing words, Alfonso offers a gesture: 'Gli rimaneva soltanto una via per isfuggire a quella lotta ...il suicidio gli avrebbe forse ridato l'affetto di Annetta' [He had only one way left to escape that struggle ... the suicide could have restored Annetta's affection for him (UV, 320)]. The suicide is an escape, the final renunciation of knowing either himself or the other. But at the same time it contains a double affirmation: the negation of the ethic of struggle *and* a last desperate invitation to a dialogue. In other words, it contains the terms of the ethical and poetic program yet to come: a confrontation between the Darwinian ideology of struggle and the desire for the other that will result in an ethic of symbiosis and contamination.

Una vita contains two movements. One is reactive, gesturing towards the past and resulting in 'uno smascheramento e una denuncia dell'illusione' [an unmasking and a denunciation of illusion (Saccone, 1977: 146)]; the other is an as yet ineffective rejection of the ideology of struggle, gesturing towards the other, towards a still uncertain future, in an insistent attempt to articulate the rationality of one's difference. In *Una vita*, this attempt fails. The embodiment of this failure is the figure of Annetta 'in mantiglia nera' [in a black cloak], who, pale and silent, disappears into the crowded streets of Trieste – a grieving figure who mourns the unfulfilled possibilities of a common story (a foreshadowing of the mourning Ada who sails reproachfully out of Zeno's life). In the suicide Alfonso and the narrator are together, to the extent that they both fail before Annetta' silence. Her silence becomes the repository of the beyond that motivates the novel, that keeps it in opposition to the Social Darwinism and naturalism that dominate the world it narrates, the *what is*. Annetta's original offer of collaboration and her final silence are the only, yet overwhelmingly powerful, gestures towards *what ought to be*.

Alfonso's 'ostinata passione di essere l'altro, di sostituirsi agli altri' [obstinate passion to be the other, to substitute oneself for the others (Saccone 1977: 151)] is the 'trampoline da cui *Senilità* si stacca' [the trampoline from which *Senilità* leaps out (145)]. The second novel will closely, and almost incestuously, focus on the contamination of the 'man who waits' with strong and weak others, and on the artistic representation of that symbiosis. From this perspective, Alfonso's ending is no ending at all since it marks the beginning of 'the adventure of difference' (Buccheri 1986–7: 85), a poetic contamination that heralds, beyond Darwinian and naturalist narratives, the modernist dream.

chapter four

The Crying of the Statues: Art and Women in *Senilità*

'Je m'adore dans ce que j'ai fait.'[1] Pygmalion's words in front of Galathea's statue can be heard as an insistent echo in Svevo's second novel, *Senilità*, a text that, more than any other by Svevo, obsessively uses the metaphor of figural representation. The two artists, sculptor Stefano Balli and writer Emilio Brentani, seek, like Rousseau's Pygmalion, a representation of the other, the living Angiolina and Amalia, that would help them achieve a successful self-production.[2] Even though the dreams of Emilio and Stefano differ radically, both artists are in search of a body to incarnate them. In *Senilità*, however, Galathea lends her body only to walk away from the artist, leaving behind a shattered dream. Both Angiolina, objectified as a body without dreams, and Amalia, a body consumed by dreams, participate as subversive agents in this figurative process.

In his uneventful life, Emilio 'abbisognava di puntelli per sentirsi sicuro' [needed props to feel safe].[3] One of these crutches is Stefano Balli, who 'era men colto, ma aveva sempre avuto su [Emilio] una specie d'autorità paterna' [was not as educated, but always held over Emilio a sort of paternal authority (S, 335)]. This friendship, that was 'piú intima di quanto Emilio per prudenza avrebbe desiderato ...' [more intimate than Emilio's caution would have desired (S, 336)], grew from a common interest in the 'arti rappresentative nelle quali andavano perfettamente d'accordo perché in quelle arti esisteva una sola idea, quella cui s'era votato il Balli' [representational arts about which they were in perfect agreement because in those arts only one idea existed, the one to which Balli subscribed (S, 336)]. Later, when the friendship with Stefano becomes rather strained because of Emilio's love for Angiolina, the narrator explicitly notes: 'L'arte del Balli era veramente l'unico punto di contatto fra i due amici [Balli's art was really the only point of contact between the two friends (S, 456)]. Art seems to substitute for a true intimacy, not only between the two friends but also between Emilio and the other crutch in his life, his sister Amalia.

Emilio's literary interest has shaped the solitary and grey relationship with his sister, with whom he used to spend uneventful evenings studying and reading. Life breaks into their monotonous existence with the same glitter and promises to be found in the first enticing pages of a novel. Thus, when Emilio narrates his encounter with Angiolina, Amalia listens intently:

> col medesimo aspetto, [con cui] ella aveva letto quel mezzo migliaio di romanzi che facevano bella mostra di sé, nel vecchio armadio adattato a biblioteca ... (S, 337)

> [with the same attitude she had when reading those five hundred novels, elegantly shown off in the old armoire that had been converted into a library ...]

But the narrator immediately specifies that Amalia 'non era passiva ascoltatrice, non era il fato altrui che l'appassionasse' [was not a passive listener, it was not somebody else's destiny to move her (S, 337)]. Collaborating with Emilio in the 'artificial construction' of Angiolina, Amalia surreptitiously lives her own 'romanzo': 'ella guardava dentro di sé sorpresa ch'essendo fatta cosí, non avesse desiderato di godere e di soffrire' [she looked inside herself and was surprised that although she was made in that way, she had not desired to suffer or enjoy life (S, 337)]. The image of Angiolina projected by Emilio's dream dispels Amalia's 'senilità.' The unconscious state of renunciation in which she had lived is replaced by the consciousness of a different self, championed by Angiolina, a woman 'che abbatteva tutti gli ostacoli e somigliava ad Amalia stessa' [who overthrew all obstacles and resembled Amalia herself (S, 382)]. Amalia's 'romanzo' is a self-discovery. The resigned 'senilità' that has enclosed and isolated brother and sister in their own thoughts is challenged by the common project of an unattainable representation of life. Emilio and Amalia enter into the same adventure, but with the difference that Amalia's 'senilità' cannot be sublimated, being a 'tristezza senza parole' [sadness without words (S, 418)], for 'la parola non guariva Amalia' [the word did not heal Amalia (S, 421)]. While Emilio will stubbornly project his plot on to Angiolina, Amalia, unable to represent her life, or, rather, prevented from doing so, will be consumed by the 'corsa vertiginosa dei suoi sogni' [vertiginous race of her dreams (S, 495)]. The repressed word will leave behind only an unconscious monologue, the delirious words of a dying woman.

Angiolina is the fourth and pivotal member of the quartet. Her story remains outside the text, the invisible loom on which the threads of the story of Emilio, Amalia, and Balli merge into a figure. The free and seductive 'figlia del popolo' [daughter of the people (S, 447)] is the surface upon which the eye of the sculptor, the dream of the poet, and Amalia's desire for 'life' project their images and illusions. But only the two artists, the sculptor Balli and the writer Emilio, have the prerogative of representing their dreams, thanks to the possibility of giving them a body, the body of the woman.

The dionysian Balli and his melancholic friend are separated not only by temperament but by two conflicting artistic credos, two conflicting modes of self-production. While Emilio, revels in a 'sentimentalità da letterato' [sentimentality of the man of letters (S, 342)] that continuously embellishes Angiolina's image to create a romantic and unlikely *Ange*, Stefano aims to regain '[la] semplicità o ingenuità che i cosidetti classici ci avevano rubate' [the simplicity or ingenuousness that the so-called classics had robbed from us (S, 336)]. As a first programmatic gesture, he clips the wings of Emilio's *Ange*, who then precipitates to earth as a vulgar *Giolona*.

> Chi avrebbe potuto far capire ad Emilio che la fantasia dell'artista s'era fermata su quell'oggetto, proprio perché in tanta purezza di linee ci aveva scoperta un'espressione indefinibile, non creata da quelle linee, qualche cosa di volgare e di goffo, che un Raffaello avrebbe soppresso e ch'egli tanto volentieri avrebbe copiato, rilevato? (S, 452)

> [Who could have explained to Emilio that the fantasy of the artist rested on that object, precisely because in such a purity of lines he had discovered an indefinable expression, something vulgar and awkward not created by such lines, that a Raphael would have suppressed and that he so willingly copied and put into relief?]

Balli's attraction to Angiolina runs counter to Emilio's; while the latter pursues an ideal representation of the woman, Stefano's eye is caught by the reality that persistently reasserts itself to pollute the perfection of the ideal, an allegory which he wants to represent in the work of art. Stefano's aesthetic, in contrast to the confused dreams of Emilio, is articulated as an artistic manifesto at the beginning of the novel:

> aveva continuato a correre la sua via dietro a un certo ideale di spontaneità, a una ruvidezza voluta, a una semplicità o, come egli diceva, perspicuità d'idea da cui credeva dovesse risultare il suo 'io' artistico depurato da tutto ciò ch'era idea o forma altrui. (S, 335)

> [for all his life he had run after a certain ideal of spontaneity, a desired roughness, simplicity or, as he put it himself, perspicacity of idea from which he thought his artistic 'self' should have emerged cleansed of other people's ideas and forms.]

The roughness pursued in Balli's artistic ideal will guarantee the triumph of his subjectivity over any 'otherness,' whether of form or content. In art as in life Balli seeks a strength that is self-contained and uncontaminated by the world.

The whirl of contrasting passions that envelopes the four protagonists of the novel is filtered both by the second-rate writer Emilio and his sculptor friend through narcissistic acts of representation. Through Angiolina and Amalia, Svevo keenly uncovers the artists' desire to transfigure, the compulsion to represent the self in the other and worship that self in the other. Angiolina and Amalia, whose desire is conveniently ignored or frustrated by the male characters, do not passively lend their bodies to the artists' dreams, but rather resist and indirectly critique them. As a result, the male dream and the women's resistance to it engender a hybrid artifact, a screaming statue.

What Is Hidden in a Statue?

The scene in Balli's studio when Angiolina poses for a sculpture frames, through Emilio's eyes, the representational act that obsessively invests the woman throughout *Senilità*. Despite the opposing strategies followed by Emilio and Stefano in the project of reading and writing the self, and the different media used, the sculpting session articulates an intersubjective relationship between the artist and his object that functions as a leitmotif in at least two other crucial scenes of the novel: namely Amalia's death and Angiolina's final assumption into Emilio's artistic pantheon.

> Su una base informe poggiava inginocchiata una figura quasi umana, le

due spalle vestite, evidentemente quelle d'Angiolina nella forma e nell'atteggiamento. Fatta fino a quel punto la figura aveva qualche cosa di tragico. *Pareva fosse sepolta nell'argilla, facesse degli sforzi immani per liberarsene.* Anche *la testa* su cui qualche colpo di pollice aveva incavate le tempie e lisciata la fronte, *appariva come un teschio coperto accuratamente di terra acciocché non gridasse.* – Vedi come *la cosa* sorge – disse lo scultore, gettando un'occhiata, una carezza su tutto il lavoro. – L'idea c'è già tutta; è la forma che manca. (S, 455; emphasis mine)

[On a shapeless base an almost human figure rested kneeling, both shoulders dressed, obviously Angiolina's in shape and attitude. Modelled to that point the figure conveyed a tragic sensation. *It seemed to be buried in clay, and to be exerting itself desperately to emerge to freedom.* Even the *head*, on which a few thumb strokes had hollowed out the temples and smoothed over the forehead, *appeared like a skull carefully covered with earth to prevent its screaming.* – See how *the thing* rises – the sculptor said, throwing a glance like a caress over the whole work. – The idea is all already there, only the form is missing.]

The living Angiolina, under the weight of the idea, kneels down, encased in dead matter like an obedient *thing*. The head, shaped by the violent touch of the sculptor, has been reduced to a skull silenced as if to prevent a scream. In order to achieve form, the 'I' of the artist, his 'pure and transparent' idea, has killed the living body, has suffocated the other.[4] Pygmalion's anxieties before the living Galathea are unknown to Balli's unproblematic search for self-recognition. The contrasting perceptions of the work-in-progress continue to unfold, moving between Balli's illustration of his idea and the narrator's – and Emilio's – critical view of it:

Ma l'idea non la vedeva che lui. Qualche cosa di fine, quasi inafferrabile. Doveva sorgere da quell'argilla una prece, la prece di persona che per un istante crede e che forse non avrebbe creduto mai piú. Il Balli spiegò anche la forma che voleva. La base sarebbe rimasta grezza e la figura sarebbe andata affinandosi in su fino ai capelli, che dovevano essere disposti con la civetteria del parrucchiere piú modernamente raffinato. I capelli erano destinati a negare la preghiera che la faccia avrebbe espressa. (S, 455)

[But he was the only one to see the idea. It was something subtle, almost intangible. A prayer had to emerge from the clay, the prayer of a person that for a moment has faith and who perhaps will lose it forever. Balli also explained the form that he wanted. The base would remain rough and the figure would become more and more refined up to the hair, which would be made up following the coquetry of the most modern and exquisite hairdresser. The hair was destined to negate the prayer that the face would express.]

Totally absorbed in his 'idea,' which is invisible to Emilio, Balli does not see the violence involved in his allegory. It is Emilio's gaze that reveals the distorted limbs of the woman disguised under the beautiful surface of the 'finished' figure. The scream of pain rising from the buried figure will reach human ears only sublimated in a 'pure' transcendent voice: from the silenced skull will rise only an unutterable prayer.

Since initially 'ad Emilio non parve che l'argilla riproducesse alcun tratto della faccia d'Angiolina' [for Emilio the clay did not seem to reproduce any trait of Angiolina's face (S, 456)], the sculptor teaches him how to 'look.' As a result 'Emilio vide quella somiglianza evidentissima' [Emilio saw that evident resemblance (S, 456)], a resemblance that interestingly is perceivable only 'quando si guardava quella testa da un solo punto' [when one watched that head from one single point (S, 456)], namely Balli's uncontaminated perspective. Angiolina does not recognize herself in the shapeless clay. From the beginning of her posing for the sculpture, she is far from being contained in Balli's concept. In fact, the sculptor notices with disappointment and 'disgust':

> Quella beghina non sapeva pregare. Piuttosto che rivolgerli piamente, ella lanciava con impertinenza gli occhi in alto. Civettava col signor Iddio. (S, 455)

> [That hypocrite did not know how to pray. Rather than piously look to the sky, she glanced up with impertinence. She flirted with God.]

Angiolina's face, notwithstanding Balli's directions, holds an expression of challenge rather than supplication, ultimately defying his fantasy. At the end of the session, the artist covers the statue's sleeping face; this Angiolina will never awake from his dream.

The molding of Angiolina's statue constitutes a powerful metaphor of the violence involved in the production of the 'figure' of the woman. The scene of Amalia's agony, because of the anaesthetizing gaze that Stefano and Emilio cast on her body, constitutes an actualization of the violence contained in the sculpting session. The scream suffocated in

Angiolina's statue finds a voice in the dying Amalia, even as her death is sublimated into an aesthetic experience.

> Amalia era livida; la sua faccia aveva il colore del guanciale su cui si proiettava. Il Balli la guardò con evidente ammirazione. La luce gialla della candela si rifletteva luminosissima sulla faccia umida d'Amalia, tanto che pareva luminosità sua; *il nudo così brillante e sofferente gridava. Pareva la rappresentazione plastica di un grido violento di dolore.* [...] Il Balli disse: – Pareva *una buona dolce furia.* Non ho mai visto qualche cosa di simile – . S'era seduto e guardava in aria con quell'occhio da sognatore con cui cercava le idee. Era evidente, ed Emilio ne provò soddisfazione: Amalia moriva amata dell'amore più nobile che il Balli potesse offrire. (S, 495; emphasis mine)

> [Amalia was livid: her face had the color of the pillow on which her shadow was projected. Balli looked at her with evident admiration. The candle's yellow light was brightly reflecting on Amalia's wet face, so that it seemed to be her own luminosity; *the naked skin so brilliant and suffering was crying out. It seemed the plastic representation of a violent scream of suffering.* ... Balli said: – She seemed *a good sweet Fury.* I have never seen anything like it – He seated himself and looked in the air with that dreamy eye in search of ideas. It was obvious: Amalia was dying loved by the purest love that Balli could offer. Emilio felt satisfaction.]

'It seemed the plastic representation of a violent scream of suffering,' directly recalls the previous description of the statue. While Emilio critically discerns an image of death in the 'thing rising' from Balli's hands, he willingly participates, in the case of Amalia's scream, in the transfiguration of the dying woman. The living form approximating death titillates the artist's imagination, but his representation, as in Angiolina's statue, strives to cover up the fundamental reality of death. Thus, Amalia, the ignored messenger from the realm of the dead, is exorcised into a paradoxically unthreatening Fury ('a good sweet Fury'). In both cases, the artistic gaze effaces the woman, art competing with death in its powers of erasure.

Angiolina eventually escapes from both the 'mortuary sheet' imposed upon her by Balli and the suffocating dream of Emilio. On the other hand, Amalia, thrust back into Emilio's stifling 'senilità,' dies literally suffocated in the inconsistent clay of her dreams. A similar control over the two women is exerted within the narrative structure through the manipulation of the narrative point of view. While the inaccessibility of Angiolina's point of view creates a shadow where her subjectivity is hidden *and* protected from any manipulation, Amalia's thoughts, as they emerge in the narration, occasion her imprisonment in the shadow of Emilio's adventure. His story not only hides Amalia's in his 'cono d'ombra' [the cone of his shadow (Benedetti 1991: 206)], but it co-opts it for his own search for meaning.[5] From the moment Amalia's softly spoken dream of happiness is overheard by Emilio and betrayed to Balli, the narration represents the progressive ravaging of Amalia's interiority. As the 'illness' strips her of all her clothes, revealing her fragile nudity, the narration lifts away the layers of her consciousness one after the other, leading her to death 'misconosciuta e vilipesa' [misunderstood and vilified (S, 484)]. In the final babbled and broken words of her agony, she, too, is left as a screaming statue, an object for the gaze of the two artists.

For the guilty Emilio, Balli's 'purest love' constitutes a white shroud, the last beautifying and redeeming act that accompanies the woman into the silence of death. The aggressive love of the older woman for Balli, 'una seconda Angiolina che lo veniva a turbare nelle sue abitudini, ma un'Angiolina che gli faceva ribrezzo' [a second Angiolina who came to disturb his habits, but an Angiolina who repelled him (S, 415)] is again transfigured by the sculptor to simultaneously capture and suppress the scream. The mold of a *good sweet Fury*, imposed by Balli's 'dreamy eye' onto Amalia, forever hides the menacing sexuality of the other, a disturbing and embarrassing desire which threatens to disrupt the stories of Stefano and Emilio.

The cold ennobling 'love' of the artist, a necrophilic love for the object, taints Emilio's love for Amalia as well. Confronted with her death, Emilio casts *his* 'artistic eye' on his dying sister in the search for a beautifying image.

> Guardò a lungo Amalia sperando di poter nuovamente piangere. L'analizzò, la scrutò, per sentire tutto il suo male e soffrire con lei. Poi guardò altrove vergognandosi; s'era accorto che nella ricerca di commozione era andato *alla ricerca di immagini e di traslati.* (S, 492; emphasis mine)

> [He looked at Amalia for a long time hoping to be able once again to cry. He analysed her, he scrutinized her to feel all her pain and suffer with her. Then he looked away with shame; he realized that in the attempt to be moved, he had gone *in search of images and metaphors.*]

Sempre guardandola egli pensò: – Ella morrà! – Se la *figurò* morta, quietata, priva d'affanno e di delirio. Ebbe dolore di avere avuta quell'idea poco affettuosa. (S, 493)

[Still looking at her he thought: – She will die! – He *imagined* her dead, still, without pain and delirium. He was pained to have had such an unloving idea.]

No prayer that would transcend the reality of death and absolve the guilty Emilio rises from Amalia's bed, only a 'humble protest,' immediately translated into 'il lamento della materia che, già abbandonata, disorganizzandosi, emette i suoni appresi nel lungo dolore cosciente' [the moaning of matter which, already abandoned, on the way to decomposing, emits the sounds learned in long conscious suffering (S, 500)]. Her scream finds an articulation as the voice of silent and shapeless *matter*.

But in the moment that death carries Amalia's story away into silence, its materiality scornfully defies any act of representation on the part of the two artists. Death, simultaneously evoked and hidden in Stefano's 'transparent' allegory of Angiolina's statue, comes to the surface here with a vengeance. The dream of the artist is cast off; matter refuses all disguises and relapses into its chaos. The spectacle of death stages the unveiling of the naked truth: that the two artists live vicariously through the body of the woman. If Angiolina, as some critics have repeatedly observed, metaphorically stages the elusiveness of life (Saccone 1977: 275), Amalia stages the materiality of death; one, following her own desire, disappears in the blinding light of the city, the other in the shadows of a long ceaseless night.

Seeing Grey: Emilio's Artistic Senilità

Balli's representational violence unveils the violence inherent in Emilio's repression of Amalia and her threatening desire, his egotistical preoccupation with perpetuating an image of his sister that is neither problematic nor menacing: 'Non aveva saputo tutelare la vita della sorella; avrebbe ora tentato di conservarne intatta la riputazione' [he had been unable to protect his sister's life; he would try now to keep her reputation intact (S, 497)]. Nevertheless it would be a mistake to assimilate Emilio's desire with Balli's dream of mastery and his pursuit of the idea as a faithful mirror of the self (Robinson 1971). Art is for Emilio a delicate collaborative project, an effort to dream symbiotically with the other.[6] It is Emilio's desire to *collaborate* with the woman (a desire also implicit in his preoccupation with the 'tutela' and education of Amalia and Angiolina) that radically separates him from Balli. While Angiolina, as we will analyse later, resists Emilio's symbiotic dream, Amalia, because of her own desire for a 'story,' participates in Emilio's creation, though, in the process, subverting it with a silent but radical critique.

> ad Emilio piacque di aver creata nella sua mente un'Angiolina ben diversa dalla reale. Quando si trovava con la sorella, amava quell'immagine, l'abbelliva, vi aggiungeva tutte le qualità che gli sarebbe piaciuto trovare in Angiolina, e quando capí che anche Amalia *collaborava* a quella costruzione artificiale, ne gioí vivamente. (S, 381; emphasis mine)

> [Emilio was pleased to have created in his mind an Angiolina very different from the real one. When he was with his sister, he loved that image, he embellished it, he added all the qualities that he would have liked to find in Angiolina, and when he understood that even Amalia *was collaborating* in that artificial construction, he deeply enjoyed it.]

Amalia is a precious partner; thanks to her, a much longed for 'sweetness' is insinuated into Emilio's adventure. In the shadow of Amalia, Emilio can endlessly enrich and correct his fantastic idyll like a work of fiction through collaborative dreaming with her sister, and, exactly like the man in the shadow of the compliant mammoth, live his private dream in the world. As in the fable, the story of association and mutual contamination is also a story of betrayal, as the man, in pursuit of his desire, abandons the faithful mammoth.

From the moment Emilio starts an intimate relationship with Angiolina, the 'senilità' that united brother and sister and allowed their symbiotic dream of a more energetic life becomes so burdensome to Emilio that he shies away from Amalia as if from 'una persona inquietante, di cui si doveva evitare la vicinanza' [an unsettling person, whose closeness had to be avoided (S, 496)]. Even after Amalia's death, Emilio will unconvincingly reiterate the distance separating him from his sister: 'Amalia stessa era stata insignificante nella sua vita' [Amalia herself had been insignificant in his life (S, 501)]. But the poet's symbiotic contamination with his sister survives this last rejection and betrayal, growing instead in significance with the unfolding of the novel. It is 'the ennobling thought of Amalia' that finally will grant a fictional fulfilment to Emilio's love (life) story.

Shockingly for Emilio, the mammoth has desires too, and even though it eventually dies, the presence of its unwritten story opens a powerful critique of the weak and unfaithful man. Even if contained in Emilio's story, Amalia's voice, when heard, reveals the silences on Emilio's part and advances her own interpretation of 'senilità.'[7] During the night at the opera, Amalia's thoughts emerge independently in the narration stirred by the music of Wagner's *Die Walküre*:

> Ma, assorbito da quella musica, il suo grande dolore si coloriva, diveniva ancora piú importante, pur facendosi semplice, puro, perché mondato d'ogni avvilimento. [...] Mai non s'era sentita tanto mite, liberata da ogni ira, e disposta a piangere lungamente, senza singhiozzi. [...] La magnifica onda sonora rappresentava il destino di tutti. La vedeva correre giú per una china, guidata dall'ineguale conformazione del suolo. Ora una sola cascata, ora divisa in mille piú piccole, colorite tutte dalla piú varia luce e dal riflesso delle cose. (S, 428)

> [But, absorbed in that music the sorrow gained color, became even more important, although simpler and pure because cleansed of any humiliation. ... She never felt so peaceful, freed from any anger, and willing to cry for a long time, without sobbing ... The marvellous wave of sound was representing everybody's destiny. She saw it running down a hill, guided by the uneven formation of the ground. Now a single waterfall, now divided into a thousand smaller ones, all colored by the most varied light and the reflection of things.]

Amalia, now betrayed and abandoned to her solitude, wilfully embraces Wagner's grandiose celebration of the impassivity of destiny and finds there that artistic sublimation of her sorrow she cannot otherwise attain. Emilio, on the other hand, still in the swing of his passion, maintains a detached critical eye on the performance. Unaddressed by the narrator, the story of *Die Walküre* – the doomed incestuous love between the siblings Siegmund and Sieglinde – hovers over the estranged brother and sister. Although incestuous overtones are present in the relationship of Amalia and Emilio, the core of their drama is their different attitudes towards destiny. While Amalia resigns herself to fate, and, unlike Sieglinde, is finally crushed by it, Emilio refuses to submit to an idea of destiny, that is, to confront the limitation of his character, namely, that 'senilità' that binds him in a metaphorical incest with his sister.

It is only later on, on the eve of his loss of both Amalia and Angiolina, and at the sight of a truly Wagnerian sea storm, that Emilio reaches an insight into his weakness similar to Amalia's at the opera:

> Al sibilare del vento si univa imponente il clamore del mare, un urlo enorme composto dall'unione di varie voci piú piccole. [...] Ad Emilio parve che quel tramestío si confacesse al suo dolore. Vi attingeva ancora maggiore calma. *L'abito letterario* gli fece pensare il paragone fra quello spettacolo e quello della propria vita. Anche là, nel turbine, nelle onde di cui una trasmetteva all'altra il movimento che aveva tratto lei stessa dall'inerzia, un tentativo di sollevarsi che finiva in uno spostamento orizzontale, egli vedeva l'impassibilità del destino. Non v'era colpa, per quanto ci fosse tanto danno. [...] Emilio pensò che la sua sventura era formata dall'inerzia del proprio destino. (S, 487–8; emphasis mine)

> [The hissing of the wind was joined by the imposing clamor of the sea, a huge cry made of the union of various smaller voices. ... Emilio had the impression that such noise suited his sorrow. He gained an even greater peace from it. *Literary habit* made him draw a comparison between that spectacle and the one of his own life. Even there, in the eddy, in the waves that transmitted from one to another the movement that subtracted each of them from the initial inertia, an attempt to rise that ended in a horizontal movement, he saw the impassiveness of destiny. Even in the midst of such destruction there was no guilt. ... Emilio thought that his misfortune was due to the inertia of his own destiny.]

Brother and sister think the same thoughts as if they were contrapuntal and diachronic stages of the same consciousness. Emilio's reflection – 'se gli fosse stato imposto di forzare con la propria voce i clamori del vento e del mare, egli sarebbe stato meno debole e meno infelice' [If it had been imposed on him to confront with his own voice the roar of the wind and sea he would have been less weak and unhappy (S, 488)] – echoes Amalia's slightly more passive interrogation: 'Piccola e debole, ella era stata abbattuta; chi avrebbe potuto pretendere ch'ella reagisse?' [Little and weak, she had been knocked down; who could have expected a reaction from her? (S, 428)]. Amalia is able to reflect on and question her own 'senilità' when her brother does not have the insight to do so, and her consciousness lucidly precedes her brother's in her final realization: 'Nella sua vita non c'erano però catene; ella era del tutto libera, e nessuno le chiedeva né risoluzione, né forza, né amore' [In her life there were no longer any chains; she was totally free, and no one asked of her either resolution, strength, or love (S, 382)].

Although Emilio's resignation to destiny before the tempest is similar to Amalia's after the concert, there is at least one important difference. While for Amalia 'the marvellous wave of sound' *purifies* her sorrow of any humiliation, for Emilio the 'impassiveness of destiny' is simply a way to *disguise* individual responsibilty: 'even in the midst of such destruction there was no guilt.' These different moral reactions find an explanation in Amalia and Emilio's different view of their 'senilità.' In coherent pursuit of his self-deception, Emilio eagerly shares his 'guilt' for their sad existence with Amalia: 'Come erano stati colpevoli lui e Amalia di prendere la vita tanto sul serio!' [How guilty he and Amalia had been in taking life so seriously! (S, 487)]. Amalia, on the other hand, gave earlier on in the story a very different reading of her own 'senilità':

> Ella aveva parlato altre volte d'amore, ma altrimenti, senz'indulgenza, perché non si doveva. Come aveva preso sul serio quell'imperativo che le era stato gridato nelle orecchie sin dall'infanzia. Aveva odiato, disprezzato coloro che non avevano obbedito e in se stessa aveva soffocato qualunque tentativo di ribellione. Era stata *truffata*! (S, 376; emphasis mine)

> [She spoke other times of love, but differently, without indulgence, because one should not. How seriously she took that imperative that had been shouted in her ears since her childhood. She had hated, despised those that did not obey and she had suffocated in herself any attempt at rebellion. She had been *cheated*!]

The significance of 'senilità' for brother and sister diverges, but not because it splits into the opposing terms of resigned old age and youth (Saccone 1977: 178). If Emilio recognizes their 'senilità' as a choice and a guilty one, Amalia's reflection reveals surprisingly that 'senilità' for her is an imposed trait, something that she had been tricked into, a repression of her desire. While Emilio embraces 'senilità' as a self-defence, Amalia sees herself as deceived into a false religion.

Beguiled by Emilio's example of 'voluntary resignation to the same sad destiny,' Amalia awakens to dreams induced by the passions of Emilio and Stefano. Nevertheless, she is deprived of the means to project her own story, which, repressed, finally finds a powerful, if resigned, staging as inescapable 'destiny' in Siegmund and Sieglinde's story. Unable to attain an affirmative sublimation independently, Amalia yields to Wagner's representation, and, once more, although this time willingly and consciously, she embraces somebody's else destiny, 'the destiny of everybody.' If it is true that 'ella non esce dal sistema, non mette in discussione il mondo che l'ha prodotta' 'she does not escape the system, she does not put in question the world that produced her (Saccone 1977: 180)], Amalia's 'silent revolution' (Benedetti 1991: 210) still manages to unveil Emilio's disguises and the illusion that art stands above the pain of life as a universal and ideal consolation. 'L'arte [...] che canta ed eleva il destino di questi vinti' [The art ... that sings and ennobles the destiny of these defeated (Saccone 1977: 180)] seals Amalia's destiny as if it were a shroud. 'Era nata grigia' [she was born grey (S, 336)] comments the artist Balli, thus essentializing a 'greyness' to which the narrator already from the start condemned Amalia 'piú vecchia per carattere o forse per destino' [older by character or perhaps by destino (S, 329)]. If there is any consolation in the sublimation of art, it is a privilege only to be shared by the artist for whom the spectacle of ruin and destruction entails aesthetic enjoyment *and* the added pleasure of seeing his responsibility dissolved. Thus Emilio reflects after Amelia's death: 'Era passata la morte, il grande misfatto, ed egli sentiva che i propri errori e misfatti erano stati del tutto dimenticati' [Death had passed by, the final misdeed, and he felt that his mistakes and misdeeds had been totally forgotten (S, 500)].

Amalia's death simultaneously stages an artistic, moral, and material erasure. But confronted with the spectacle of her death, the artists' sublimation miserably pales. Emilio as well as Balli will not accomplish a representation either of life (Angiolina) or death (Amalia). Significantly, Emilio's final allegory of the crying Angiolina, a last fragmentary artistic disguise, is obtained only by re-enacting the passage of death, and killing Amalia one last time: '[Angiolina] conservò inalterata la sua bellezza, ma acquistò anche tutte le qualità d'Amelia che morí in lei una seconda volta' [Angiolina kept her beauty intact, but she acquired too the qualities of Amalia who died in her a second time (S, 505)]. The only sublimation the morally bankrupt artist will fully enjoy will be the one afforded by the other's death.

Sporadic as they are, Amalia's reflections further our understanding of her condition; unlike her brother, she does not usually indulge in the creation of mystifying images. Nonetheless, following the night at the opera, Amalia surprises her brother by putting on a disguise in an attempt to escape her destiny. Emilio finds her slowly strolling in the sunny streets wearing 'dei colori azzurri, chiari, su una stoffa grezza' [clear blue colors on a rough fabric (S, 429)]. Her thin figure awkwardly stands out on the Corso, the stage of Angiolina's triumphant walks. She is as incongruous an apparition as the rough linen against the cheerful color of the dress. Amalia's disguise fails to erase the 'destiny' inscribed on her thin body by Emilio, who brings her back home to the 'vestito abituale, grigio come la sua figura e il suo destino' [everyday dress, grey as her figure and her destiny (S, 429)]. On the other hand Emilio's body never objectifies him; he can carry his sadness around the city without being essentialized in the greyness of a dress. It is rather a subjective perception of the other, one that 'ved[e] grigio e sent[e] grigio' [sees grey and feels grey (S, 400)], the whole world, his sister included.

The inertia and sense of defeat that condemns Amalia finds in Emilio'case a convenient and dignified disguise in his 'abito letterario.' While Amalia, at the *Walküre*, reaches a kind of self-knowledge, Emilio searches in that same music for a suitable moral disguise for his subjectivity.

> Egli credeva che il suo amore e il suo dolore si sarebbero presto *travestiti* nel pensiero del genio. No. Per lui si movevano sulla scena eroi e dei, e lo trascinavano con sé lontano dal mondo ove aveva sofferto. Negl'intervalli egli cercava invano nel ricordo qualche accento che avesse meritato *un travestimento* simile. L'arte forse lo guariva? (S, 428; emphasis mine)

> [He believed that his love and his sorrow soon would have been disguised by the mind of the genius. No. For him heroes and gods were moving on the stage, and taking him away from the world where he had suffered. In the intermissions he searched vainly in his memory for some feeling that deserved such *a disguise*. Was art healing him?]

Seen in this context the novel's first tentative title, *Il Carnevale di Emilio*, acquires its full meaning, shedding light on *Emilio's 'senilità.'* From such a Carnival, the 'sosia,' the uncanny double, must be banned: Amalia is unable to masquerade, because she *is* one of the masks Emilio wears, the stark reminder of an existential complicity that 'the artist,' pursuing his sunny muse, has to suppress.

'Per sognare in due': The Poet's Symbiosis with the Muse

The complicity between Emilio and Angiolina is of a totally different nature and lies exactly in that 'artistic' territory from which Amalia is excluded. Although the same desire for a collective dream with the other punctuates the poet's relationship with his muse, Angiolina, unlike Amalia, is baffled by Emilio's desire for collective fantasizing. Before such a desire, she opposes an indifferent resistance:

> La donna ch'egli amava, *Ange*, era sua invenzione, [...] essa non aveva *collaborato* a questa creazione, non l'aveva neppure lasciato fare perché aveva resistito. (S, 358; emphasis mine)

> [The woman he loved, *Ange*, was an invention of his, ... she did not *collaborate* on this creation, she didn't even let him pursue it for she resisted it.]

Ironically, to overcome such a resistance and live his fantasy, 'pur di renderla dolce' [more in the manner of Amalia] 'e indurla a entrare in quelle idee, *per sognare in due*' [in order to make her sweet and induce her to enter those ideas, *to dream together* (S, 447; emphasis mine)], Emilio will be the one *collaborating with the other's dream*, making Angiolina's lies his own. Started as an attempt to appropriate the other, Emilio's desire for a symbiotic dreaming will yield an unexpected surprise: Emilio will be the one appropriated. An ironic example of this collaboration at a parodically degraded 'artistic' level is the letter Emilio and Angiolina write to the tailor Volpini, the only collective creation of their relationship and the meeting point of the well-packaged lies of the rhetorician and Angiolina's 'lies': 'Angiolina era potuta sembrare superiore nell'interpretazione della lettera del Volpini; la risposta colò intera dalla penna esperta di Emilio' [Angiolina might have seemed more insightful in the interpretation of Volpini's letter; the reply flowed entirely from Emilio's skilled pen (S, 464)]. Beyond the failed attempt to dream together, it is in the ambiguous relationship between the artist and the muse that the complicity between Emilio and Angiolina lies, a complicity that starts from the moment Emilio enters into his artistic adventure.

Emilio's literary ambition, a senile *and* adolescent expectation of an unspecified future, waltzes arm in arm with Angiolina in the narration, and, thus, from the very beginning of the text, the problem of self-representation and the representation of the other are one and the same thing. If Balli molds reality, Emilio seems to be waiting for a mold from the outside, a mold that would give form and direction to his life and his art.

> Viveva sempre in un'aspettativa, non paziente, di qualche cosa che doveva

venirgli dal cervello, l'arte, di qualche cosa che doveva venirgli dal di fuori. ... (S, 330)

[He lived always in an impatient expectation of something that should have come to him from the mind, art, or something that should have come from the outside. ...]

Angiolina represents that hoped-for mould. The encounter with Angiolina, 'l'evento che segna uno scatto nella *senilità* di Emilio' [the event that marks a change in Emilio's *senilità* (Palumbo 1976: 71)], is immediately interpreted as the possibility of living a long-awaited dream, of 'composing,' of uttering well-rehearsed words.

Fece piovere sulla bionda testa le *dichiarazioni liriche* che nei lunghi anni il suo desiderio aveva maturate e affinate [...]. Ebbe il sentimento che da tanti anni non aveva provato, *di comporre, di trarre dal proprio intimo idee e parole*: un sollievo che dava a quel momento della sua vita non lieta, un aspetto strano, indimenticabile, di pausa, di pace. *La donna vi entrava*! (S, 330–1; emphasis mine)

[He showered the blond head with all the *lyric declarations* that his desire had matured and refined through the years ... He felt, as he had not felt for many years, *as if he were composing, drawing ideas and words from his interiority*: a relief that gave to that moment of his not too happy life a strange aspect, unforgettable, of pause, of peace. *The woman was entering it*!]

We enter the narration *because* Angiolina, the muse, enters it, opening the floodgates of Emilio's fantasy. But from the first moment, Angiolina plays the paradoxical functions of both a mould (the idealized 'musa' or 'dea') and an artistic and sexual object to be moulded by the artist. The poet is therefore caught in an unresolved tension between two opposite desires: to enclose the woman in an unspecified artistic ideal and to dream symbiotically with the muse. *Senilità* narrates the failed attempt to share an already written romance with an unsuspecting muse, the failed making of a 'romanzo' (both love story and novel). It is exactly in the gap that separates the 'romanzo' already written and interpreted by a unified subjectivity (the idyll rehearsed for years in Emilio's mind) and the living flesh and blood of the experience that Emilio's story unfolds. 'Senilità' is the paradoxical yearning for an already written story. In this sense Emilio's adventure is truly quixotic, Emilio being the last hero of a now impossible romance, and therefore possibly the initiator of a new genre, the modernist novel that represents not Emilio's time past 'ma un tempo che egli sa bene di non aver mai posseduto, ma solo *sognato, sperato*' [but a time that he knows well he never possessed, but only *dreamed* and hoped for (Saccone 1977: 191)].

Nevertheless, both Emilio's striving for a symbiotic dream and the Balli-like attempt to enclose the muse in an image fail before Angiolina's indifference. A kaleidoscopic number of images are worn and cast off by Angiolina as she *resists* representation with the defiance of an impenetrable mask: 'aveva sulla faccia una *mancanza assoluta di espressione*' [she had on her face an absolute lack of expression (S, 396; emphasis mine)]. Emilio deploys all his rhetorical weapons to reduce the threatening indifference of the woman to a reassuring and frozen dream image: 'le vedeva la compostezza e la serietà della buona infermiera dolce e disinteressata' [he saw her with the composure and seriousness of a good nurse, sweet and disinterested, (S, 437)] a decorous posture that recalls the dignified corpse of Amalia. In flight from the familial nest where he is attended by the grey vestal, Emilio tries to recreate with Angiolina the same reassuring nest, inhabited though by a golden muse (expressed, for example, in his dream of the mountain).

In this sense, Angiolina is radically different from the woman tiger, protagonist of Emilio's first novel, a hybrid creature that contains the woman within the male fantasy and through which Emilio can vicariously suffer and rejoice. Angiolina is rather the *indifferent* woman whose resistance threatens to annihilate both the man and the artist. As Sarah Kofman notes when reflecting on the figure of woman in Freud's writings: 'What makes woman enigmatic here is no longer some 'inborn deficiency,' some sort of lack, but on the contrary her narcissistic self-sufficiency and her indifference; it is no longer the woman who envies man his penis, it is he who envies her for her unassailable libidinal position, whereas he himself – one may wonder why – has been impoverished, has been emptied of this original narcissism' (1985: 52). Not only Angiolina, the narcissistic beauty, but Amalia as well represents such a threat: 'Amalia non gli apparteneva nel delirio; era ancora meno sua che quando si trovava nel possesso dei suoi sensi' [Amalia did not belong to him in delirium; she was even less his than when she was in full possession of her senses (S, 482)]. Pygmalion's narcissistic contemplation and perpetuation of his self in the other is now only possible for Emilio *with* the collaboration of the other. But unlike Galathea, Angiolina pre-exists the dream of the poet. Ungraspable, she walks in the world with all the color and warmth of his fantasy, an irrepressible other without whom there is no representation for the self, but whose presence also disrupts that representation.

Along with Angiolina, the medium has to be held partly responsible for the ambiguous and ungraspable character of Emilio's representations. While clay obediently yields under the ordering gesture of the artist, words seem to arrange themselves around gravitational points beyond the will of the writer. The first paragraph of *Senilità* attracts our attention to this immateriality and ambiguousness of language, by opening with the cautious *prime parole* that an unspecified 'he' addresses to an equally unspecified 'she.' [8]

> Subito, con le prime parole che le rivolse, volle avvisarla che non intendeva compromettersi in una relazione troppo seria. Parlò cioè a un dipresso cosí: – T'amo molto e per il tuo bene desidero che ci si metta d'accordo di andare molto cauti – . La parola era tanto prudente ch'era difficile di crederla detta per amore altrui, e un po' piú franca avrebbe dovuto suonare cosí: – Mi piaci molto, ma nella mia vita non potrai essere giammai piú importante di un giocattolo. (S, 329)

> [Immediately, with the first words he addressed to her, he wanted to warn her that he did not intend to compromise himself with too serious a relationship. Thus, he spoke more or less as follows: – I love you a lot and for your own good I want us to agree to move very cautiously–. The word was so prudent that it was difficult to believe it was said for somebody else's sake, and if it would have been a little more sincere it should have sounded like this: – I like you a lot, but in my life you will never be more important than a toy.]

Given the abstraction of the dialogic situation and its actors, this *incipit* could be read as a classical invocation of the muse, yet one which, when transcribed into the secular world of *Senilità*, becomes an unabashed act of seduction. At the same time it is an invocation of and a careful distancing from the muse's power to make the poet go astray from his comfortable if mediocre path.

But another effect of this opening paragraph is to concentrate all attention on the 'first words,' as if they were the real protagonists of the story. The first action is a word, a word uttered to distance oneself, a step backward from a yet invisible other. As Emilio steps backward from his engagement with Angiolina, from the start torn between desire and caution, the narrator, 'che è tutt'altro che ai margini o dietro la storia che sta narrando [who is far from being at the margins or hidden behind the story that he is telling (Palumbo 1976: 96)], steps away from his character by laying bare Emilio's complex defence strategy in the pursuit of a safe passion. But the narrator steps down as well, though less noticeably so, from his role as a writer who could univocally narrate the story. The narrator's insistence on approximating the phrasing of Emilio's intentions amounts to a denunciation of the word as an opaque screen, a manoeuver which, even more importantly, acknowledges his own participation in the deceptiveness of discourse.[9] Emilio's desire for truth proceeds with the narration, and, with the narration, is constantly sidetracked into detours and disguises. Where could Emilio find a better fellow traveller than Angiolina in the undertaking of this insidious adventure?

There is an intrinsic contamination between the travesties and deceptions of the artist and the muse's disguises. Here lies the fundamental complicity between Angiolina and Emilio. John Locke puts his finger on the founding trait that ties the artist to the woman: 'Eloquence, like the fair sex, has too prevailing beauties in it to suffer itself ever to be spoken against. And it is vain to find fault with those arts of deceiving wherein men find pleasure to be deceived' (cited in Johnson 1989: 38). No other words could be a more appropriate admonition for Emilio. The poet's rhetoric and the woman's beauty compete in creating parallel worlds, losing themselves in a merry-go-round of deception. So if Emilio states over and over that 'la menzogna doveva essere tanto connaturata in quella donna, ch'ella non se ne sarebbe liberata mai' [lying must have been such a second nature to that woman that she would never have been able to free herself from it (S, 402)], the narrator immediately corrects the statement by saying:

> Egli dimenticava quanto in altri momenti aveva percepito tanto chiaramente, cioè il fatto ch'egli aveva stranamente *collaborato* a vedere in Angiolina ciò ch'ella non era, ch'era stato lui a creare la menzogna. (S, 402; emphasis mine)
>
> [He forgot what in other moments he had perceived so clearly, that is the fact that he had strangely *collaborated* in seeing in Angiolina what she was not, that he had been the one to create the lie.]

Angiolina's own travesties neatly mirror the rhetorical masquerades Emilio uses to disguise his feelings, each corresponding in its turn to new biographies of Angiolina. The impossibility of representing the other, the woman, because of her active resistance, really amounts to the impossibility of representing oneself announced in the very *incipit* of *Senilità*. It should not be any surprise to Emilio then that 'Col Balli che non la possedeva, ella si *smascherava*, con lui no!' [With Balli who did not possess her, she *unmasked* herself; with him, no! (S, 458)] Emilio's complicity with Angiolina is marked by his sense of guilt, but Angiolina, unlike Amalia, is no victim of Emilio's moral self-chastising. To his mystifications she opposes 'il riso forte delle Baccanti' [the strong laugh of the Bacchanti (S, 385)]; 'lieta, ingenuamente perversa' [happy, ingenuously perverse (S, 359)] she dissolves Emilio's ambiguous juggling with truth and lies into a Dionysian celebration of joy beyond innocence and guilt.

Jacques Derrida, in his reading of the inscription of woman in Nietzsche's texts, explores the complicity between woman, life, and seduction, referring to it as a constellation of 'the veiled and veiling effects' enacted by femininity, and the 'veiling' performed by the artist. While for women the veiling is merely 'an affair of decency and modesty,' for the poet, who is involved in the deceptive choreographies of truth and untruth, the veiling becomes the fundamental act of creating meaning (Derrida 1979:51). In *La coscienza di Zeno* these two movements are intricately woven together during Zeno's dream of Carla, when he indulges in the all too familiar pleasure of Svevo's 'artists' of painting on the joyful and indifferent surface of the woman's face the depth of sorrow, 'una lotta fra la letizia e il dolore' [a struggle between happiness and sorrow (CdZ, 665)]. Once confronted with the reality of Carla, Zeno comes to the conclusion that she lives on a smooth surface oblivious to any profundity:

> la *bellezza femminile simula dei sentimenti coi quali nulla ha a vedere.* Così la tela su cui è dipinta una battaglia non ha alcun sentimento eroico. (CdZ, 665; emphasis mine)
>
> [*Feminine beauty simulates feelings with which it has nothing to share.* Similarly the canvas on which a battle scene is depicted has no heroic feeling.]

Nor may we assume does the painter.

The world of appearance and deception in which the woman lives, rather than being inherently her own, is the defining domain of artistic production. Woman is trapped on the surface; if she cannot live on that surface and reflect the deceptions of the eye of the other (the male artist and creator), she is refused any possibility of survival, and, like Amalia, must disappear into the unformed world of matter. In this system only the woman as artist, an artist that competes with the male artist for control and the ability to create her own fiction, could survive. The woman is artistic, or (a much more troubling possibility!) the artist is truly feminine. If Angiolina's language and gestures are traces, signs of other men, this very mimetic character unites her with Emilio: 'Emilio subí l'influenza dell'amico persino nel modo di camminare, parlare, gestire' so that 'il Balli [...] quando si trovava accanto il Brentani, poteva avere la sensazione d'essere accompagnato da una delle tante femmine a lui soggette' [Emilio suffered the influence of his friend even in his way of walking, speaking, gesticulating [so that] Balli ... when he was near to Brentani could have the sensation of being accompanied by one of the many women he had subjugated (S, 336)].

In this context it is interesting that the first time Emilio feels he is possessing the Angiolina of his dreams is when he, at the moment of abandoning her, succeeds in getting a cry of anguish out of her, of painting sorrow on her face, leaving his trace – or better, finding the trace of Amalia.

> Gli camminava accanto la donna nobilitata dal suo sogno ininterrotto, da quell'ultimo grido d'angoscia ch'egli le aveva strappato lasciandola, e che per lungo tempo l'aveva personificata tutta; persino dall'arte, perché ormai il desiderio fece sentire ad Emilio d'aver accanto la dea capace di qualunque nobiltà di suono o di parola. (S, 434)
>
> [They walked along, the woman ennobled by his uninterrupted dream, and by that last cry of anguish that he elicited by leaving her. That last cry completely personified her for a long time. Emilio's desire transformed her into an artistic symbol; he felt next to him a goddess capable of every noble sound or word.]

Once again a cry ennobles the woman, taming her in the image of a 'crying beauty' ('donna amante, sempre però donna triste e pensierosa' [the woman lover, always though a woman sad and thoughtful (S, 505)]), an image that recalls the 'sweet Fury' whose cry sublimates an obtrusive and uncontrollable passion. The tension between the self (of the artist) and the other, namely an attempt to contain the threat of the overwhelming sexuality of the Beauty and the Fury, finds in these oxymorons a concise but ambiguous rhetorical formulation. Emilio's muse is a hybrid creature: Angiolina's inspiring beauty *needs* Amalia's sweetness and sorrow to grant the fulfilment of his dream.

In the final symbol of Angiolina standing on the altar, the poet accomplishes the painting of sorrow (the veiling) on the indifferent surface.

> Egli la vide dinanzi a sé come su un altare, la personificazione del pensiero e del dolore [...]. Ella rappresentava tutto quello di nobile ch'egli in quel periodo avesse pensato od osservato. (S, 505)

> [He saw her in front of him as if on an altar, the personification of thought and sorrow .... She represented everything noble that he thought or observed in that period.]

It is notable that, in order to achieve a final representation of his experience, the 'letterato ozioso' [idle man of letters (S, 505)] has to resort to a statuesque image to try and save himself from the snares of words, and this final image of Angiolina brings back, curiously re-elaborated, Balli's screaming statue. With a striking inversion, Angiolina, the former kneeling worshipper before the 'priest' – 'nel suo lungo mantello di tela [Balli] aveva un aspetto sacerdotale' [in his long cloth cloak [Balli] had a priestly look (S, 456)] – becomes the goddess on the altar, while the artist, powerless worshipper, now stands before her. Has Emilio thereby achieved his dream of collaboration? Is he giving up the 'disguises'? Or is this only the ultimate disguise?

In the fragmentary story 'In Serenella,' the character dreams of a gigantic pietà emerging from the horizon, representing '[la] Donna che consola l'Uomo inginocchiato e riposante nel suo grembo' [the Woman who consoles the Man kneeling and resting on her lap (1968: 356)]. This dream, which Emilio repeatedly tried to impose on Angiolina, finds its ironic actualization in *Senilità*'s final image.

> Sì! Angiolina pensa e piange! Pensa come se le fosse stato spiegato il segreto dell'universo e della propria esistenza; piange come se nel vasto mondo non avesse più trovato neppure un *Deo gratias* qualunque. (S, 505)

> [Yes! Angiolina thinks and cries! She thinks as if the secret of the universe and of her own existence had been explained to her; she cries as if she did not find any *Deo gratias* in the whole wide world.]

If Angiolina is the one in need of consolation, we could observe that the artist, absent from this final representation, plays the role of the '*Deo gratias* qualunque.' Nevertheless, in spite of Emilio's desire to be needed, the final transfiguration of Angiolina is but another attempt to hide her indifference. The divinity/muse is no *mater dolorosa* and definitely she *does not need* the worshipper. Thus, unable to accomplish his dream of symbiosis with Angiolina or Amalia, Emilio is left only with the consolation of being able to represent it: he finally elevates the ideal symbiosis between *senilità* and life on to an altar.

The question remains open regarding the relation between woman's 'truth,' living on the indifferent surface, and the truth of the poet, the veil of sorrow that redeems the woman. Derrida, commenting upon Nietzsche's text, describes the relation in these terms: '"Truth" can only be a surface. But the blushing movement of that truth which is not suspended in quotation marks casts a modest veil over such a surface. And only through such a veil which thus falls over it could 'truth' become truth, profound, indecent, desirable. But should that veil be suspended, or even fall a bit differently, there would no longer be any truth, only 'truth' – written in quotation marks. *Le voile/tombe*' (1979: 59).

Is Emilio's representation of truth with or without quotation marks? 'Perché circondare quell'avventura di tanti particolari e pensieri strani? Era un'avventura solita ...' [Why surround that adventure with so many details and strange thoughts? It was a common adventure ... (S, 391)] – so Emilio reflects, and, after so doing, keeps on laying veils over the surface, thereby introducing profundity, indecency, and desire into the 'avventura solita.' In Emilio's case the suspicion arises that the poet's intent in dropping the veil, however, is not to create profundity and indecency but rather to cover it. For him, the *opacity* of the surface is what is indecent, putting him closer to Hofmannsthal – 'Truth *is hidden* in the surface' – than Nietzsche. The 'simbolo alto, magnifico' [noble, splendid symbol (S, 505)] therefore constitutes the final veil, but a veil which, by hinting at a hidden profundity, creates the truth of the surface. The indifferent surface of Angiolina's face teaches the secret of the universe, of existence. Tears roll down her indifferent cheeks as if no veil could piously cover her indecent *pudendum*. Thus 'truth,' woman's belief in the superficiality of existence, exposes the poet's truth at the conclusion of *Senilità*, and as a result *the veil is suspended between meaning and its negation*. Svevo, through the representation of Angiolina, transcends the logic of the enchantress (truth) turned hag (non-truth), opting for Derrida's third affirming woman, 'a dissimulatress, an artist, a dionysiac. And no longer is it man who affirms her. She affirms herself, in and of herself in man' (1979: 97).

* * *

While Balli experiences the artifact only as the frozen embodiment of his idea (his self), Emilio experiences the shock of the unpredictable life of the other as it escapes, like Galathea, from the marble of a reified imagination. As in Rousseau's *Pygmalion,* the artistic creation epitomizes for Emilio the repetitive vacillation of character rather than the Bildungsroman's teleology of selfhood. While in Rousseau's *Pygmalion* the artist creates the woman out of nothing – it is in coming to life that Galathea questions the artist's subjectivity – in *Senilità,* and despite Emilio's boast of knowing Angiolina 'come se l'avesse fatta lui,' [as if he made her himself (S, 453)], Angiolina and Amalia refuse to revert to the stillness of the dream, and by so doing they call it into question. Although Emilio creates out of his fantasy the woman-tiger, a hybrid figure similar to Pygmalion's goddess, a *monstrous* concatenation of self and other – 'Aveva sofferto e goduto con essa sentendo a volte vivere anche in sé quell'ibrido miscuglio di tigre e di donna' [With her, he suffered and loved, and at times he felt that hybrid mix of tiger and woman living within his very self (S, 430)], the woman, the radical other in *Senilità,* pre-exists any such 'figure.' Even the final hybrid of Angiolina and Amalia is but a reflection of Margherita, Balli's lover, whose face expresses 'vivacità e sofferenza' [liveliness and pain] an allegory not of mastery but of recognition and desire, the unavoidable and sought after *complicity* of the subject with its object, of artist and woman, in the form of an ambiguous symbiosis. The oxymoron is but the expression of a utopian contamination between self and other, a contamination called love.

The creative act, which, once played out, reveals the unavoidable contiguity and promiscuity of self and other, is not quite accomplished by either Stefano or Emilio. Emilio's 'simbolo alto e magnifico,' the 'figure,' the rhetoric within which he has enveloped his dream throughout the narration, ends up covering, like the sheet Stefano drapes over the unfinished statue of Angiolina, the unknowable contours of the woman, and, conversely, the unknowable contours of the self as a 'lenzuolo mortuario' [death shroud]. *Le voile/tombe.*

chapter five

Leading the Pedagogue by the Hand

Eppure sarebbe tanto bene ch'io sapessi spiegarmi. Invece che spiegare ti racconterò. [It would be so good if I could explain myself. Instead of explaining I will tell you a story.]

Italo Svevo, La rigenerazione

L'uomo ubbriacatosi a chi lo accompagna: La testa mi balla in modo che mi sembra di essere te cui balla sempre. [The drunken man to the one who is leading him: My head is swaying in such a way that I have the impression of being you whose head is always swaying.]

Italo Svevo, 'Frammento'

Woman between Biology and Pedagogy

In a diary entry under the rhythmical date of 30–9–99, Ettore Schmitz records some reflections on marriage and the different desires leading man and woman into it; he concludes with these words:

> è certo che piú onesto di tutti è l'animale che essendo castoro abita sulla riva dei fiumi, essendo elefante nei boschi, essendo talpa sotterra, ed essendo donna accanto ad un marito in una casa sua da ordinarsi, da regolarsi magari da rovinarsi.[1]

> [certainly the most honest animal is the one that being a beaver lives on the banks of the rivers, being an elephant in the forest, being a mole underground, and being a woman next to a husband in a house of her own to fix, order, and possibly to ruin.]

By comparing woman's desire to that of beavers, elephants, and moles, Ettore reduces it to a univocal instinct: the unconscious search for her 'natural' environment. Woman's search for that environment leads her to desire marriage because husband and house stand metonymically for one another. On the other hand, the man (Ettore?) renounces the 'honesty' of the mole and the elephant by formulating his own desire in a way that evades definition: 'L'uomo quando vuole il matrimonio vuole la donna' [When man wants marriage he wants the woman] – but, as Ettore well knows, beyond the affirmation of the instinct, the question remains: What is a woman?

The nature of man's desire is, using Teresa de Lauretis's words, 'distanza, assenza, il tendere a' [distance, absence, the striving towards (1976: 146)], an ontological condition that allows him to live in a space of delayed potentiality. Thus, the husband, who does not seek in marriage the house or the wife but rather the woman, expresses what Anthony Wilden defined as the 'desire of a desire' (1969: 103). By giving an historical and evolutionary perspective to this desire, Zeno defines the humanization of the animal instinct as a complication and a falsification, which he illustrates by the male's effort 'di evocare [in una capigliatura femminile] una luce che non c'è' [to evoke (in a woman's hair) a light that is not there (CdZ, 644)]. 'Woman' belongs to the beyond evoked by desire, a realm of dream and rhetoric.

In 'L'uomo e la teoria darwiniana,' a fable that shares a common imagery with this passage from the diary, man's desire finds a more problematic articulation. In the association of the primitive man with the mammoth, a symbiotic relationship akin to marriage, man entered into the union not as the result of a choice inspired by desire, but rather as a response to need. The failed recognition of this founding reality of desire is at the core of man's 'weakness.' Following Ettore's metaphor to its ultimate consequences, woman, like the animals in adapting to a particular environment, has an incredible advantage over man: she *knows* her desire is grounded in need. Woman's strength in weakness unveils the ambiguous nature of man's 'superiority' as one built upon unrecognized weaknesses. Man's dream of mastery emerges from the experience of slavery, the need for the other's desire.

In 1899, after three years of marriage, Ettore seems to have capitulated to the conventional belief in a necessary, natural order presiding over sexual difference, a somewhat comforting, yet impossible faith for a writer obsessed with the dis/order of things. 'Tutto è fuori di posto' [Everything is out of order (1969: 560)] exclaims Giovanni in Svevo's last play *La rigenerazione*. As for the newlywed Ettore, the question of woman and man's positioning is a source of trouble for the old man. Now it is the disrupted physiology of desire rather than the youthful idealism that keeps displacing the woman. Because of this disruption, she emerges out of the safe beyond where male desire exiled her to question in turn man's own position.[2] Giovanni's final words to Anna – 'E lavoro per te' [And I work for you (*La rigenerazione*, 562)] – find an echo and a critique in Clelia's words, the character in an earlier play, *Terzetto spezzato*, who, to the husband's statement ' – Lavoro per te, *sono* tutto ai miei affari' – replies – E *dove saresti* se io non ci fossi? [I work for you, *I am* all in my work – And *where would you be* if I were not here? (Pds, 1968: 823)].

Knowing that 'il danno viene tutto dal sesso' [all harm comes from sex (*La rigenerazione*, 518)], Giovanni sets himself to work in the dream that closes the play, driven by the anxious yet hopeful realization that 'Questo è uno stato di cose che bisogna cambiare' [This is a state of things that needs to be changed (*La rigenerazione*, 560)].[3] But this confused recognition of the need to change the relations between the sexes still remains bound to marriage, as both a norm and an occasion for transgression. The ensuing desire to educate the woman constitutes at the same time the symptom of a disorder and a timid attempt at correction. At the head of a long procession of self-proclaimed pedagogues, the newlywed Ettore Schmitz inaugurates the pedagogical adventure. The endless number of reflections, sermons, treatises, disquisitions – and, not least, novels – directed towards educating, convincing, and bringing wives, sisters, and lovers to know themselves, have to be understood as tentative detours on the road to mutual change.

Reading Svevo's scattered notes on marriage, woman appears ironically as both the prisoner and upholder of bourgeois society. Svevo wrote in 1897 in the 'Cronaca della famiglia': 'Il mondo' for Livia 'dunque è una bella e buona costruzione ideologica dove ognuno ha il suo posto e merita il rispetto del suo posto e deve rispetto agli altri posti' [The world (for Livia) is therefore a beautiful and good ideological construction where everybody has his own place and deserves respect for that place and owes respect to the other's places].[4] At that time Ettore, describing himself as 'sempre ammirato di quello che potrebbe essere e mai ossequiente a quello che è' [always in admiration of what could be, and never obsequious to what is ('Cronaca,' 67)], and thereby apparently rejecting any biologistic conclusions, approached his marriage as 'un nuovissimo esperimento di sociologia' [a newest sociological experiment ('Cronaca,' 67)]. Armed with Schopenhauer, Marx, and Bebel's *Woman under Socialism*, he undertook the education of Livia:

> certo che se uno dei due avesse cambiato, quello non sarei stato io! Anzi volevo cambiare un po' mia moglie nel senso di *darle la libertà* e *insegnarle a conoscere sé stessa*. ('Cronaca,' 67–8; emphasis mine)

> [convinced that if any one of us had to change, that one would not have been me! Rather, what I wanted to do was to change my wife a little, *to give her freedom and teach her to know herself.*]

The emphatic opening declaration that he will not be the one to change puts the supposedly disinterested project of educating Livia in an ambiguous light. Why should the pedagogue *proclaim* his unshakable position when undertaking the pupil's instruction? The suspicion arises that marriage is not so much an objective sociological experiment as a developing struggle for control: Ettore wants to win over Livia, paradoxically by liberating her. In a letter dated 24-5-98 he expresses unmistakably, under the sway of one of his famous attacks of jealousy, the Pygmalion-like intent to create the woman in his own image:

> soffro intensamente quando mi scontro in te in idee che io non amo. Ne soffro come un artista che lasciandosi andare abbia messo nel suo proprio lavoro delle pennellate scolorite e volgari. Queste pennellate non possono farmi amare meno il mio caro quadro ma – se ne avrò il potere – queste pennellate le annullerò ... (1966: 110)

> [I suffer intensely when I clash with ideas of yours that I do not love. I suffer like an artist who, when not paying attention, put into his work some vulgar and discolored brushstrokes. These brushstrokes cannot make me love my dear painting less but – if I have the power to do so I will erase them ...]

But just as Emilio Brentani fails in *Senilità* to convert Angiolina to socialism, discovering that 'la figlia del popolo teneva dalla parte dei ricchi' [the daughter of the people sided with the rich (Svevo 1993: 447)], Ettore, for similar reasons, fails to educate Livia:

> Già per quella borghese la cosa essenziale è di viver in buona pace con tutti e tenersi le proprie idee nella piccola testa difesa da tanti capelli; *non le importa di convincere*. ('Cronaca,' 68; emphasis mine)

[After all for that bourgeiois the essential thing is to live in good peace with everybody and keep her own ideas in her little head protected by her thick hair; *she does not care to convince.*]

The failure of his attempt to proselytize Livia teaches Ettore that the other is impermeable to change, but what disappoints him is not her indifference to his teachings per se, but rather her indifference about participating in them ('she does not care to convince,' that is, in this case, *to teach herself*). This reveals how the agonistic desire formalized in the pedagogic pose is, more than a struggle for control, a desire for engagement, for reciprocal contamination.

Livia refuses to enter the rhetorical arena Svevo and his characters inhabit. Moving in a world where words are harmless, everyday tools endowed with a simple use-value, Livia is beyond the reach of Ettore's educational project. Frustrated in his effort, Ettore must finally recognize, with mixed admiration and spite, that: 'Ella non convinse nessuno ma la mia casa *somiglia* piú a lei che a me' [she did not convince anybody, but my house *resembles* her more than me ('Cronaca,' 68; emphasis mine)]. Contamination happens in unexpected ways. By refusing to engage in the fight, Livia affirms her authority; rather than being changed (convinced), she changes the house, and, we may presume, by metonymical extension, the husband as well.

But earlier on, in the 'Diario per la fidanzata,' started on 1 January 1896, during Ettore's engagement with Livia, Ettore's view of man's 'association' with the woman had been cast in very different terms. There Ettore expresses a desire quite the opposite of the one voiced in the 'Cronaca della famiglia,' to change himself and resemble Livia: 'Scrivendo ho le lacrime agli occhi dal dolore *di non somigliarti di piú*' [As I write my eyes fill up with tears from the regret *of not resembling you more*; emphasis mine].[5] The desire for change is now cast in terms of a desire for a common language; Ettore's yearning for the difference of the other is a yearning for Livia's 'parola franca e semplice' [honest and simple word ('Diario,' 784)]. But immediately despairing of his own change, he warns Livia against 'il *terribile rètore* che in me è sempre in guardia' [*the terrible rhetorician* who in me is always awake ('Diario,' 784; emphasis mine)]. The rhetorician, who later will confidently undertake the woman's education, is described now as a sort of evil spirit that threatens at any moment to take hold of Ettore and falsify his dialogue with Livia. To express both his desire to change himself and its unlikeliness, Ettore writes: 'Per diventare uguale a te con la tua semplicità d'espressione non mi basterebbe neppure di divenire sano e forte!' [In order to become like you with your simplicity of expression it would not even suffice to become healthy and strong! ('Diario,' 783–4)]. This is the very desire and hope Zeno has 'di poter finire col somigliare ad Augusta che era la salute personificata' [to end up resembling Augusta who was the personification of health (CdZ, 645)]. As in Zeno's case, Ettore's sickness, the intersubjective desire to change or to be changed, separates him from Livia. This sickness coincides with language, namely a way of expressing himself '(che accarezza) sempre piuttosto l'idea che il sentimento!' [(that favors) always the idea over the feeling ('Diario,' 784)]. After all, Ettore as well as Svevo's 'uomini in abbozzo' – 'tutti apostoli di qualche idea o del *nulla*!' [all apostles of some idea or of *nothingness*! ('Cronaca,' 68)] – do have a fixed and crystallizing environment: they swim like fishes in a sea of discourse.

The pedagogical project, a soapbox for the rhetorician, is therefore defined by two opposing though complementary tendencies: a predatory desire to change the other, and a subterranean desire to be changed, to be educated. The pedagogue, while enamoured of his own word, searches for the wisdom (health) of the pupil, the quiet knowledge of the one who does not want to teach. In both cases it is in the rhetorical sphere, an ambiguous dimension where deception and illumination intersect and blur into one another, that Svevo and his characters strive for self-knowledge: in the gesture of teaching the other to know herself, the original desire to know one's own self is disguised, and, as we shall see, perhaps even realized.

This ideal history of the progress of Ettore's ideas on the association of man and woman, is reversed once we look at the biographical passages chronologically. From the first desire, voiced in the 'Diario per la fidanzata,' to emulate the difference of the other, Ettore comes to perceive Livia's difference as a lack that inspires his decision 'di darle la libertà' [to give her freedom] by teaching her 'a conoscere se stessa' [to know herself]. But the desire to change Livia is soon transformed from a project of enlightenment into an attempt to proselytize – that is, to save the self put in question by the difference of the other – and finally settles into the very traditional desire of molding the wife in the husband's image. The pedagogical impulse submits to the reliable bounds of social convention. But however we want to read such a progression, it is indisputable that the association of man and woman is the stage throughout Svevo's fictional production of a conflicted consciousness, torn between a persistent 'malcontento' concerning the relations between the sexes and a resigned but soothing irony, one that allows an elegant if ephemeral synthesis of irreconcilable desires.

Mario Lavagetto, commenting on the failure of Ettore's educational project with Livia, observes:

> La moglie non è un personaggio letterario: non si lascia plasmare, né sedurre; si pone agli antipodi della letteratura insieme ai contratti, agli impegni, ai 'valori' che Svevo cercherà di condividere. (1986: 16)
>
> [The wife is not a literary character, she does not let herself either be molded or seduced; she stands at the antipodes of literature, together with the contracts, commitments and 'values' that Svevo will try to share.]

While Lavagetto makes a plausible assessment of Livia's resistance to pedagogy, it remains doubtful whether the literary characters, the fictional women, let themselves be molded, seduced, or convinced by the male characters any more than Livia does. Ettore's ambiguous economy of pedagogy is carried over to the fictional world where it is mercilessly scrutinized for its both naive and calculating self-deceptions. Svevo's writers, in performing the 'apostolic' task of educating and seducing women, yield simultaneously to Pygmalion's desire to mold and create the other and to the desire, even need, for a truly intersubjective relationship, a reciprocal contamination.

* * *

The literary *pendant* to Svevo's project of educating Livia is Emilio's attempt in *Senilità* to change Angiolina while making sure that his own life remains quiet and unchanged. Since the time of Plato's *Symposium*, education has unfolded as seduction, and *Senilità* openly stages the pitfalls of such an education, bringing the dimension of sexual desire to the foreground. 'Non sarebbe stato meglio di renderla meno onesta e piú astuta?' [Would it not have been better to make her less honest and somewhat more cunning? (S, 339)] reflects Emilio soon after encountering Angiolina and 'Fattasi questa domanda, gli venne la magnifica idea d'educare lui quella fanciulla' [He had no sooner asked himself this question, than he had the wonderful idea of educating the girl himself (S, 339)]. Like the good old man of the 'Novella,' Emilio climbs on a grand moral pedestal from which he can seduce without being seduced (into any moral responsibilities). 'Cessò di baciarla [...] e, per insegnarle il vizio, assunse l'aspetto austero di un maestro di virtú' [He stopped kissing her ... and, in order to teach her depravity, he took on the austere countenance of a teacher of virtue (S, 340)]. But because of the pupil's readiness to absorb the lesson in support of loose conduct ('Ella era in verità come egli l'aveva voluta, e gli dava l'amore senza legami, senza pericolo' [In truth she was exactly how he wanted her to be; she was offering him a love without ties or dangers (S, 350)], Emilio's aroused jealousy dictates a new and inverted 'educational' strategy.

The suspicion that Angiolina might have attended other 'schools' prompts the desire in Emilio to recreate an Angiolina 'onesta,' so that he can be lulled by the reassuring illusion 'd'essere stato lui il corruttore della fanciulla' [of having been the one to corrupt the girl]. The impossible – thus incredibly desirable – actualization of this dream would amount to true possession. In an attempt to undo the earlier extravagant sermons on the shortcomings of honesty, this approach 'doveva consistere nel farle sentire che dolcezza sia il rispetto per darle il desiderio di conquistarselo' [would consist in making her feel how sweet it was to be respected and therefore give her the desire to win such respect (S, 384)]. But far from being molded by this modern Pygmalion, Angiolina chooses, as an intelligent and discriminating pupil, the teachings that best suit her. Seen through Emilio's eyes, Angiolina remains unknowable. But what is truly unknowable is what Emilio ultimately wants her *and therefore himself* to be.

Pedagogy in Emilio's hands is a highly versatile, though ultimately ineffective means of asserting control over the woman. If the education as seduction guarantees him a noncommittal possession, her promiscuity leads him to use education as a pious veil to recreate her virginity. To further this end, religion, long banished from his life, is enthusiastically embraced as a possible seal of Angiolina's virtue, as a handy disguise for a too disquieting woman – 'La religione addobbava la donna desiderata' [Religion adorned the desired woman (M, 252)], observed another Svevian pedagogue. In the frantic activity of covering up a feared 'essence' that would reduce his dreams to dust, Emilio acts like Nietzsche's ridiculed pedagogue who 'procures artificial limbs, wax noses, spectacled eyes' for the unfortunate pupil.[6] The final abortive result of this education as pastiche is the reassuring chimera of the crying Angiolina at the end of the novel.

Once education fails as disguise, Emilio reaches for a conception of woman borrowed from scientific and naturalist discourses:

> Perché disperarsi, perché indignarsi di leggi di natura? Angiolina era stata perduta già nel ventre della madre [...] vittima essa stessa di una legge universale. Rinasceva finalmente in lui l'antico naturalista convinto. (S, 395–6)

Leading the Pedagogue by the Hand 135

[Why despair, why be indignant against the laws of nature? Angiolina was already lost in the womb of her mother ... a victim herself of a universal law. The old fervent naturalist was finally reborn in him.]

Thus disillusioned about the possibility of molding Angiolina, Emilio reverts to the objectifications of physiognomy. Even a sham scientist like Franz Joseph Gall, the founder of phrenology, is a handy tool for a last attempt to control Angiolina:

> Ella portava la testina eternamente inclinata sulla spalla destra. – Segno di vanità, secondo il Gall – osservava Emilio, e con la serietà di uno scienziato che fa degli esperimenti, aggiungeva: – Chissà che le osservazioni del Gall non sieno meno errate di quanto generalmente si creda? (S, 351–2)

[She held her gracious head eternally bent over the right shoulder. – A sign of vanity, according to Gall – observed Emilio, and with the seriousness of a scientist performing an experiment, he added: – May it be possible that Gall's observations are less erroneous than is commonly believed?]

This essentialized definition of both female and physical character sanctions Angiolina's imperviousness to the influence of education while protecting Emilio from her threatening difference. But Emilio's desire, as well as Svevo's, does not rest with such an image. Svevo's obsessive focus on the economy of pedagogy and seduction works exactly against such an ideology of sexual difference, investigating instead the mutual contaminations of educator and educated, seducer and seduced.

The belief that woman is beyond education will find a highly influential theorization, shortly after the 1898 publication of *Senilità*, in Otto Weininger's 1903 book *Geschlecht und Charakter*. For Weininger woman is endowed with great 'imitative powers' but no original capacity that would distinguish her from the world; man, on the other hand, possesses a strong unified consciousness that if cultivated can attain genius. Ironically, Emilio, who lives in constant pursuit of a *Bildung*,[7] seems to be, like the Weiningerian woman, beyond education. If Stefano Balli in his self-assurance, impervious to any external influence, constitutes an embodiment *avant la lettre* of Weininger's ideal male, Emilio displays, in Weiningers' words, a 'weak' identity, one that waits for an external mold to define itself.[8] For Emilio education coincides with imitation. Like all Svevian characters, he cultivates his own dream of genius while pursuing an infinite education in the shadow of others.

In the shadow of Balli, Emilio will try to learn his strength. The painful 'cena dei vitelli' [calves' supper], attended by the two friends and their respective lovers, was organized to give Emilio, according to Balli's intention, 'una lezione in piena regola' [a full-fledged lesson (S, 367)]. Following a system 'che pareva dovesse essere la brutalità' [that apparently consisted in brutality (S, 367)], Balli humiliates and abuses the women without sparing his timid friend. The cruel lesson does nothing, however, but reiterate Emilio's weakness, a weakness that makes him more than ever akin to the women.

In the aftermath of this failure, the idea of *Bildung* is eventually substituted by the idea of *cure*. Balli's teaching is meant to start a healing process – 'Il Balli s'era proposto di *curare* definitivamente l'amico' [Balli resolved to *cure* his friend for good (S, 407; emphasis mine)] – whose goal is to restore the impaired man to his male wholeness and individuality.[9] But such a cure is finally unattainable, and, more importantly, undesirable. Emilio eventually recognizes that

> non avrebbe saputo contenersi altrimenti perché gli pareva che *la dolcezza* fosse la condizione essenziale per poter godere. (S, 374; emphasis mine)
>
> [he could not have behaved otherwise because he felt that *sweetness* was the essential condition for being able to take pleasure]

'Dolcezza' is the very form of Emilio's desire and as such is beyond healing and education. This founding 'weakness' that unites Svevo's man to the women characters, and which was at first dreaded as a crippling inferiority, will eventually be recognized and accepted – under the name of 'malattia' – as 'quello che [l'umanità] ha di meglio [the best part of humanity (1966: 859)]. The pedagogical enterprise can be correctly understood only within this existential economy as a strategy for the pursuit of 'dolcezza,' the desire expressed during Emilio's ambiguous socialist sermon to Angiolina '[di] sognare in due' [about dreaming together].

A successful *Bildung*, one that would eventually afford a ground for the pedagogue's activity, depends on the stability of the subject position, or, in Weiningerian terms, on an independent 'essence.' But Emilio's 'essence,' his 'feminine' weakness, his desire for 'dolcezza,' is inextricably interwoven from the start with the supposed 'essence' of the other. This founding contamination between self and other finds its formalization in the pedagogic act, which is, as we saw, a deeply contradictory enterprise that simultaneously structures the intersubjective relation and strives to repress and hide it. These contradictions result in the failure of the character's *Bildung*, a failure to achieve both self-knowledge and knowledge of the other. As a result, the education of man is displaced into the education of the woman, the only education man can have.

In the 'Profilo Autobiografico,' Svevo writes that 'molti capitoli [di *Senilità*] furono scritti con l'intento di preparare l'educazione di Angiolina' [many chapters of [*Senilità*] were written to prepare Angiolina's education (1968: 804)]. Conceived as a more or less calculated sermon for Giuseppina Zergol, the 'real' Angiolina, *Senilità*'s educational impetus overflows the borders of the fictional work. We don't know to what extent the instructional manual failed or succeeded in its attempt to enlighten the woman, but its pedagogical usefulness was not exhausted there. It pops out again during Livia and Ettore's honeymoon as essential reading for the young bride. What kind of lesson did Ettore expect to impart to her? Perhaps more than a lesson, what this act reveals is the search for a physically present female reader, Ettore's desire to make a confession, a confession that might teach him, while teaching the other, about himself.

Senilità constitutes a powerful critique and distantiation from any pretence of changing the woman under the guise of education, and in the process it unveils the driving forces behind such a desire. Assuming that the woman does not know what she wants, the man wants to teach her; but paradoxically it is the teacher, in search of recognition, that needs the pupil and not vice versa. The woman *is* (albeit someone unknown, who, in order to allow the free unfolding of desire, has to remain unknown), she does not need to convince. The contradictions inherent in the pedagogic project lead back to woman's conflicted position: if, at the level of the plot (whether as sister, mother, wife or lover), she is simply a manipulated object of sexual desire, in the intersubjective sphere of writing, she is the instance occasioning the dialogue that inaugurates the novel.[10] The desire to 'educate' Angiolina cannot be reduced to a ploy, albeit a highly roundabout one, to conquer her; rather it betrays, as the biographical occasion for the novel confirms, the search for an interlocutor, an other indispensable for the pursuit of self-knowledge. Svevo's persistent need to share his experience points to the desire for a dialogue that nonetheless remains a monologue. Between the words of the rhetorician (teacher and writer) and the inscrutable silence of the other (pupil and reader), the Socratic imperative 'know thyself' hangs suspended as an ironic reminder of the illusory hierarchies of education.

Who Will Educate the Educators?

The 'giovane indebolito' [weakened young man], aging protagonist of 'La Novella del buon vecchio e della bella fanciulla'[11] (The Story of the Good Old Man and the Beautiful Girl), lives at many years' distance the same adventure as Emilio, 'il vecchio giovane' [the young old man]. Surely the old and the young display different styles in the pursuit of 'love': the young, carried by passion, 'gettano per aria almeno la loro casa credendo che per andare a letto con una donna occorra prima conquistare, creare o distruggere' [turn their homes upside down, believing that, in order to sleep with a woman, you must first conquer, create or destroy (NB, 23)], while the old 'vi si abbandonano in piena consapevolezza ed entrano nel letto della colpa solo con debito riguardo ai raffreddori' [abandon themselves to passion in full awareness and enter the bed of guilt only with due regard to colds (NB, 23)]. Nonetheless, both lovers make the same mistakes. 'Come tutti i vecchi e i giovani, [il buon vecchio] fece quello che gli piacque pur sapendo meglio' [Like all the old and young [the good old man] did what he liked although he knew better (NB, 27)].

Like Emilio before him, the old man seduces the woman while assuming the becoming pose of the benevolent pedagogue ('Che scopo c'era ormai di conservare l'aspetto odioso del seduttore?' [What was the use now to keep the odious attitude of the seducer? (NB, 28)]. Then, when the presence of other men threatens his 'schooling,' he undertakes to actually educate her by prefacing his love-making with sermons:

> Guai se si fosse fidata di altri come s'era fidata di lui. Nella gelosia faceva capolino la propria colpa. E' perciò che a compensare il proprio iniquo esempio, il vecchio s'abituò a predicare la morale proprio quando faceva all'amore. (NB, 31)

> [God forbid that she came to trust others as she had trusted him. In his jealousy glimmered a sense of guilt. That is why, in order to amend his bad example, the old man took up the habit of preaching morality exactly when he was making love.]

By seducing (*se-ducere*, to lead apart) and educating (*ex-ducere*, to take out) the old man maintains the illusion, as Emilio had before him, of carrying the young woman along his path. But not unlike Angiolina, it is in fact 'la fanciulla in cenci colorati' [the girl in colorful rags] who, walking through a Trieste emptied by the war, imperiously enters the life of the old man, himself resting anxiously, like the deserted city, on the verge of a dramatic change. The old man 'conquiso' [conquered (NB, 23)] by the childish eye of the girl follows her 'con il passo del conquistatore' [with the step of the conqueror]. The paradoxical reversals investing the bond between the seducer-pedagogue and the woman, only partially explored in *Senilità*, here structure the plot which relentlessly explores the ambiguous economy of pedagogy with the detachment and sober irony of an eighteenth-century 'conte philosophique.'

In light of Svevo's previous narratives, Daniela Bini reads this late story as 'un racconto [...] particolarmente emblematico della dicotomia contemplazione-azione' [a story ... particularly emblematic of the dichotomy contemplation-action (1978: 353)]. But this opposition finds quite a different configuration in the life of the old man; after all things have changed since Emilio's exploits with Angiolina. Following the uncertain beginnings of the good old man's adventure, the narrator reflects on the differences separating old and young lovers:

> I giovani dopo un poco di esperienza od anche prima di averne alcuna trovano tutto quello che occorre mentre il vecchio è un amatore disorganizzato. La macchina per fare all'amore manca in essi di almeno una rotella. (NB, 25)

> [Young people, after having some experience or even before having any, find everything that is needed while an old man is a disorganized lover. The machine for making love in them is missing at least one wheel.]

The context soon clarifies the nature of this missing wheel. When still on the trolley under the indiscrete eyes of the crowd, the good old man gropes for a word or gesture that would assure him of the complicity of the woman without betraying his desire: 'Infine il vecchio non inventò ma ricordò' [Finally the old man did not invent but remembered (NB, 25)]. The love of the old man is not carried by the upsurge of instinct, nor does it follow the geometry of reason; instead it finds a voice from far away, a memory of the instinct, a fragment of another life, filtered through reason. Action and contemplation are collapsed in memory, every action being already the remembering of a past one. The adventure just starting is a late and unexpected memory of youth conjured up by the woman: 'il vecchio sentendosi deliziosamente colpevole e deliziosamente giovine [pensò]: – "La gioventù ritorna"' [the old man feeling deliciously guilty and deliciously young [thought]: – 'Youth is coming back' (NB, 23)]. In this configuration, any clear-cut distinction between action and contemplation or instinct and reason is undermined, if it ever existed; the opposite terms merge into one another, creating the scene of what Svevo fittingly called the wild old age (Pds, 844)].[12]

To the extent that the gestures and desires of the old man are remembrances, they constitute an inheritance, always a burdensome one, of the young man's experience. Svevo noted in his diary: 'Ho il dubbio però che mutando di desideri non mi muto essenzialmente. Forse l'essenziale è il modo' [I have the doubt that although my desire changes, I essentially do not change. Perhaps what is essential is style (Pds, 828)]. The unfolding of the good old man's adventure exposes the 'modo essenziale,' the familiar ritual by which all Svevian characters seek to fulfil their desire: the 'falsificazione' of the 'avventura comunissima' [very common adventure]. 'Ecco una giovinetta ch'io comprerò ... se è in vendita' [Here it is a girl that I will buy ... if she is on sale (NB, 24)]. This crude but honest initial statement of the old man's intention, if pursued as such, risks reducing his adventure to a hurried business transaction. To avoid this danger, the intention is immediately 'corrected,' and thereby hopelessly complicated, by the desire to have a '*vera* avventura [...] un'avventura in cui c'entri anche il cuore' [*true* adventure ... an adventure in which the heart plays a part as well (NB, 23; emphasis mine]). But the old man's correction of the common adventure differs significantly from that of the young man.

Emilio's adventure with Angiolina is a metaphorical pursuit of life. Once Emilio lets the woman go, he can take safe refuge in the 'senility' of nostalgic dreams in which he is lulled by the thought of her unattainability. 'Ci pensava come un vecchio alla propria giovinezza' [he thought about her like an old man of his youth], thereby creating 'senilità,' the distance of old age. On the other hand, for the old man the pursuit has become way too literal; for him there is no escape left in Emilio's metaphorical 'senilità,' by now a crystallized old age.[13] 'Desideroso di vivere e di agire' [eager to live and act (NB, 41)] the old man has only one direction he can go against a current that wants to carry him further and further away from life. He cannot afford to lose the young girl, and thus his 'falsification' will be formalized into a theory, an ethical treatise on the relations between youth and old age, a bond that will grant him an extended youth as long and unfinished as writing itself.

The *legame* between the 'bella fanciulla' and the 'buon vecchio,' a bond created by seduction and education, can be best understood in structural rather than ethical terms. Usually in Svevo's works the striving for authority is cast in terms of superiority and inferiority, but in the case of the old man the preoccupation is rather one of leading and following; what appears to be at stake in the relationship is the physical position of the actors, and even more importantly for Svevo, the affirmation of the necessity of such a positioning, the inalienability of the bond.

During the time of their physical encounters, the pedagogue-seducer has the comforting sensation of being the one who sets the pace of the *liaison*: 'la giovinetta camminava di conserva col vecchio' [the young girl walked along together with the old man (NB, 31)]. But the sudden visitation of sickness confines him to his room, where, while sitting by the window looking enviously at life passing by and disappearing around the corner, he catches sight of his young woman walking with a 'zerbinotto' [fop]. The old man is immediately overwhelmed by jealousy and above all by the sensation that life is leaving him behind: 'Non era piú la vita altrui che passava per quella via, era la propria' [It was no longer somebody else's life that walked by in that street, it was his own (NB, 37)]. In order to lead again, the old man 's'(attaccò) ad una manifestazione di forza,' [(stuck) to a manifestation of strength]:

> Le avrebbe dato del denaro. Quanto? Due ... tre ... cinquecento corone. Il denaro bisognava darlo se non altro per acquisire il diritto di educare. Poi l'avrebbe messa in guardia contro gli amori disordinati. (NB, 39)

> [He would have given her money. How much? Two ... three ... five hundred crowns. The money had to be given for no other reason than to acquire the right to educate. Then he would have warned her against disorderly love.]

Thus the old man's sickness initiates a new phase in his relationship with the girl, one in which he will strive to mend the moral damage he has perpetrated in order to lead once again.

But immediately after voicing his resolve to educate the girl, a task fitting his new invalid condition, the old man witnesses a scene that will constitute the *tableau-vivant* of what we could call the old man's anxiety of position:

> Un fanciullo di forse otto o dieci anni, scalzo, scendeva la via traendosi dietro per mano un uomo evidentemente ubriaco. Pareva che il fanciullo

fosse conscio della sua responsabilità. Procedeva con un passo piccolo ma risoluto. Guardava di tratto in tratto dietro di sé il grande uomo che pareva convinto di dover seguirlo, eppoi guardava dinanzi a sé per vedere la propria via. *Certo egli sapeva di dover consigliare e dirigere.* [...] il fanciullo scese dal maraciapiedi per camminare meglio e non fu subito seguito dall'uomo. Perciò avvenne che le loro braccia allacciate andarono a cozzare contro il colonnino di un fanale. Non subito il fanciullo intese che avrebbe dovuto retrocedere per accompagnarsi all'uomo. Aveva fretta e probabilmente fece male all'ubbriaco premendone la mano sul colonnino. Costui fu preso da un improvviso furore. Si svincolò dal fanciullo e subito gli menò un calcio atterrandolo. (NB, 39; emphasis mine)

[A boy, perhaps eight or nine years old, barefoot, was coming down the road leading a man, evidently drunk, by the hand. The boy seemed conscious of his responsibility. He went along with tiny but determined step. Now and then he looked behind at the big man who seemed convinced that he had to follow, and then he looked ahead to his road again. *Clearly he knew that he had to advise and lead* ... The child stepped down from the sidewalk to walk easier and the man did not immediately follow. So it happened that their locked arms hit a lamppost. The boy failed to understand that he had to step back to go along with the man. He was in a hurry and perhaps he hurt the drunk by pressing his hand against the little column. The man got furious. He disengaged himself from the child and kicked him to the ground.]

This scene, that Tibor Wlassics defines as 'la scena-mito' [the mythical scene (1971: 251)] will lead to the writing of the treatise 'Dei rapporti fra vecchiaia e gioventù' ['Of the Relations between Old Age and Youth'], the last self-reflexive turn of the old man's story. But at the time the scene's meaning escapes the 'buon vecchio.' It is only a dream he has the following night that 'reveals' to him the symbolic import of the child and the drunken man for his own adventure:

camminava al sole tenendo per mano la bella fanciulla, proprio come l'ubbriaco teneva per mano il ragazzo. Anch'essa lo precedeva di poco [...] ad ogni suo passo risonava il campanello d'allarme come quel giorno sul viale di Sant'Andrea. Il vecchio che fino allora era proceduto con il suo passo lento, si sforzò di raggiungere la giovinetta. [...] Poi fu subito stanco e volle sciogliere la sua mano da quella della giovinetta. Non vi riuscì che quando esausto cadde a terra. La giovinetta come un automa si allontanò da lui senza neppure guardarlo ... (NB, 40–1)

[he was walking in the sun holding the beautiful girl by the hand, precisely as the drunk did with the boy. She as well slightly preceded him ... at every step of hers the alarm bell rang like that day on the Sant'Andrea Boulevard. The old man who until then advanced with his slow step, forced himself to keep up with the young girl. ... Then he was immediately tired and wanted to disentangle his hand from that of the girl. He did not succeed until, exhausted, he fell to the ground. Like an automaton, the girl moved away without even looking at him.]

Reflecting upon the two scenes, the old man draws the obvious parallel between the powerless child and the girl, and then, anxious to hide his moral responsibilities, between the drunken man and the 'zerbinotto.' The former 'corruptor' of the girl, now fully engaged in his new role as philanthropist-pedagogue, shrugs off his possible identification with the villain: 'Volle sorridere al paragone impossibile' [He tried to smile at the impossible comparison (NB, 41)]. Even in the dream a compromise is struck: the old man does occupy the position of the drunk, but far from being a brutal aggressor, he is, like the child, the one who falls helpless to the ground.

Wlassics concludes, after comparing these two scenes and questioning the moral responsibility of the actors, that 'le similitudini sono dissimilitudini [...] boia e vittima si confondono e si fondono' [the similitudes are dissimilitudes ... torturer and victim are fused and confused with each other (1971: 254)]. It is only when the dream and the scene in the street are read as representations of the old man's anxiety of position, however, that they become metaphorically consistent. In both cases the adult, whether intoxicated by wine or age, *follows* the youth who leads as if she/he knew 'di dover consigliare e dirigere' [had to advise and lead]. The scene in the street and its oneiric 'correction' stage, not so much Wlassics' 'identità del tormentatore e tormentato' [identity of tormentor and tormented (1971: 255)], as the *reversibilità di educatore e educato* [the reversibility of educator and educated]. The dream reveals, through the reversal, the self-interestedness inherent in the position of the pedagogue. The child, who behaves like a good pedagogue 'conscio della sua responsabilità' [conscious of his responsibility], is transformed into the indifferent girl who, inebriated by the ring of her own step, walks away from the weak pupil. The suspicion arises that the educator, whoever he/she may be, rather than educating the other is perhaps simply pursuing 'come un automa' his/her own path, his/her own desire. This implication constitutes a chastisement and a warning for the old man who seduced the girl and who is now pursuing her education in the hope of being led to a 'cure.'

The images the old man considers for the illustration of his volume reveal the tension in the relative positions of educator and educated, as well as old age and youth. First he thinks of a drawing representing '[la] piattaforma della Tramvia con la giovinetta al freno e un vecchio che la strappa al lavoro' [the platform of the tramway with the girl at the brake and an old man that steals her away from work (NB, 54)], then, discouraged by the possibility of rendering the idea visually (an idea charged with damning implications), he has a sudden inspiration: 'la vignetta doveva rappresentare un fanciullo decenne che conduce un vecchio ubriaco' [the illustration should represent a ten-year-old boy leading an old drunk (NB, 54)]. In both instances youth is represented as morally in the right, while the old man, whether leading or following, appears in need of guidance. The old man chooses the second image; if before he could neither physically follow nor morally lead the young woman, now, by following the child appearing on the cover of his volume, he hopes to lead not only her but an army of youth and old men in need of moral example. How did the old man arrive at this grandiose yet perversely dimininished position?

Like the protagonist of *Il vegliardo*, Svevo's fourth and unfinished novel, the 'buon vecchio' dives into his adventure because 'non vuole sottostare alle leggi mediocri di natura e di morale e tenta l'avventura del ringiovanimento' [he does not want to yield to the mediocre laws of nature and morals, and so he attempts the adventure of rejuvenation (Contini 1980: 136)]. Dictated and justified by the natural clock, the old man's behaviour is supposedly beyond good and evil. Invoking such a justification, however, constitutes a two-edged sword since it becomes an admission that he is beyond the laws governing the living, beyond education, and finally beyond life itself. For this reason, 'l'avventura del ringiovanimento' needs to coincide with the writing of the educational treatise, a way to re-enter youth as a wise man.

> In genere è certo che la maggior parte dei vecchi crede di aver molti diritti e soli diritti. Sapendo di non essere più raggiungibili da un'educazione, credono di poter vivere proprio come il loro organismo domanda. Il buon vecchio s'assise al tavolo con un desiderio d'assimilazione che gli ricordava la vera gioventù. Beato, pensò: – '*La buona e bella cura comincia.*' (NB, 26; emphasis mine)

[Generally it is a fact that most old people think they have many rights and only rights. Knowing that they are beyond the reach of education, they believe they can live exactly as their organism dictates. The good old man sat down at the table with a desire for assimilation that reminded him of real youth. Blissful, he thought: – *The good and beautiful cure has begun.*]

Thus, for our good old man, the *cure*, the restoration of a lost youth, has to be at the same time 'beautiful' (that is pleasantly self-indulgent) *and* 'good,' meaning good for health, but above all morally good. The 'buona e bella cura,' if successful, would assure the old man the enviable position of being an example to society while living outside its laws, a position of absolute authority similar to the one pursued by Giovanni in *La rigenerazione*: 'Tu sei il padrone di tutti perché sei vecchio, perché sei giovane' [You are everybody's master because you are old, because you are young (1969, 537)]. But both the cure and the project of education need the presence of the woman: a pupil who will lead the old man as in the dream beyond the end of his adventure and thus beyond himself. With the 'bella fanciulla' lies the true lesson, the lesson the old man refrains from learning.

In Svevo's late production, the most privileged relations of his protagonists are with the child;[14] the woman (with some significant exceptions) retreats to the horizon, together with the struggles, responsibilities, and tasks of everyday life happily abandoned by the old man. In the character of the old man, childishness mingles with the convoluted self-deceptions of senility. Like childhood, old age belongs less to the openness of the streets than to the safe intimacy of interiors, the spaces to which the good old man is confined like a sick child:

> Si sedeva davanti alla stufa e amava di gettarvi dei pezzi di carbone che guardava poi bruciare. Poi chiudeva gli occhi abbacinati e li riapriva per riprendere lo stesso gioco. (NB, 36)

> [He sat in front of the stove. He loved to throw in pieces of coal that he then watched burning. Then he closed eyes blinded by the fire and opened them again to resume the same game.]

The old man shares with the child the timeless space of play, but the deepest commonality of experience is the powerlessness that finds equal expression, as Wlassics points out, in the 'urlo muto' [silent scream] of the child abused in the streets and of the old man before the violence of death (Wlassics 1971: 251). The 'fanciulla in cenci colorati' participates in this realm as well, in her the child and the woman coexist even more significantly and actively, creating a hybrid figure of otherness. She enters the story playfully, like a tomboy.

> essa era tanto infantile che riusciva a convertire il lavoro in un giuoco, e le piaceva di correre cosí e di far rumore con quella macchinetta ingegnosa. Tutti i bambini amano di gridare quando corrono. Era vestita di cenci colorati. Causa la sua grande bellezza sembrava travestita. [...] Guardando la sola sua testa si sarebbe potuta credere un maschietto ... (NB, 22)

> [she was so childish that she succeeded in transforming the work into a game, and she liked to run so and to make noise with the ingenious little machine. All children love to shout when they run. She was dressed in colorful rags. Because of her great beauty she seemed to be in disguise. ... By looking only at her head, one could have taken her for a boy ...]

The magical woman-child, first represented while pressing the alarm bell on the trolley car, makes a foreboding entrance: she seems disguised, a hermaphroditic boy who entices the old man, carrying him over to the next stage of his life. With the progression of the narration, she will undergo a series of metamorphoses that mark successive stages in the adventure of the old man.

'In fondo il rimorso non è altro che il risultato di un dato modo di guardarsi in uno specchio' [In the last analysis, remorse is nothing but the result of a certain way of looking at oneself in the mirror (NB, 48)], muses the narrator of the story. The young girl is that mirror. Her metamorphosis throughout the story represents a *mise-en-abîme* of the old man's stumbling progression from seduction to education and finally to the writing of the treatise. Thus, for instance, the initial 'amori disordinati' of the old man become a reality only when mirrored in the loose behavior of the young woman. Then, like a repentant incestuous father (Almansi 1972), the old man seeks to erase his guilt by changing the girl, that is by educating her: 'Bisognava salvarla *mutandola* in modo da farla ridivenire la buona cara fanciulla, che – purtroppo! – era stata sua' [It was necessary to save her by *changing her* so that one could transform her again into the good dear girl, who – unfortunately! – he possessed (NB, 52; emphasis mine)]. The girl who gave up 'cenci colorati' for the 'calze di seta' [silken socks] of the fetishized doll – a living testimony to the egotistical desire of the seducer-pedagogue – is restored to her pristine condition, but not before bearing a progeny for the old father: out of the incestuous relationship pure theory is born. The sermons, a grandiose reflection on why he should not have done what he did, miraculously resurrect 'la fanciulla' who can preside over the old man's thoughts and wisely lead him as a 'vera madre della teoria' [true mother of theory (NB, 56)].

In trying to subordinate his weaknesses to the ordered and timeless geometry of theory, the good old man is the character who comes the nearest to recognizing, if only abstractly and in the form of an unsolvable conundrum, the reversals and pitfalls of pedagogy. The pretence to educate and change the other, behind which Svevo's other characters, and Emilio among them, hide, openly transforms itself into the pursuit of his own education, namely his rejuvenation. The final attempt to codify and control the fluid and disordered relations between educators and pupils, youth and old age, runs aground on a shoal of unanswered questions. The old man's interrogation, 'Da chi ha da cominciare la morale?' [With whom should morality start?] – and by extension *education* – echoes the reflection on pedagogy in Marx's 'Theses on Feuerbach': '*it is essential to educate the educator himself*' (1978: 144). While the acceptance of this self-critique, which finds an indirect representation in the anxiety about leading and following, would strip the pedagogue of his authority, its refusal would sever him from youth and life. Thus, the folder entitled 'Da studiarsi quando l'educazione del vecchio ha da cominciare' [To be studied when the education of the old should start (NB, 61)] will remain unaddressed, cast away with other questions that suggest a transformative practice still to be undertaken by the old man and Svevian man in general.

The woman and the child indeed play a similar role in the Svevian world. Both are subjects-in-becoming in which the Svevian man seeks himself, only to deny the discovered resemblance. Their constitutive 'weakness' is an intrinsic trait of the 'dolcezza' he secretly cherishes. Woman and child – to apply to the particular an observation Svevo makes about human nature – 'portano in sé i germi di tutti i caratteri' [carry within them the seeds of all characters ('Del sentimento in arte,' 1968: 670)]; they share with the 'uomo in abbozzo' a space of *potentiality*, of unspoken possibilities, but in a way different from him because they are deprived of his consciousness and live restricted within the confines of society. Their relationship with Svevian man is a symbiotic association that, although organized as a hierarchy of the more and the less 'evolved,' threatens to undergo a radical mutation: the 'potential consciousness' of the other (more feared than recognized in the case of the woman) could transform the pacific mammoth into a Trojan horse. Thus, a great anxiety is attached to these figures, for they remind the man, and particularly the old man, of the potential loss of his own consciousness.

The 'ringiovanimento'/re-education of the Svevian 'vecchione' does not arrest the irresistible current that carries him and the envied youth in the same direction. It is just an illusory detour allowed by the presence of the woman. While leading the old man by the hand, the young woman undergoes a last paradoxical reversal: if at first she is a desired connection to life, she ultimately reveals herself to be the mysterious *trait d'union* with death. Like the first 'Annina' invented by Doctor Menghi, 'la bella fanciulla' works like a *pharmacon* that intensifies the vital functions, thereby leading the old man more rapidly to death (his 'gioventù non era altro che una corsa pazza alla vecchiaia' [youth was nothing else than a mad run towards old age (1968: 532)]. Thus, the young girl, the healthy youth who should educate old age, is an infernal ferrywoman, an unrecognized Charonte who conducts the old man to the end of his line. By casting off the disguise, the 'cenci colorati' [colourful rags] that misguided the old man, the 'bella fanciulla' reveals herself not as the messenger from a forgotten past but rather as the herald of the great mutation awaiting him in the near future. Emilio's 'simbolo alto e magnifico' [noble, splendid symbol] of a crying Angiolina, becomes here the unrepresentable otherness of death, beyond correction, beyond 'senilità.'

The Death of the Pedagogue

As if to underline the perspectival error made by the good old man in theorizing the youthfulness of old age, Roberto, the protagonist of 'La morte,' dedicates himself to the extreme lesson to be had for an old man: the experience of death. Roberto declares himself ready for the irreversible change and confidently undertakes his final education, the preparation for death, by teaching his wife Teresa how to die. Once again, but for the last time, a character sets himself forward as an example for the woman sustained by the consoling thought that he has greater self-knowledge than she does.

Unlike 'La Novella,' which focuses on the one-way bond between the good old man and the beautiful and unknown girl, 'La morte' dramatizes the resumption of a dialogue that forces husband and wife to look at each other again after years of silence and indifference. Their marriage, characterized by a reciprocal respect based on misunderstanding, recalls Zeno's description of his association with Augusta:

> La nostra fu e rimase una relazione sorridente perché io sorrisi sempre di lei, che credevo non sapesse e lei di me, cui attribuiva molta scienza e molti errori ch'essa – cosí si lusingava – avrebbe corretti. (CdZ, 649)

> [Ours was and remained a smiling relationship because I always smiled about her, whom I thought did not know, and she about me, to whom she credited much knowledge and many mistakes that she – so she deluded herself – would have corrected.]

Similarly, at the moment of joining their lives, Roberto and Teresa had both secretly entertained the desire to change the other: Teresa wanted to convert her husband to religion, and Roberto, the last 'apostolo del nulla' [apostle of nothingness], 'le corse dietro per distruggere la legge di Vesta' [ran after her to destroy the law of Vesta].[15] Now with great surprise they recognize that 'tutto quello che avrebbe dovuto dividerli li aveva riuniti' [everything that should have divided them instead brought them together (M, 252)]. Thus, without smoothing the differences that divided them in their youth, old age creates a space outside the 'struggle' to change the other, in which the original dissonance of thoughts is transformed into a soothing and intimate confession made perceptible to the reader in the mixing of the voices in the third-person narration. The detached love of old age reopens a dialogue where the imperative 'know thyself,' left suspended in the experience of youth, can be addressed once again.

But very soon the intimacy and honesty of personal recollections that created this shared space is brusquely interrupted by Roberto, who, in search of an ornate expression to describe Teresa's religion, sententiously declares: 'Eternamente forse la mitologia resterà la sorte della donna' [Perhaps for eternity mythology will be the destiny of woman (M, 252)]. The intimate dialogue is abandoned and from now on the rhetorician will dominate the conversation, resuming his lifelong 'struggle' to define the other. To explain his previous words to the offended Teresa, Roberto goes on:

> C'era la morte a questo mondo e solo i forti potevano affrontarla. Per le

donne la lotta era priva di speranza se la religione non le soccorreva. 'E' vero' disse lei convinta della propria debolezza. (M, 252)

[In this world there was death and only the strong could face it. For women the struggle was hopeless if religion did not support them. 'It is true,' she said, convinced of her own weakness.]

Naturally the rhetorician is numbered among the 'strong,' while the woman, because of her supposed biological weakness, is defeated from the start in the decisive confrontation with death. But Teresa's conviction of her weakness means acceptance, and acceptance is strength, a lesson that the male protagonist, dazzled by his rhetoric, fails to learn. His self-proclaimed strength will constitute his real weakness: the denial that even for him history (and a supposedly self-made history at that) will revert to mythology.

As if to signify a narrative disclaimer about Roberto's statement that mythology is the exclusive domain of the woman, Teresa's name appears at that moment for the first time in the story. The short story which had begun in Svevo's usual third-person point of view, with omniscience limited to the thoughts of the male character – with the exception of the already mentioned mixing of Roberto and Teresa's consciousness in the opening paragraph – from now on will shift more and more to Teresa's thoughts, with which, significantly, the narration will end. Thus, Roberto's attempt to explain Teresa's religion as a way of thinking and living outside time – one destined to a repetition without correction, namely without understanding – is highly ironic, since in the end it is he who by exiting the story/history will be barred from understanding.

But for the time being Teresa retreats again from the scene, becoming a silent and complacent listener to Roberto's confession of his lifelong preparation for death – 'anche nella salute piú perfetta [aveva] pensato alla morte' [even in the most perfect health he thought about death (M, 253)] – a revelation that surprises Teresa, who realizes that she did not know her husband. Lacking the self-irony displayed by Zeno in his judgment of Augusta, Roberto indulges in the belief that Teresa lacks knowledge, and so he keeps expounding a sermon, which, according to him, will offer the weak Teresa a much needed guidance: 'Era per lei ch'egli costantemente si preparava alla morte. [...] Doveva *servirle d'esempio*' [It was for her that he prepared constantly for death. ... He had *to be an example for her* (M, 253; emphasis mine)].

Apparently freed from the contradictions that characterized the education-as-seduction that Emilio and the good old man wanted to impose on the woman, Roberto can hold himself up as a model for the woman's education, an ideal example beyond the influences of life, change, and error. Nevertheless, even in Roberto's case this supposed disinterestedness is contradicted by the actual process through which he reaches self-understanding. Strength is built on the other's weakness, and knowledge is measured against the other's assumed ignorance; the 'example' is still the result of the pedagogue's hidden mirroring of the pupil. Just as the good old man feels remorse for his conduct because he perceives it in the changed presence of the 'bella fanciulla,' Roberto forgets the reality of his own self and body and reflects on old age only through the mirror image of Teresa:

> Quando le parlò essa lo guardò con un mite, debole sorriso. 'Molto vecchia' pensò con uno stringimento di cuore, lui ch'era tanto piú vecchio di lei. (M, 251)

> [When he spoke to her she looked at him with a gentle, weak smile. 'Very old' he thought with a heart pang, he who was much older than she.]

The distance which allows the male character to live vicariously through the other also grants him the authority to speak, write, and above all teach. The jolt for Roberto comes, when, to his surprise, he discovers this condition to be his very own. This mechanism reveals the instability of the pedagogue: concentrating on the task of watching and leading the other, he thinks he is standing on the firm ground of his authority – his understanding of the general law – which is nothing more that a complex self-defence built on words.

Inspired by the conviction that 'il pensiero della morte deve essere quello dell'uomo sano' [thought about death had to be that of a healthy man (M, 253)], Roberto's preparation for death unfolds as a rhetorical construction:

> Non occorreva il cielo per divenire buoni e misericordiosi. Il pensiero della morte mitigava tutto. L'ardore della lotta per la vita si mitigava nella decisione di prepararsi alla morte. (M, 253)

> [The presence of heaven was not necessary to become good and compassionate. The thought of death mitigated everything. The ardor of the struggle for life subsided in the decision to prepare for death.]

Before the silent Teresa he criticizes the mindless dismissal of death inspired by religion, to which he opposes the stoic determination of a man who can look his destiny in the face. But Roberto is looking once again at destiny *in the face of the other*, gaining a confirmation of his own strength at the sight of Teresa's 'weakness.' From Roberto's point of view, Teresa lacks the sound defence of his rhetorical rationalizations and is thus left alone and helpless before death. But she does not need to worry, because all along he has been altruistically preparing for *her* encounter with it: 'Io volevo proprio prepararmi alla morte. Per me, per te, per tutti' [I wanted indeed to prepare myself for death. For me, for you, for everybody (M, 254)]. After this rhetorical demonstration of superiority, Roberto goes to bed reassured about his own education but preoccupied about Teresa:

> pensò: 'La morte non minaccia me. Io sono forte. Come sopporterà lei la mia morte? [...] Saprà imitare la mia rassegnazione? Ma come potrà lei sentire che nella legge generale non può esserci dolore né spavento?' (M, 254)

> [he thought: – 'Death does not threaten me. I am strong. How will she bear my death? ... Will she be able to imitate my resignation? But how will she be able to feel that before the general law there cannot be either pain or fear?']

Nevertheless, and as the following events will show, the theoretical knowledge of the law does not amount to knowing how to live it. Exactly that pitiful and ridiculous image that Roberto's long preparation was intended to exorcise, 'i movimenti scomposti dell'animale quando il coltello del macellaio lo raggiunge' [the unseemly movements of the animal when the butcher's knife reaches him (M, 254)], is the one that will return to haunt him. This foreboding image, which makes Teresa shiver, marks the ironic limit of the pedagogue's 'dotta ignoranza' [learned ignorance].

Sickness sneaks up unexpectedly on Roberto. 'L'ammalato [sebbene] ben educato da anni di preparazione' [the sick man (although) well trained by years of preparation (M, 260)] dramatically experiences his powerlessness before a pain that imposes grotesque distortions on his body, a pain he hoped to have exorcised with his reflections:

> Ora appena avvicinata la testa alla finestra socchiusa essa la vide scomposta

da uno sberleffo di dolore che vi si formava e spariva per riformarvisi. [...] Ci fu una pausa dovuta ad uno sberleffo violento imposto dal dolore e che s'estese dalla faccia a tutto il corpo. [...] Girò l'occhio vago come se avesse cercato di ricordare ma anche quello sforzo era interrotto dallo sberleffo cui era costretto. (M, 260–1)

[Now, as soon as he turned his head towards the half-closed window, she saw it distorted by a grimace of pain that appeared and disappeared only to return again. ... There was a pause after a violent grimace imposed by pain had extended from his face to the rest of his body. ... He turned his eye hazily as if he were trying to remember, but even that effort was interrupted by a forced grimace.]

These 'sberleffi' [grimaces] ironically punctuate his final pathetic sermon to Teresa, distorting the words which he thought so powerful. Even though he is conscious of his weakness, recognizing that 'Non pensai tutto quando questo dolore non c'era e feci male' [I did not think about everything when this pain was not here and that was a mistake (M, 261)] Roberto still requires Teresa to remain in the room and learn: *'Resta tranquilla con me a guardarmi e ad apprendere'* [Remain calm here with me, look at me and learn (M, 261; emphasis mine)]. But immediately after this exhortation, like an ultimate 'sberleffo' that finally undermines his pretence of control, the pain stops.

Ed egli guardò attorno a sé privo di dolore e privo di eroismo. [...] Le sue parole eroiche miseramente assumevano l'aspetto di una vanteria. (M, 261)

[And he looked around him without pain and without heroism. ... His heroic words acquired the miserable aspect of a boasting.]

The pedagogue's intention to display an exemplary death turns into exactly what he wanted to avoid, namely a wordless convulsion of fear. Theoretical conviction disappears in a cold sweat, while the word that should have sheltered him from the pain is revealed to be an empty husk: 'Stava morta accanto al dolore vivo, attivo che egli si sforzava di lasciare imperversare su di lui senz'ascoltarlo.' [It lay dead near the live, active pain that he was trying to let rage on him without listening to it (M, 261)]. Roberto's powerful self-defence, a castle of convincingly piled words, has crumbled, leaving the rhetorician as weak and helpless as a child:

> Fu un pianto violento che gli tolse il respiro come avviene ad un bambino castigato ingiustamente o anche per una ingiustizia evidente anche a lui. Parve che il pianto avesse impedita la parola. Le lacrime furono interrotte [...] [da] un suono strano che a Teresa dapprima parve ancora piú infantile del singhiozzo. Era il rantolo. (M, 263)

> [He had a violent crying spell that took his breath away like that which comes over a child unjustly punished or for an unjustice evident even to him. It seemed as if the crying had obstructed the word. The tears were stopped ... [by] a strange noise that to Teresa seemed at first even more childish than the sob. It was the death rattle.]

Once again, as in 'La Novella' of the good old man, the pedagogue dies in the ignorance of a child. He experiences death as a regression to the inarticulateness of infancy.[16]

As the pedagogue dies, defeated in his will to teach by the reality of wordless fright, the silent pupil Teresa is left alone on the stage. In a last ironic reversal she rewards, like a good teacher, the courage and accomplishment of her unexpected pupil:

> Ecco ch'egli irrigidito, appariva forte e sereno come un soldato che rispondesse all'appello. E lei, per cui la morte non finiva nulla pensò cercando una consolazione a tanto strazio: 'Ecco che prendi la tua rivincita. Come sei bravo!' (M, 263)

> [Now that he was stiff, he looked strong and serene as a soldier who answers to the roll-call. And she, for whom death did not put an end to anything, thought, looking for some consolation in such misery: – 'Now you get your second chance. How good you are!'

Now frozen in the posture of an obedient yet inarticulate pupil, Roberto finally seems to have attained the strength and serenity he could not win with intellectual preparedness.

After Roberto's death the narration resumes on a familiar note, pursuing the same old questions: Who has changed? Who has learned? The struggle for identity continues after the passage of death, maintained by a narrator obsessed with the hierarchical positioning within that symbiosis called marriage:

> L'associazione tanto intima di due persone d'indole tanto differente per

quanto mitigata dal desiderio e dal rispetto deve finire con l'impartirle la fisionomia di uno dei due associati. Quella di Teresa e di Roberto portava le linee della faccia di Roberto. (M, 263)

[The very intimate association of two people of such different temperaments, although mitigated by desire and respect, must end up assuming the physiognomy of one of the two associates. That of Teresa and Roberto bore the lines of Roberto's face.]

Why? The narrator does not explain. Instead he goes on to tell how the separate faiths enclosed in the hearts of Roberto and Teresa, 'mancando [loro] la chiara intelligente manifestazione,' [lacking a clear and intelligent manifestation (M, 263)] ended up shrivelling and losing significance. In fact, desire and respect – the smile that accompanies the relationship of Augusta and Zeno, for example – are precisely what prevents the actors in the association from knowing each other, thus requiring a hidden struggle for control. If their marriage had the outlines of Roberto's face during his life, after his death 'tutto quello che restò di Roberto sulla terra cioè nel cuore di Teresa si convertì [...] silenziosamente' [everything of Roberto that remained on earth, that is in Teresa's heart, was silently converted (M, 263)]. The woman was changed, and then the man was changed, but in this silent process their paths crossed without their meeting for a last time.

The impossibility of presenting the woman's point of view creates a silence which raises the question of who the other in the association is, a question the text urgently poses but leaves unanswered. In fact, the story does not even conclude, perhaps because of the narrator's difficulty in writing from Teresa's perspective or perhaps because Ettore Schmitz's death interrupted its composition.[17]

These scenes of misrecognition between male and female characters are crucial to Svevo's thought; they are the tempered edge of his cutting insight. In 'Corto viaggio sentimentale,' his penultimate fiction, written, like 'La novella del buon vecchio,' after 1925, he explores once again the relationship between an old couple. The elderly Signor Aghios, also afflicted with Roberto's self-assurance, remembers and regrets the quite brutal and intolerant instruction of his wife. Suddenly the thought dawns on him that she might be as free in her thoughts as he.

Invece essa invecchiava peggio di lui, perché essa poi mancava del suo libero pensiero. Poverina! Non era però suo l'ufficio di darle tale pensiero.

In passato egli invece aveva fatto del suo meglio per toglierglielo. Anzi, appena sposati, la sua morale era stata dura e imperiosa. Che rimorso! [...] Ma se invece in lei tale pensiero fosse ora altrettanto libero che da lui? Poteva essere che, come essa non l'indovinava in lui, cosí lui non lo scoprisse da lei.[18]

[Instead she was aging worse than he was, because after all she lacked his free thought. Unlucky! It was not his task to give her such thought. On the contrary, in the past he did his best to take it away from her. In fact, as soon as they got married, his ethics had been hard and imperious. What a remorse! ... But what if instead thought were now as free for her at it was for him? It could have been that, just as she could not imagine it in him, he could not detect it in her.]

The suspicion arises in these last texts of Svevo that man and woman have been divided by a gross misunderstanding. For the first time, even if only at the speculative level, the woman is allowed a perspective on the man, and as a result the previously neutral point of view is exposed as specifically that of the man. In fact, the increasing use of first person narration after *La coscienza di Zeno*, in stories and then in the fragments of *Il vegliardo*, might be read as a recognition of the specific positioning of the male perspective and a desire therefore to overtly narrate from such an 'eccentric' view of the world.

As long as woman remains excluded, exiled to the margins of consciousness as the other that allows consciousness, she is unable to be a friend, an equal, forever barred from the dialogue the male pedagogue inscribes on her 'indifferent' skin. In *Thus Spoke Zarathustra*, Nietzsche captures in epigrammatic form the tension represented, criticized, and left unresolved in Svevo's reflection on man and his other: 'All-too-long have a slave and tyrant been concealed in woman. Therefore woman is not yet capable of friendship: she knows only love [...] Woman is not capable of friendship. But tell me, you men, who among you is capable of friendship?' (1978: 57). The struggle in which the pedagogue engages with the world finds a miniaturized representation in the struggle to educate and convince the woman. In both cases, the man is forced, as Signor Aghios is well aware, to recognize the impossibility of the true friendship Nietzsche talked about: 'Poi ricordò che neppure fra uomini ci si intendeva, se non ci si spiegava, come era da lui e sua moglie' [Then he remembered that among men, as also between him and his wife, there was no mutual understanding, if they did not explain themselves to each other ('Corto viaggio,' 161)]. As the effect of the departure of the only lady in Aghios train compartment suggests, this mutual understanding depends upon the woman, for without her presence the system of signification that holds men together is doomed to collapse: 'Senza quel piedino [...] i quattro uomini rimasti avevano perduto ogni contatto fra di loro. Erano divenuti dei *veri stranieri scialbi e muti*' [Without that little foot ... the four remaining men lost every contact among themselves. They became *true strangers, mute and insignificant* (161; emphasis mine)]. Thus, the true tragedy would not be men's disappearance from the world, as Aghios imagines with self-importance a few lines before – 'Guai a noi se l'uomo non ci fosse' [Heaven help us if man did not exist] – but rather women's.

It is time to return to the initial question raised by the association of Ettore and Livia, namely: what does a woman signify? or rather what is her function in the male economy? Clearly she offers the man the opportunity to teach, to lead, the possibility of seeking and losing himself in a less evolved creature, or at least someone he thinks he knows: '"Ti conosco perché sei bella"' ['I know you because you are beautiful' ('Corto viaggio,' 158)]. But in the intersubjective relationship, Svevo's dialogue between man and woman, the woman is more than a passive listener; she is a witness to a search disguised as seduction, education or 'tutela.' It is again Signor Aghios, who, while discussing the moral obligation of the husband towards the wife, suddenly questions himself on the identity of his interlocutor:

> discutere [...] Con chi? Non con la moglie, che nei suoi sogni mai apriva bocca, ma con quell'essere non precisabile, ma che pur deve esserci in qualche luogo, nell'etere forse che si suppone sia dappertutto, che sovrintende alla legge morale. ('Corto viaggio,' 159)

> [to discuss ... With whom? Not with the wife, who in his dreams never opened her mouth, but with that unspecifiable being, that nonetheless has to be there some place, perhaps in the ether that one supposes to be everywhere, that being that oversees the moral law.]

How can we speak of intersubjectivity when (as Aghios admits) the woman does not speak? We might observe that if the wife 'non apriva mai bocca' [never opened her mouth] the other indescribable interlocutor, despite its advantage of being 'non precisabile' [indeterminable], is certainly no more loquacious. It might very well be that the woman and the abstract embodiment of the law are not as distinct as they seem, since in the end they perform the same function, namely to listen to the 'dialogue' of the male character.

This dialogic instance between man and woman recalls the transference of the psychoanalytic session. The querulous pedagogue, in his inexhaustible desire to explain himself, to expound his convictions, is the patient, who, while lying on the couch, is thinking of sitting in the analyst's chair – very much like Zeno, who, by becoming both patient and analyst, gains complete control over his narrative. Education is a psychoanalytic dialogue with a silent other who does not actively participate, *but needs to be there* in order to allow the patient to construct his narrative. But the danger for the pedagogue, as for the patient – or psychoanalyst – is to fall in love with his own desire for a story, and, in the obsession to interpret, lose any understanding. The pedagogue expounds his arguments, but he pays the not-negligible price of losing the truth he searched for and being convinced instead, if not by any argument of the other, by the inescapable logic of reality.

If Svevo achieved through his characters an education (an understanding), his characters, intent on doing the talking, just barely learn how to listen. The final renunciation of convincing, the throwing in of the towel in the struggle to lead, only comes, as for the old man and Roberto, before the absolute otherness of death. When the word is consumed, nothing is left to be taught and it is too late to listen. What the pedagogue failed to learn in his life is finally taught in the encounter with death: 'Le sue ultime parole già irrorate di lacrime furono: – "Io non sapevo"' [His last words already wet with tears were: – 'I did not know' (M, 262)].

But if death and ignorance get the last word, alternative narratives remain partially expressed by the presence and functioning of the women characters in the structure of the text. All the women characters who attend school with Svevo's men, far from being convinced – that is, from being molded – simply defend their silence. What Bebel defined somewhat disparagingly as 'the neglected culture of woman' (1971: 114), and which inspires the pedagogue's zeal, is once again a construction, a myth that justifies his intervention. Angiolina, Carla, Augusta, and finally Teresa are not even allowed the chance granted to the dog, Argo – protagonist of Svevo's story 'Argo e il suo padrone' – when undergoing the same pedagogic violence, of becoming 'il primo filosofo di sua gente' [the first philosopher of his people (Svevo 1968: 314)].

After all, theirs would be a much more embarrassing diary to record. Nevertheless, woman's silence, so rarely broken in Svevo's narrative, is far from passive and yielding. The narrative, in dealing insistently with this repression, brings it fully to light, so that even in her silence woman reclaims her 'neglected culture,' thus achieving what, though disguised, cannot be repressed, namely, to lead the pedagogue by the hand.

Jane Gallop, reflecting on the troubled marriage between feminism and psychoanalytic theory, draws a similar comparison based on the psychoanalytic session: 'the one who does all the listening is not necessarily in the subordinate position, [...] knowledge and authority in certain ways derive from the one who does all the listening. Perhaps, after all, psychoanalysis has been doing all its talking in relation to the knowledge it presumes feminism (or women) to have. That may be why feminism has been so willing to listen. But the other story, the influence of feminism on psychoanalysis, remains to be told' (Gallop 1987: 324). If, in the telling of the pedagogue's story, the other story, the story of the woman, remains untold, Svevo could and did tell of the silence and listening of the other that allowed his story to come into being. He clearly and dispassionately represents the tricks, self-deceptions, and violence of the 'pedagogic' project, expressing at the same time a nostalgic envy 'per la parola franca' [for the honest word] of the other, a seemingly lost or perhaps eternally unreachable condition. The site of this tension emerges in clearer relief when placed beside the insights of psychoanalysis on the configuration of love and servitude, most provocatively articulated by Jacques Lacan in 'The Mirror Stage': 'psychoanalysis alone recognizes [the] knot of imaginary servitude that love must always undo again, or sever. For such a task, we place no trust in altruistic feeling, we who lay bare the aggressivity that underlies the activity of the philantropist, the idealist, the pedagogue, and even the reformer' (Lacan 1977: 7).

Svevo's tale of pedagogues and pupils, while laying bare the aggressivity that underlies their relationship, simultaneously affirms, by contrast *the inalienability of the altruistic feeling*, a feeling based on a founding need that pre-exists the entering into language: the need for the other. 'In complesso abbiamo bisogno di tutelare o di essere tutelati,' writes Svevo, 'Altrimenti la nostra mente non vede uno scopo della vita' [All in all we need to protect or to be protected. Otherwise our mind sees no goal in life (Pds, 828)]. For Svevo, imaginary knots cannot and perhaps should not be severed, not even – and Zeno would argue particularly not – by psychoanalysis, but they certainly can be tied and untied in a literary text that shares with them the same inescapable and elusive strings. *La coscienza di Zeno*, because of its first-person narration, will tell the tale of the intricate interweaving of altruism and aggression with even more focus through Zeno's pursuit of a symbiotic contamination with the other. Here alone will a character, declining any pretence of knowledge, narrate his love of the other's poison, his need and desire for 'tutela.'

chapter six

Out of the Shadow of the Mammoth: Zeno and the Story of the Other

In complesso abbiamo bisogno di tutelare o di essere tutelati. Altrimenti la nostra mente non vede uno scopo della vita. [All in all we need to protect or to be protected. Otherwise our mind sees no goal in life.]

Italo Svevo, '25 Ottobre 1917'

E scrivo ancora di questi due anni perché il mio attaccamento a lui mi sembra una chiara manifestazione della mia malattia. ... *Una vera e propria manfestazione di malattia o di grande bontà, due qualità che stanno in rapporto molto intimo fra di loro. [And I am still writing of these two years because my attachment to him seems to me a clear manifestation of my sickness. ... A genuine manifestation of sickness or great goodness, two qualities that stand in very intimate relation.]*

Italo Svevo, *La Coscienza di Zeno* (emphasis mine)[1]

In the last pages of the *Coscienza*, Zeno, freed from the stifling 'tutela' [protection] of the psychoanalyst, becomes more and more solitary, wandering along the metaphysical banks of the Isonzo River, up to when the war separates him permanently from all those ties, obligations, and social expectations that had wrapped him in their dense web. The solitude with which Zeno, alone in his study, began the narration of memory returns in the intimacy of 'raccoglimento' [meditation] in the final chapter, entitled 'Psico-analisi' [Psychoanalysis]. In between, the narrator unravels the arrhythmic story of consciousness. It is around the story of Zeno's associations with the other that *La coscienza di Zeno* organizes itself both at a thematic and a structural level, in the intersubjective nature of the narrative enunciation, suspended in the address of an *I* to a *thou*.[2] It is around the oscillation between 'tutelare' and 'essere tutelati' [the demand for and offer of protection] that Svevo's subject constitutes himself.

Even though, as Gabriella Contini notes, 'Manoscritti e pagine preparatorie del romanzo non ci sono pervenuti' [no manuscripts or preparatory pages of the novel have reached us (1996: 45)], Svevo's Darwinian fables, 'La corruzione dell'anima' and 'L'uomo e la teoria darwiniana,' are key texts for reading not just the final pages of *La coscienza*, but for understanding the text in its entirety. Zeno, as criticism has now repeatedly stressed, is the fictional personification of the 'uomo in abbozzo,' whose endlessly unfolding desire can be defined with Zeno's words as 'un impetuoso conato al meglio' [a strong impulse to become better (CdZ, 536)]. This sense of virtuality is exemplified in the first chapter, 'Il fumo' [The last cigarette], by Zeno's ever-renewed resolution to quit smoking. Zeno marks every 'last cigarette' with a date that announces his desire to begin a new and better era in his life. But no cigarette for Zeno is ever the last, because what matters in the end is the feeling, granted by the chronic breaking and renewal of the resolution, 'di credersi grande di una grandezza latente' [of believing in one's own latent greatness (CdZ, 516)]. The comical *mise en abîme* of the 'last cigarette' provides the overture for the series of relationships with the other, which will, in a much less mechanical way, repeat and increasingly problematize this originary impulse. Like the primitive man in 'L'uomo e la teoria darwiniana,' Zeno spends his life in the shadow of a healthier, stronger other, who, because 'finished' (like the mammoth), grants him the possibility of endless development. Once read in the light of the fables, Zeno's virtuality – the evasion of the present to live under the reign of potentiality – appears as relational, played out intersubjectively with an other in whose shadow Zeno can be dissolved and redrawn.

Both men and women characters are mammoths that grant Zeno the ceaseless rebirth of his desire, 'la vita più intensa,' that he on one occasion compares to the sound of the wave 'che, dacché si forma, muta ad ogni istante finché non muore!' [that from the moment it is born incessantly changes till its death (CdZ, 561)]. But differently from the cigarettes that lend themselves to flawless repetitions and returns, the mammoths, and particularly those who are women, oppose the pacing of Zeno's desire, the telling of his story, introducing their own temporalization, and thus a story of their own. Far from being an appendage of Zeno's subjectivity, the other of the symbiotic relationship constitutes his founding instance. In this sense, *La coscienza di Zeno* marks the limit and the correction of the Darwinian fable. The characters of Ada, Carla, and Teresina, far from being silent mammoths, eventually turn their backs on Zeno's desire and leave him 'finished' in the shadow of himself. The 'uomo in abbozzo,' imprisoned in the shadow in which he had thought only to hide, unexpectedly creates a shadow for a new possibility: the 'unfinished woman' ['la donna in abbozzo'].

In the Shadow of the Doctor

Carla Benedetti observes that 'la distorsione per Zeno è un'attività necessaria, "connaturata" al suo manifestarsi come soggetto' [distortion is a necessary activity for Zeno, innate to his manifestation as a subject (1984: 125)]. Of all the numberless doctors consulted by Zeno in his life, no one more than the psychoanalyst Dr S. can address Zeno's propensity for distortion. But, at the same time, and because of the compulsive and rhetorical nature of this distortion, no cure is so desired and so resisted by Zeno. At the root of this ambivalence, stands the profound similarity linking psychoanalytic discourse, where, according to Zeno, 'non si ripetono mai né le stesse immagini né le stesse parole' [the same images and the same words are never repeated (CdZ, 876)], to Zeno's own discourse where each word becomes 'un avvenimento a sé [...] e perciò non poteva essere imprigionata da nessun altro avvenimento' [an event in itself ... and therefore could not be imprisoned in any other event (CdZ, 574)]. Like that of psychoanalysis, the word of Zeno is a performance that 'costruisce un mondo parallelo, simbiotico o forse parassita rispetto a quello comune' [builds a parallel, symbiotic or parassitical world to the common one (Savelli 1998: 57)]. Symbiosis and parasitism, while defining the intersubjective instance of both the analytic method and the subject's discourse, extends to encompass the rhetoric of both patient and doctor. Indeed, symbiosis is the name of Zeno's rhetorical distortion.

The ambiguous dependence on the other is brilliantly dramatized by Svevo in the structuring frames of the novel, where Dr S.'s introduction, Zeno's 'Preambolo,' and his conclusion fight to contain and outwit each other. Ultimately, Zeno's discourse aspires to a cognitive position equal to that of the 'talking cure.'

It is in the shadow of Dr S. that Zeno unfolds the writing of his memory. The figure of the psychoanalyst (simultaneously reader, interpreter, and listener) combines all the nuances of the symbiotic relationship that ties Zeno to his other. Without this symbiosis there would be no writing, and, as it becomes clear at the conclusion of the novel, outside it there is only great, vast, uninterrupted health, a condition that can be described only in the sense of a Nietzschean *Jenseits*. Dr S., in his initial condition of presence-absence, offers Zeno what Lacan defined as 'the mirage of the monologue' – as opposed to the 'forced labour' of the Freudian *durcharbeiten* that Zeno escapes (1977: 41) – and thus guarantees the manifestation of the word as desire, apparently a completely narcissistic one. In the shadow of psychoanalysis, Zeno willingly makes himself the doctor's 'slave' in order to write his story.

But to complicate the doctor-patient association, Zeno's need to *know* his illness, which makes him a privileged subject for psychoanalysis, is inextricably tied to the desire to convince. As such it repeats the classical Socratic gesture of seducing the other, in this case the subject 'who is presumed to know.' All Zeno's writing could be read as an effort to convince the doctor of his sickness, a sickness that was born from a description to a doctor. Already with the doctor who used electricity to cure his patients, Zeno 'correv[a] a quelle sedute nella speranza di convincere il dottore a proibir[gli] il fumo' [ran to those sessions in the hope of convincing the doctor to order [him] to give up smoking (CdZ, 519)]; 'E fu per convincerlo ch'io feci quello ch'egli non volle fare e studiai la mia malattia raccogliendone tutti i sintomi' [it was in order to convince him that I did what he had neglected to do and studied all the symptoms of my disease in detail (CdZ, 520)]. For this reason his relation with Dr S. is doomed to deteriorate into open struggle when, after Zeno abandons the writing of his memories, the 'caressing' eye of the doctor unexpectedly rests on his story. Like the hated Dr Coprosich who assisted his father, the glance of the listener and interpreter of Zeno's speech is intolerable because it is beyond Zeno's reach: 'i suoi occhi accecati guardavano accanto o al disopra del suo interlocutore e avevano il curioso aspetto degli occhi privi di colore di una statua, minacciosi o, forse, ironici' [His blinded eyes looked around and above his interlocutor and were strangely like the colorless eyes of a statue, threatening or perhaps ironical (CdZ, 548)].[3] The threat contained in the glance of the other materializes when, with an inversion of roles, the psychoanalyst undertakes the 'rieducazione' [convincing (CdZ, 871)] of the patient. From being the subject of the word, Zeno ends up occupying the uncomfortable position of object, which the doctor intends, in his own way, to 'costruire intero' [make whole].

By parodying the piercing glance of the doctor in the last pages of his diary, Zeno exorcises his power and removes himself from his uncanny 'tutela.' It is with a sense of victory and relief that Zeno addresses Dr S. as 'bestione' [big animal (CdZ, 873)], a mammoth in whose shadow he wrote and remembered, but from whose servitude he emancipated himself when he was at risk of being transformed from the man of infinite possibilities – that is, the one with a story of endless potential interpretations – into a finished animal, a mammoth, whose story, the Oedipus myth, had already been written for centuries. Left to himself, the psychoanalyst gives voice (in the famous preface) to his own frustrated desire, a desire that can no longer be satisfied, because it has been deprived of the founding shadow of the other.

When the doctor eventually takes hold of Zeno's story in the 'Preface' to the published manuscript, his own desire for interpretation expresses itself in the form of 'revenge' on the patient who cheated him of the fruits of his long analysis (CdZ, 509). Whoever holds the key to Zeno's truth, it is unquestionable, as Saccone observed, that 'medico e paziente [...] hanno bisogno l'uno dell'altro – e il medico, sembra, forse anche piú del paziente' [doctor and patient ... need each other – and the doctor, it seems, perhaps even more than the patient (1973: 56)]. Now it is the doctor who desires to live in the shadow of Zeno's story in order to let his own truth emerge. Although invoked in the doctor's discourse – 'Se sapesse quante sorprese potrebbero risultargli dal commento delle tante verità e bugie ch'egli ha qui accumulate!' [If he only knew how many surprises would come to him if somebody set about to comment on the truth and lies he has collected here! (CdZ, 509)] – truth remains a 'reading effect,' forever suspended in the dialogue between an *I* and a *thou*.

At the end of the novel, Zeno – threatened with terminal health by the interpretation/cure of the doctor – escapes from the dangerous symbiosis. But the ambiguous hierarchy between narrator and narratee is still being dramatized over and over again by a text suspended in the intersubjectivity of a failed dialogue. After Dr S. publishes his story the symbiosis extends outside the limits of the text, and, re-enacted at every new reading, reaches the shadow in which we ourselves are reading it (Savelli 1998).

Finished and Unfinished Men

If the chapter on smoking can be considered the dramatization of the lifelong association between Zeno and his doctors, the second chapter on the death of his father plunges us directly into the story of the earliest association with the other. '15.4.1890 ore 4 1/2. Muore mio padre. U.S.' [4:30 a.m. My father dies. L.C. (CdZ, 534)]. With this annotation Zeno opens his recollections about his father. To exorcise the finality of this moment, Zeno marks with the letters 'L.C.' – last cigarette – the event, but in this instance it is the event itself that threatens to mark the end of the sweet chain of resolutions: 'Lui morto non c'era piú una dimane ove collocare il proposito' [His death destroyed the future, the natural horizon of my resolutions (CdZ, 535)]. Confronted with the death of old Cosini, Zeno, who defines his dreams of strength and balance as 'un impetuoso conato al meglio' [a strong impulse to become better (CdZ, 536)], feels dangerously close to the completion of his potential.

> la morte di mio padre fu una vera, grande catastrofe. Il paradiso non esisteva piú ed io poi, a trent'anni, ero un *uomo finito*. (CdZ, 535; emphasis mine)

> [My father's death was an unmitigated catastrophe. Paradise had ceased to exist for me, and at thirty I was a *finished man*.]

Within Zeno's system the father is a 'finished man.' But what does it mean exactly to be a finished man? And how does the father's disappearance curtail Zeno's future?

The description of old Cosini, who 'aveva [...] quiete nella sua casa e nell'animo suo' [had ... peace in his house and in his soul (CdZ, 536)], affords a definition of that much dreaded condition:

> Per lui il cuore non pulsava e non v'era bisogno di ricordare valvole e vene e ricambio per spiegare come il suo organismo viveva. Niente movimento perché l'esperienza diceva che quanto si moveva finiva coll'arrestarsi. Anche la terra era per lui immobile e solidamente piantata su dei cardini. (CdZ, 537)

> [As far as he was concerned the heart did not beat, and he had no need to remind himself of valves and veins and metabolism to explain why he was alive. No need to think of movement, since experience taught that whatever moved eventually had to stop. For him even the earth was motionless and securely poised between its poles.]

Totally unaware of the changes in the world and in his body, Zeno's father is 'finished' like the mammoth in the essay 'L'uomo e la teoria darwiniana,' which in its unconsciousness is imperceptibly brought to extinction.

> Non è lui che si evolve perché già perfetto rinunziò alla vera vita. [...] Intorno a lui la natura si modifica ed egli non se ne accorge neppure se tali mutamenti implicano per lui la morte. Muore con lo stesso aspetto (e certamente la stessa convinzione) che avrebbe morendo perché un suo organo non piú funzionò ... (UT, 640)

> [He is not the one to evolve because, already perfect, he renounces the real life. ... Around him nature mutates, and he does not realize it even if such changes imply his death. He dies with the same aspect (and certainly the same conviction) that he would have had if an organ of his stopped working ...]

'Così è fatto l'animale privo d'anima' [So it is made, the animal without a soul (UT, 640)]. Like the mammoth crystallized in his unshakeable certainties, caged in an eternal present, the father 'viveva perfettamente d'accordo sul modo come l'avevano fatto' [lived perfectly in tune with the way he had been made (CdZ, 536)].

Zeno – the conscious, active and 'malcontento uomo' – had claimed, beside his pacific and unconscious father, a position of strength.

> Insomma io, accanto a lui, rappresentavo la forza e talvolta penso che la scomparsa di quella debolezza, che mi elevava, fu sentita da me come una diminuzione. (CdZ, 538)

> [Near to him, I therefore represented pure strength, and sometimes I think that the disappearance of that weakness, which put me in relief, resulted in a personal diminishment.]

Till this moment, Zeno's virtuality (the dreams of strength) represented true strength, while adaptation (the actuality of strength) coincided with weakness. The death of the father has the catastrophic effect of chasing Zeno out of the paradise enclosed by such a consoling dialectic. The disappeareance of the elder Cosini reveals to Zeno how his strength is predicated on the other in whose shadow he had lived. For this reason, the mourning, occasioning a further motive for remorse, is directed more at the loss of the defining shadow than at the loss of the father: 'Piansi molto, ma piuttosto su me stesso' [I shed many tears, but mostly for myself (CdZ, 558)]. The death of the other taught the 'uomo in abbozzo' something about the nature of his desire, namely that it does not exist as an absolute, but only as the effect of a comparison.

Death surprisingly redefines the nature of the finished man as well. Separated in life, father and son – finished mammoth and unfinished man – are brought dangerously close together by death. The father's final *consciousness* of his impending end marks an unexpected event: the birth of the mammoth's soul. Far from being 'l'animale privo d'anima' [the animal without a soul (UT, 640)], the elder Cosini struggles to express the meaning of existence to his skeptical son before the onset of final unconsciousness.

> – 'Quello ch'io cerco non è complicato affatto. Si tratta anzi di trovare una parola, una sola e la troverò!' (CdZ, 544)

> [– 'What I am looking for is not at all complicated. It is only a question of finding a word, a single word, and I will find it!']

While death endows the father with the soul the son refused him, it paradoxically marks the reification of the survivor, limited in his being by the disappearance of the weakness of the other. In fact, the astounding emergence of a mammoth with a soul constitutes a realization of those very dreams of 'balance and strength' that Zeno religiously pursued from resolution to resolution.

The last image of the father's body – 'che giaceva superbo e minaccioso' [lying there proud and menacing (CdZ, 559)], an image of absolute strength – will forever dominate Zeno's memory. Death leaves the 'uomo in abbozzo' with the regret of having missed the chance of recognizing his father and of being recognized by him. To suffocate any such remorse, Zeno abandons himself to a final corrective fantasy that extends the symbiosis beyond death, thus negating the reality of his own finitude:

> Poi, al funerale, riuscii a ricordare mio padre debole e buono [...]. Divenni buono, buono e il ricordo di mio padre s'accompagnò a me, divenendo sempre piú dolce. Fu come un sogno delizioso: eravamo ormai perfettamente d'accordo, io divenuto il piú debole e lui il piú forte. (CdZ, 559)

> [Then, at the funeral, I succeeded in remembering my father weak and

good ... I became very kind and the memory of my father never left me and grew sweeter to me. It was like a delightful dream: we were now in complete agreement, I having become the weaker and he the stronger.]

The consoling dream, like Angiolina's symbolic representation as the weeping beauty at the end of *Senilità*, only manages to maintain the symbiotic relationship by scrambling its terms. The other, who withheld the final word, now occupies the last horizon of Zeno's future, the ultimate depository of his 'anxious hope,' as a benign presence to preside over Zeno's continuing efforts to better himself.

Zeno, who perused the future 'indagando per trovare perché e per chi [avrebbe] potuto continuare i [suoi] sforzi di migliorar[si]' [in search of why and for whom [he] could have continued [his]efforts of self-improvement (CdZ, 557–8)], ultimately avoids the threatened finitude by finding a new father. Giovanni Malfenti, his future father-in-law, is a finished man in whose shadow he can live and whose strength and health, now that he is conscious of the 'weakness' and 'sickness' that ties him to the other, he can try to imitate:

> Lui [...] era un grande negoziante, ignorante ed attivo. Ma dalla sua ignoranza gli risultava forza e serenità ed io m'incantavo a guardarlo, invidiandolo. [...] Le poche idee che gli si movevano nella grossa testa erano svolte da lui con tanta chiarezza, sviscerate con tale assiduità, [...] da divenire *sue parti, sue membra*, suo carattere. (CdZ, 562; emphasis mine)
>
> [He ... was an important businessman, ignorant and active. His ignorance gave him strength and serenity. I was fascinated by his sight, and I envied him his qualities. ... The few ideas that revolved in his big head were exposed with such clarity, unravelled with such tenacity, ... that they became *part of his very self, his limbs*, his character.]

Malfenti is the animal who, by favoring the complete development of a part of his body – that is, of his *ideas* – has become crystallized, but in that very process has obtained the strength and assurance that the 'uomo in abbozzo' is lacking. It will be only at the end that Zeno, the war profiteer, will successfully embrace this economy. 'Come tutte le persone forti,' he muses, certaintly thinking back to his father-in-law, 'ebbi nella mia testa una sola idea e di quella vissi e fu la mia fortuna' [Like all the strong people, I had in my head only one idea and I lived through that and it was my fortune (CdZ, 893)].

But for the time being, Zeno pursues a mimetic desire for Malfenti's strength, and in order to learn his finitude, he lives in his shadow.

> Quando io ammiro qualcuno, tento immediatamente di somigliargli. Copiai anche il Malfenti. Volli essere e mi sentii molto astuto. (CdZ, 563)

> [When I admire someone I at once try to be like him. So I began to imitate Malfenti. I desired to be and, indeed, I started feeling very astute.]

And yet strength is not the true object of Zeno's desire. Dreading his own 'arrested development,' Zeno, like the 'uomo in abbozzo,' is constantly overtaken by a compulsion to change, to resemble the other, a chameleon-like desire that reaches comic levels: 'quando leggo un giornale, mi sento trasformato in opinione pubblica' [when I read the papers, I become metamorphosed into public opinion (CdZ, 565)]. Therefore the pursuit of strength is nothing but the desire to guarantee his unfinished character by living two lives at once (Saccone 1977). Zeno's desire for finitude – i.e., 'health' – unfolds as a defence of his unfinishedness – his 'sickness.'

It is not surprising, therefore, if his mourning for the loss of Malfenti, this stronger other, is once again tinged by a sense of having lost his own subjectivity:

> Alla sua tomba come a tutte quelle su cui piansi, *il mio dolore fu dedicato anche a quella parte di me stesso che vi era sepolta*. Quale *diminuzione* per me venir privato di quel mio secondo padre, ordinario, ignorante, feroce lottatore che dava risalto alla mia debolezza, la mia cultura, la mia timidezza. [...] Chissà come mi sarei conosciuto meglio se egli avesse continuato a starmi accanto. (CdZ, 567; emphasis mine)

> [At his grave, as at all the ones on which I cried, *my sorrow was directed as well to that part of myself that had been buried there*. What a *diminution* it was for me to be deprived of that second father, that ordinary, ignorant, fierce fighter who put into relief my weakness, culture, timidity ... How much better I might have known myself if he kept on living beside me.]

Once again the word *diminuzione* returns, as after the death of the father, and points out how Zeno's 'coscienza' is inseparable from a consciousness of the other. Symbiosis is Zeno's mode of self-knowledge.

On a similar note, Zeno writes after Guido's death: 'l'intera mia vita mi sembrò vuota poiché tanta parte ne era invasa da lui e dai suoi affari' [my whole life seemed empty because so much of it was taken over by him and his business (CdZ, 752)]. The bond linking Zeno and Guido develops on a very different and much more ambiguous level than the earlier ones. Zeno's association with Guido has the qualities of a life experiment like the one described by the passenger of the 'Diario di bordo' who follows the explorer Riottison to the North Pole: 'come e perché due nature così dissimili come la mia e la sua si trovino unite è facile dire' [how and why two natures so different as mine and his are tied together is easily said (481)], he muses, 'Io mi legai a lui per vedere se vivere una vita come è la sua sia più divertente che vegetare la mia' [I bound myself to him to see if living a life like his would be more fun than vegetating in mine (1968: 481)]. 'La storia di un'associazione commerciale' [A Business Partnership] is such an experiment in contamination between two radically different existential economies. In the association with Malfenti, the latter's superiority, business wisdom, and strength are unquestioned, and Zeno dutifully sets about to learn them. But the association with Guido is born under the sign of a comparison, 'to see if' one man is stronger or weaker, superior or inferior, finished or unfinished with respect to the other. While the relationship with Malfenti held no surprises, Zeno embarks on his association with Guido as if on an adventure. As in the 'Diario di bordo,' Guido is the captain, Zeno the passenger writing the travelogue of the other's trip as his own voyage of self-discovery.

Guido will not reach the Pole, but Zeno, who beside him '[si] fece molto inerte' [made (himself) very inert (CdZ, 755)], that is, mammothlike, does get a chance to challenge Guido. After the death and financial ruin of Guido, now literally a finished man, Zeno will finally emerge from the shadow in which he had been waiting and live a moment of full health, switching from the reign of potentiality and sickness to that of action by recuperating singlehandedly half the patrimony that Guido squandered. The mourning of Guido's death, in the opening of the narration of the business association, as loss – a 'diminishment' like the one Zeno experienced at his father and Malfenti's death – is now scandalously celebrated as a chance to conquer strength and health.

> Ero tutta salute e forza. La salute non risalta che da un paragone. Mi paragonavo al povero Guido e salivo, salivo in alto con la mia vittoria nella stessa lotta nella quale egli era soggiaciuto. (CdZ, 856)

[I was all strength and health. Health is finally only the result of a comparison. I compared myself to poor Guido and I stood tall with my victory in the very struggle in which he was vanquished.]

Even though introduced with regret, Zeno's relationship with Guido will unfold as a somewhat disguised but relentless competition, a competition that dates back to the struggle over Ada's affection. In the 'Storia di un'associazione commerciale' the Darwinian struggle dominating the world of business is powerfully projected on the small yet labyrinthine stage of Zeno's most intimate affections.

A patronizing feeling of superiority, not dissimilar to the one Zeno felt towards his father, a feeling marked by the pleasure 'di vederlo felice nella sua illusione di essere tanto forte quand'era invece debolissimo' [of seeing him happy in his illusion of strength when he was instead very weak (CdZ, 543)] inaugurates Zeno's association with Guido:

> Prima di tutto gli volevo bene e benché egli volesse sembrare forte e sicuro, a me pareva un inerme abbisognante di una protezione che io volentieri volevo accordargli. (CdZ, 749)

> [First of all I loved him and although he wanted to look strong and self-assured, to me he looked helpless and in need of a protection that I gladly wanted to grant him.]

But how can Zeno, while pursuing the never-abandoned hope of becoming a good businessman, afford any protection to Guido with whom he shares, as he did already with the father, the absolute lack of any business sense (CdZ, 536)? 'Mi pareva piú facile,' explains Zeno, 'di progredire insegnando a Guido, che facendomi insegnare dall'Olivi' [It seemed to me easier to progress by teaching Guido, rather than being taught by Olivi (his father's accountant) (CdZ, 749)]. Once again the desire of a Svevian character is to learn by teaching the pupil, to be at the same time pupil – 'unfinished' in the protective shadow of the other – and pedagogue – finished and powerful. By being with Guido, Zeno does not learn or teach how to be a good businessman – in this sense it is true, as Ada said, that Guido died for nothing – but he is able to question the ethical nature of his ambiguous symbiosis: 'Am I good or bad?' he asks himself. Like life, which he declares 'né brutta né bella, ma [...] originale!' [neither beautiful nor ugly, but original! (CdZ, 801)], Zeno refuses an essentialist truth in favor of a narrative one.

Many are the proofs brought forth during the courting of the Malfenti sisters to convince the reader and the other judge within the narrative world – Ada – of Guido's inferiority. Zeno says to Ada: 'Suona bene il violino, ma vi sono anche delle scimmie che sanno suonarlo. Ogni sua parola tradisce il bestione.' [He plays the violin well, but there are monkeys that can play it as well. Every word of his betrays the animal (CdZ, 623)]. Music, being 'lei stessa il tempo ch'essa crea ed esaurisce' [the very time it creates and exhausts (CdZ, 609)], is a perfect expression of Guido's balanced organism: 'parallelamente alla sua sicurezza sul violino, correva anche la sua disinvoltura nella vita' [his ease in playing the violin was one and the same as the confidence with which he went through life (CdZ, 767)]. Zeno envies the 'superiority' of this finitude – Guido's complete adherence to time, his *being* time – and at the same time despises the inferiority that it entails. Guido, presented through Zeno's perspective, seems, like Malfenti before him, a true 'bestione,' finished in his perfection. But his character is more ambiguous than Zeno purports it to be. Guido's repeatedly stressed 'weakness' makes him also an uncanny and dangerous double of Zeno. As a matter of fact, it is a necessity within Zeno's economy that Guido be portrayed as radically other. In order for Zeno to be and remain the 'unfinished man,' Guido *must* be the mammoth. What constituted an undisputed reality in Zeno's relationship with Malfenti – the latter's manifestation of force and superiority – will become with Guido a matter of rhetorical struggle.

After their first business transaction, Zeno arrives at an important conclusion: 'Allora credetti di scoprire la grande differenza che c'era fra me e Guido. Quanto sapevo io, mi serviva per parlare e a lui per agire' [Then I believed I discovered the great difference between me and Guido. What I knew served me for talking, and him for acting (CdZ, 752)]. The story about to be told seems to be one in which the man of virtuality, Zeno, confronts Guido, the man of action. But it is important to notice how on this occasion – by saying 'I believed' – Zeno the narrator distances himself from Zeno the character and thereby suggests that the dichotomy with Guido might in fact be a feigned one. As Zeno records the events of the story, the story silently undoes his conclusions, showing how the two friends have much more in common than Zeno himself would like to admit.

Indeed, and in direct contradiction to Zeno's assertion, Zeno and Guido are united in their love for the word and passion for pedagogy. If Zeno entered the association with the intent to teach he is soon confronted with Guido's equal desire to play the educator: 'Guido spendeva sempre una parte della giornata ad insegnare dapprima a Luciano, poi a me e quindi all'impiegata' [Guido spent a good part of each day in teaching Luciano, then me, and finally the female employee (CdZ, 753)]. Witnessing an all too familiar tendency for rhetoric in Guido's relations with his lover, Zeno acrimoniously observes: 'Guido ciarlava molto. Chissà che non sia stato attaccato a Carmen dalla sua passione per l'insegnamento piuttosto che dall'amore' [Guido chatted a lot. He might have been attached to Carmen because of his passion for pedagogy rather than his love (CdZ, 776)]. And when it is Guido's turn to play the pupil for Zeno's lesson in accounting, he is put in an equally derisive light:

> Guido restò a bocca aperta, comprese troppo bene come gli succedeva sempre e si attaccò a quella teoria che propinò a chi la volle. [...] Gli pareva addirittura che la conoscenza della contabilità conferisse al mondo un nuovo aspetto. Egli vedeva nascere debitori e creditori dappertutto anche quando due si picchiavano o si baciavano. (CdZ, 754)

> [Guido was utterly astounded. As always he understood too well and hung on to that theory which eventually he imposed on whoever he wished. ... He felt that the knowledge of bookkeeping put the world in a different light. He saw debtors and creditors everywhere, whether two people were fighting or kissing each other.]

But who more than Zeno displays the tendency to become obsessed with theories? Following Ada's sickness, Zeno develops a whole life philosophy based on the Basedow disease: 'Grande, importante malattia quella di Basedow! [...] credetti di scoprire appena allora il segreto essenziale del nostro organismo' [Great and important was Basedow's disease! ... I believed I discovered just then the essential secret of our organism (CdZ, 788)]. He even justifies his own propensity for philosophizing in grandiose theoretical terms by observing that

> da molti come da me vi sieno dei periodi di tempo in cui certe idee occupino e ingombrino tutto il cervello chiudendolo a tutte le altre. Ma se anche alla collettività succede la stessa cosa! (CdZ, 788)

> [there must be many people who, like me, go through periods in which certain ideas dominate their minds to the exclusion of all else. But does not the same thing happen with society?]

What in Guido was a sign of narrow-mindedness, in Zeno becomes the unfolding of a zeitgeist.

The trademarks of Zeno's eccentricity – the pedagogical attitude, the love for the word as performance, the singleminded infatuation with ideas – have found a worthy match in Guido. The unresolved, mysterious quality of Guido's character – 'uno strano uomo' [a strange man (CdZ, 862)] as Zeno finally defines him – is a mirroring of Zeno's own strangeness. Only after Guido's death will Zeno begrudgingly recognize their similarity when he comments to Ada – 'Hai finito con lo sposare un uomo ancora piú bizzarro di me, Ada!' [You ended up marrying a man even more bizarre than I, Ada! (CdZ, 813)].

The confrontation between Zeno and Guido, after its first climax in Guido's violin performance at Malfenti's home, has a second highly charged moment in the fable contest. In this instance, and because the narration is somewhat more removed from the monopoly of Zeno's voice, the dialogue between the fables 'invented' by the two friends generates a more objective perspective on their relationship. These, like Mario's fables in 'La burla riuscita,' are what Lavagetto defines as fable-fetishes (1986: 155): within the story, Guido openly recognizes them as such, invoking them along with the violin as a means of compensating, perhaps even substituting, for his failure in the business world. While Zeno may see them as offensive weapons in his struggle against his friend, for him too they function as fetishes in the sense that they 'occultano la realtà e la rivelano spietatamente' [at the same time hide and pitilessly reveal reality (155)]. As a result, their fetish nature is greater in Zeno's case precisely because it remains hidden from him. 'Oracoli [...] inascoltati' [unheeded oracles (155)] for Zeno, the fables afford the readers an insight into Zeno's blindness.

The first fable told by Guido belongs to Svevo himself. It is the story, already quoted in chapter two, of the little bird, who, fearing to be deprived of the freedom to go back to his cage, closes the door left open by mistake.

> La seconda trattava di un elefante ed era veramente elefantesca. Soffrendo di debolezza alle gambe, il grosso animale andava a consultare un uomo, celebre medico, il quale al vedere quegli arti poderosi gridava: – Non vidi giammai delle gambe tanto forti. (CdZ, 781)

[The second was about an elephant and it was truly elephantine. The huge beast, feeling weak in the legs, went to consult a famous doctor, who when he saw his enormous limbs exclaimed: I never saw such strong legs!]

The first fable, with its refusal of instinct and the vocation for struggle in order to embrace the limitation that creates one's own desire, is a defining parable of Svevo's subject. But despite Zeno's scorn, the second fable as well evokes themes and characters dear to Svevo, from the relativity of strength and weakness to doctors and 'mammoths,' and ironically concentrates in one 'elephantine' character both the story of Guido, 'the weak beast,' and Zeno, the man obsessed with undetectable diseases. On one level, Zeno's dismissal – 'Ritengo che la prima delle due favole non sia stata sua e che invece la seconda sia veramente uscita dal suo cervello di cui mi sembra degna' [I believe that the first fable wasn't his while the second really came out of his brain, of which it seemed a worthy product (CdZ, 780–1)] – fails to disqualify Guido's performance (much as his attack on Guido's violin recital failed). But even more profoundly, by making a gift of his own story to Guido, Svevo allows Guido an insight that, as we shall see, is of a higher order than Zeno's.[4]

Spurred by the old pains in his legs caused by Guido's success, Zeno picks up the challenge by writing a dialogue entitled 'Hymn to life,' and then a fable about a man and his fleas:

Il gamberello meditabondo: – La vita è bella ma bisogna badare al posto dove ci si siede. *L'orata,* correndo dal dentista: – La vita è bella ma bisognerebbe eliminarne quegli animalucci traditori che celano nella carne saporita il metallo acuminato. [...]

'C'era una volta un principe morso da molte pulci. S'appellò agli dei che gl'infliggessero una sola pulce, grossa e famelica, ma una sola, e destinassero le altre agli altri uomini. Ma nessuna delle pulci accettò di restare sola con quella bestia d'uomo, ed egli dovette tenersele tutte.' (CdZ, 782)

[*The prawn impaled on a hook, meditating:* – Life is beautiful but one must watch where one sits down. *The sea bass,* running to the dentist: – Life is beautiful, but one must get rid of those treacherous little animals who hide sharp metal in their tasty flesh.

'There was once a prince who was bitten by many fleas. He prayed to the gods to grant him only one flea, as big and ravenous as they liked but only one, and to distribute the others to the rest of mankind. But not one of the fleas would consent to stay alone with that beast of a prince, and he was obliged to keep them all.']

At first Zeno thinks his fables are 'splendid,' but he soon realizes his poor judgment. Guido, turning out to be not just a better storyteller but a more acute interpreter, recognizes himself immediately in the second fable and he pointedly comments: 'Non è una favola, ma è un modo di darmi della bestia' [it is not a fable, but a way to call me a beast (CdZ, 782)]. If the second fable is an open attack, the first, in light of Zeno's accompanying comment that 'L'inno alla vita fatto dal morituro è una cosa molto simpatica per coloro che lo guardano morire' [The hymn to life sung by the one who is dying is a very pleasant thing for those who watch him die (CdZ, 782)], foreshadows Zeno's future indifference towards Guido's bankruptcy and suicide.[5]

Possessed by the desire to outwit, Zeno's fables are less beautiful than Guido's. While the truth of Guido's fables lightheartedly embraces both friends, the truth of Zeno's speaks mostly of resentment towards his brother/other. All the fables move within the same Darwinian constellation, but Guido's defy Darwinian determinism, while both of Zeno's speak of the lack of freedom and the brutality of the struggle: the first in which prey and predator are equally vanquished, and the second in which symbiosis itself is reduced to parasitism, a scourge to be endured. 'Non sarebbe stato certamente l'amico che avrei liberamente prescelto' [He would not have been the friend I freely would have chosen (CdZ, 751)], says Zeno of Guido. And still, for endless overlapping reasons – because of his ambivalence about Ada, his desire and fear of the business world of struggle, his mixture of curiosity and indifference, compassion and disgust towards a man so different from him in his strength and so uncannily similar to him in his weakness – Zeno remains beside Guido, faithful as a mammoth and as treacherous as the restless man.

Augusta, or Absolute Health.

'Per la stanchezza di emettere e sentire [un'] unica nota' [Being tired of expressing and listening to only one note (CdZ, 561)], Zeno embarks upon a matrimonial adventure in which he hopes to be changed by the other.

> madre natura [...] ci dà a credere che dalla moglie risulterà anche un rinnovamento nostro, ciò ch'è un'illusione curiosa non autorizzata da alcun testo. Infatti si vive poi uno accanto all'altro, immutati, salvo che per una nuova antipatia per chi è tanto dissimile da noi e per un'invidia per chi a noi è superiore. (CdZ, 561–2)
>
> [mother nature ... makes us believe that through the wife a personal

renewal will result; a curious illusion that is not authorized by any text. As a matter of fact, people end up living one next to the other, unchanged, except for a new antipathy for the person who is so different from us and envy for the person who is superior.]

But despite emerging doubts, Zeno is overtaken during the honeymoon by 'la grande speranza di poter finire col somigliare ad Augusta ch'era la salute personificata' [the great hope of being able to finally resemble Augusta who was health personified (CdZ, 645)].

In her absolute health, Augusta summarizes the traits of both fathers, hers and Zeno's.[6] Her *Weltanschauung* thus constitutes a replay of the elderly Cosini's faith in the solidity and immobility of things:

> Essa sapeva tutte le cose che fanno disperare, ma in mano sua queste cose cambiavano di natura. Se anche la terra girava non occorreva mica avere il mal di mare! Tutt'altro! La terra girava, ma tutte le altre cose restavano al loro posto. E queste cose immobili avevano un'importanza enorme: l'anello di matrimonio, tutte le gemme e i vestiti, il verde, il nero [...] E le ore dei pasti erano tenute rigidamente e anche quelle del sonno. Esistevano, quelle ore, e si trovavano sempre al loro posto. (CdZ, 646–7)

[She knew all the things that make one despair, but in her hands these things changed in nature. Even if the earth was spinning it wasn't by any means necessary to be seasick! Quite the contrary! The earth was spinning, but all things remained in their assigned place. And these unmovable things had an enormous importance: the wedding ring, all the jewels and the dresses, the green and the black ... And the dining hours were rigidly kept as were those for resting. They existed, those hours, and always remained in their place.]

Like the pacific mammoth, Augusta lives unconscious of herself and her surroundings. She represents the 'finshed woman' who has perfected her organs and has reached the only true health, the one that belongs 'alla bestia che conosce un solo progresso, quello del proprio organismo' [to the animal that knows only one progress, the one of its own organism (CdZ, 894)]. Confronted with the fact that Augusta 'neppur sapeva come fosse fatta la salute' [did not even know how health was made (CdZ, 651)], Zeno has to refrain from studying her too closely because under his scrutiny Augusta's health gets converted into a pathology. 'E, scrivendone,' reflects Zeno, 'comincio a dubitare se quella salute non avesse avuto bisogno di cura o d'istruzione per guarire' [And while writing about it, I start doubting if that health couldn't have used a cure or instruction for healing (CdZ, 647)]. Augusta's health, with a perfection and absoluteness that nears a pathological condition, is beyond Zeno's imitation.

As Saccone notes, 'Augusta non rappresenta la guarigione, ma un compromesso. L'esigenza, ancora nevrotica come Zeno sa bene, di trovare il resto per ottenere l'intero' [Augusta does not represent healing, but only a compromise – the demand, still neurotic as Zeno knows very well, to find the remainder, to obtain the whole (1973: 103–4)]. Once he fails to imitate her health, or to make himself whole ('costituirsi intero,' as he had hoped from a marriage with Ada), Zeno strives not so much to better himself as to be continually *becoming* in the process of entering other associations. Zeno makes himself a slave of Augusta, of her ordered world, in order to win the pause that will allow the endless reinvention of his self.

With her simple and wilful words, Augusta chooses Zeno and ties her destiny to his: – 'Voi, Zeno, avete bisogno di una donna che voglia vivere per voi e vi assista. Io voglio essere quella donna' [You, Zeno, need a woman who wants to live for you and assist you. I want to be that woman (CdZ, 628)]. But after this initial affirmation, Augusta, to use Zeno's words, 'battè sicura la via per cui erano passate le sue sorelle su questa terra' [followed self-confidently the road previously trodden by her sisters on this earth (CdZ, 646)], a biological destiny that does not leave space to choice or different stories. Augusta's subjectivity will be totally absorbed into Zeno's consciousness. With the numberless women who preceded her, Augusta will share a life of silence and unquestioned devotion to the 'gloomy and dissatisfied man,' who, in that safe shadow, keeps building his endless 'ordigni' (tools).

In this instance, and contrary to the fable, it is the mammoth that makes itself the slave of the man. The question arises: in such an association, 'chi tutela' and 'chi è tutelato,' who is more powerful, 'chi tutela' or 'chi è tutelato'? A first answer is suggested by the fact that Augusta's story, like the story of the mammoth, is totally contained in the association with Zeno. Conversely, Zeno's story seen through 'her squint eyes' is naturalized as the one of the primitive man who the mammoth looks upon 'as the trees upon which it fed ... the air it breathed' (UT, 640). Zeno's story finds no challenge in Augusta's presence. As the benevolent mammoth, she lives unconsciously through Zeno's breaking of his contract, registering without understanding the effects of his betrayals, as when Zeno, abandoned by Carla, went to a prostitute: '– "Con te non ci si può mai annoiare. Sei ogni giorno un uomo nuovo"' [– 'One can never be bored with you. Every day you become a different man' (CdZ, 747)]. As the personification of health and legitimacy, Augusta grants Zeno's story the possibility of endless renewal.

Unlike Augusta's story, the stories of Ada and Carla stage the return of a remainder in which the glance of the other penetrates Zeno's story, holding him responsible for the breaking of a contract. This residue, rather than being a guarantor of the inexhaustible repetition of Zeno's desire, constitutes instead the uncanny appearance of a repressed subjectivity that returns on the scene of Zeno's writing and calls him by name.[7] Once the woman's subjectivity penetrates the story of the 'uomo in abbozzo,' it threatens to reduce him to an object, a finished man standing in his own shadow, a mammoth from whose shadow emerges the desire of the other.

Who is Carla?

Like the passenger in the 'Diario di bordo,' Zeno can say of his mammoth-like other 'Conosco meglio di lui [lei] l'animo suo' [I know better than he (she) his (her) soul (1968: 481)], and at the same time rest assured that 'Egli [ella] poi non mi conosce' [he (she) does not know me at all (1968: 481)]. If this might be true of Augusta, the 'laborious ant' whose absolute health can be studied, Carla is a 'sfinge' [sphinx (CdZ, 694)] who Zeno is not able to comprehend and who he systematically misunderstands. To live or love in her shadow is by no means a reassuring and unambiguous business: a 'sphinx' is no simple supplement to a wife. Rather she (and the sick Ada) behave like Derrida's particular concept of the *supplément* (1976: 141–64) with its double and undecidable economy of 'missing' and 'extra' pieces. Unlike Augusta ('la sana balia che non s'accorgeva affatto di quello che avveniva nell'animo mio' [the healthy nurse who did not realize at all what was happening in my heart (CdZ, 733)]) and all the other mammoths in whose shadows the 'uomo in abbozzo' lives, Carla comes to know Zeno. And once it is gained, this understanding ('Cominciava essa a intendermi?' [Was she beginning to understand me? (CdZ, 722)]) will envelope Zeno as the shadow of his finitude.

The relationship with Carla is born under that sign of philanthropy and pedagogy analysed in the preceding chapter. Upon the solicitation of his sick friend Copler, Zeno agrees to become her benefactor, and as such he witnesses a recital of her art. Against Copler's opinion that Carla's voice is made for the theatre, Zeno reflects that her voice 'apparteneva ad un ambiente piccolissimo dove si poteva gustare l'impressione d'ingenuità di quell'arte e sognare di portarci dentro l'arte, cioè vita e dolore' [belonged in a tiny environment where one could enjoy its naïve quality and dream of bringing art into it, that is life and sorrow (CdZ, 666)]. And he thus decides to become the sole inspiration and audience of Carla's 'art'; from philanthropist he becomes first a rigid pedagogue then a tyrannical mentor and lover. Carla's education, like those of Angiolina and the 'bella fanciulla,' is a way to neutralize the transgression and legitimize it. The association with the other is removed from the play of love, one in which hierarchies are dangerously fluid, and frozen in a safe pedagogical structure, one where the intent – as in the relationship with Guido – is to learn while teaching, to take while in the attitude of giving. But Carla's talent, as Zeno to his surprise will learn, goes beyond the perfect beauty of her dark braids, oval face, and pure complexion, and thus beyond his ambiguously parasitic and predatory protection. From Zeno's pedagogical failures, Carla will emerge as an independent subject that owes nothing to her 'teacher.' With a Triestine song celebrating youth's rights to love and life, she will surprise Zeno with an 'undeniable talent' that refuses manipulation, asking only 'affetto e protezione' [for tenderness and protection (CdZ, 716)].

The love story with Carla gives a visible geography to the endless temporal displacements of Zeno's 'propositi.' Pursuing his desire to live more intensely (CdZ, 715), Zeno runs restlessly from his sunny villa with a view of the sea to the other side of the city, beyond the public garden, where Carla lives in the shadow of her small and modest apartment. He walks Trieste in an interplay of innocence and remorse, betraying both wife and lover while they remain secluded in the claustrophobic space created by his desire: Augusta's healthy shadow –'[l'] ambiente di salute e di onestà in cui regnava Augusta a cui ritornavo subito col corpo e l'anima non appena Carla mi lasciava libero' [(the) environment of health and honesty over which Augusta presided and to which I immediately returned body and soul as soon as Carla left me free (CdZ, 725–6)] – and Carla's unhealthy one – '[la] piccola stanzuccia non contenente di piú di un metro cubo di aria, per sovrappiú caldissima' [(the) shaggy little room that did not contain more than a cubic meter of unbearably hot air (CdZ, 721)]. Living at the margins of Zeno's story, Carla seems 'un essere inferiore' [an inferior being (CdZ, 725)], a second, despised mammoth. But Carla is more than a mammoth. At the same time that she offers a shadow for the 'unfinished man,' she lives herself confined in the long shadow cast by Augusta's presence. There she does not simply acquiesce to Zeno's volatile passion but gives voice to her own desire; one of her surprising acts is to choose a new name, Dario, to call Zeno.

Nonetheless, Carla at first dutifully remains in the obscurity of her rooms, patiently awaiting her moody lover. Then, repeatedly confronted with Zeno's evasions, she openly rebels. First she extorts from Zeno a token of recognition, a stroll in the public gardens. But after being humiliated by Zeno's feigned indifference (upon accidentally meeting his friend Tullio), she also becomes subject to moodiness, a moodiness that reminds Zeno of his own:

> la mia amante finí col somigliarmi troppo. Senz'alcuna ragione, ad ogni istante, se la prendeva con me in scoppi di collera improvvisi. Presto si ravvedeva, ma bastavano per rendermi tanto eppoi tanto buono e docile. (CdZ, 731)

> [my lover ended up resembling me way too much. Without any reason, at any moment, she would get angry at me in sudden outbursts. Soon she came to herself, but it was still sufficient to make me very good and docile.]

Commenting upon his lover's rebellions, Zeno concedes, even if jokingly, that Carla might have become a 'subject' in her own right, so much so that he muses:

> Io temo che il dottore che leggerà questo mio manoscritto abbia a pensare che anche Carla sarebbe stata un soggetto interessante alla psico-analisi. (CdZ, 697)

> [I fear that the doctor who will read this manuscript of mine will come to the conclusion that even Carla would have been an interesting subject for psychoanalysis.]

Carla is a 'sfinge'; her psyche is as indecipherable as Zeno's own murky interiority.

The second and precipitating desire of Carla's is that of meeting Zeno's wife. Zeno's playful deception – and perhaps the sincere expression of the wish underlying the whole story of 'La moglie e l'amante' [Wife and Lover] – is to lead Carla, to meet not Augusta but Ada. Confronted with Ada's beauty and visible unhappiness – exactly that day she had discovered an affair of Guido's – Carla decides to pursue her desire, which is now a desire to respect Ada's desire, and becomes engaged with her singing teacher, the young Lali. On this occasion, Zeno's desire is chastised by both Ada and Carla, who exchange 'un'occhiata accorata di solidarietà' [a glance of sorrowful solidarity (CdZ, 733)] that pierces through Zeno's narrative. Carla's refusal to be either mammoth or accomplice for the unfinished man's pursuit of his desire, and its resulting betrayals, will free her to follow her own desire in the streets of Trieste.

A last significant detour precedes this freedom however. Zeno and Carla share a 'proposito': to betray one final time both Augusta and Carla's fiancé:

> Mormoravamo ambedue: – 'Per l'ultima volta!' Fu un istante delizioso. Il proposito fatto a due aveva un'efficacia che cancellava qualsiasi colpa. Eravamo innocenti e beati! Il mio benevolo destino m'aveva riservato un istante di felicità perfetta (CdZ, 734)

> [We both whispered: – 'For the last time!' It was a delightful moment. The communal purpose had the effect of erasing any guilt. We were innocent and blissful! My benevolent destiny reserved for me an instant of pure happiness.]

But while for Zeno this is only a 'comedy,' the eternal comedy of the last cigarette, for Carla this act of breaking faith marks with complete finality the end of her story with Zeno.

From this moment on Zeno will be running desperately after Carla in the attempt to once again regain his control:

> Era evidente che la mia donna correva via, sempre piú lontano da me. Io le corsi dietro follemente, con certi salti simili a quelli di un cane cui venga conteso un saporito pezzo di carne. (CdZ, 742)

> [It was evident that my woman was running away, farther and farther from me. I ran after her madly, with jumps like those of a dog from whom somebody withdrew a savory piece of meat.]

It would be a mistake to conclude from this image that 'per la coscienza di Zeno a questo punto Carla [è] ancora soltanto un oggetto' [for Zeno's consciousness at this point Carla [is] still only an object (Saccone

1973: 155)]. Zeno's identification with the dog makes Carla the master, withholding the longed-for morsel from the ravenous instinct of the animal. If at this point consciousness is being denied to someone, Zeno the narrator is denying it to his former self. This interpretation finds confirmation when the image of the dog returns, during the tumultuous last encounter between Zeno and Carla:

> – 'Ed egli [Lali] sa, tutto? Sa che anche ieri fosti mia?' – 'Sí' – essa disse con orgoglio. – 'Egli sa tutto, tutto.' – Mi sentivo perduto e nella mia rabbia, simile al cane che, quando non può piú raggiungere il boccone desiderato, addenta le vesti di chi glielo contende, dissi: – 'Questo tuo sposo ha uno stomaco eccellente. Oggi digerisce me e domani potrà digerire tutto ciò che vorrai.' (CdZ, 742)

> [– 'And he (Lali) knows everything? Does he know even that yesterday you were mine?' – 'Yes' – she said with pride. – 'He knows everything, everything.' I felt lost and in my anger like a dog that, when it cannot reach the desired morsel, worries the dress of the person who is standing in its way, I said: – 'This fiance of yours has an excellent stomach. Today he digests me and tomorrow he will be able to digest whatever you like.']

Here it is clear that Zeno is not only enslaved to a desire controlled by the other, but, in the passage of a few sentences, becomes even the food digested by another man. The 'uomo in abbozzo,' who momentarily abandoned the shadow and protection of the mammoth (Augusta) looking for prey, has become inadvertently a mammoth for Carla and prey for another. Thus, Carla's desire chases him back into the shadow from whence he came, forcing him into the position of a finished man, unable to endlessly pursue his changing desire.

The image of the dog returns one last time on the stairs of Carla's apartment, when Zeno runs after her: 'Avevo un grande desiderio di andarmene e ritornavo anche una volta, puro, ad Augusta. Anche il cane a cui a forza di pedate si impedisce l'approccio alla femmina, corre via purissimo, per il momento' [I had a great desire to leave and return once again pure to Augusta. Even the dog, kicked over and over to keep him away from the female, runs away very pure, for the time being (CdZ, 743–4)]. 'La femmina' is again an object of appetite, but this time it is Carla who kicks the dog (Zeno) away.

Walking by himself in the streets of Trieste, where Carla is now strolling with the man she has chosen, Zeno is struck by the irrevocability of his exclusion. In one of the few epiphanic moments that stand out clearly in the constant undertow of Zeno's rhetoric, the narrative reaches a standstill, and there drenched in a blinding light Zeno finally sees himself whole:

> Cessai di lagnarmi del mio destino e *vidi me stesso come se una grande luce m'avesse proiettato intero* sul selciato che guardavo. Io non domandavo Carla, io volevo il suo abbraccio e preferibilmente il suo ultimo abbraccio. Una cosa ridicola! Mi ficcai i denti nelle labbra per gettare il dolore, cioè un poco di serietà, sulla mia ridicola immagine. *Sapevo tutto di me stesso* ed era imperdonabile che soffrissi tanto perché mi veniva offerta una opportunità unica di svezzamento. Carla non c'era piú proprio come tante volte l'avevo desiderato. (CdZ, 747; emphasis mine)

> [I stopped lamenting my destiny and *I saw myself as if a great light projected me whole* on the pavement under my eyes. I was not asking for Carla, I wanted her embrace and preferably her last embrace. A ridiculous thing! I bit my lips to cast some pain, that is, a little seriousness, on my ridiculous image. *I knew everything about myself*, and it was unforgivable that I suffered so much because a unique opportunity of weaning myself was offered to me.]

The embrace is the morsel, the objectified woman, the piece, another of the many that Zeno was able to have up to that point. The end of the fiction of the 'donna a pezzi' [woman in pieces] coincides with Zeno's sudden vision of himself 'intero,' a vision of finitude that dispels the fiction of the man engaged in constant becoming. The great light nails the shadow of the finished pedagogue and philanthropist onto the white page, orphaned of Carla, the mammoth, as well as of Carla the 'donna in abbozzo' (the unfinished woman).

Carla, the 'sfinge,' the other whose desire faces the subject as a promise and a threat, is in the end tamed by memory. As Zeno goes back to the two years of happiness she gave him, he wonders how 'essa – essendo fatta nel modo che ora sapevo – avesse potuto sopportarmi per tanto tempo' [she – being made in the way I knew she was – could stand me for such a long time (CdZ, 768)]. But how was Carla made? This question creates a remainder that explodes Zeno's economy of desire. In the enigma of Carla, 'la vita sarebbe corsa via, ricca bensí di godimenti, ma anche piú di sforzi per migliorarsi' [life would have run along rich in pleasures, but even more in efforts to better oneself (CdZ, 736)], but knowing her meant dissipating the shadow in which he had

186   In the Shadow of the Mammoth

hidden and thus coming to know himself as well (seeing himself as if projected whole). Carla, who gave Zeno a new name, concluded by giving him an unbearable suspicion of finitude.

The Voice of Ada

> Poi sempre con la sua voce seria, aliena da ogni musicalità, un po' piú bassa di quella che si sarebbe aspettata dalla sua gentile personcina, raccontò che le donne in Inghilterra erano tutt'altra cosa che da noi. [...] Diceva semplicemente, con poco calore, senz'alcuna intenzione di far meravigliare o ridere. (CdZ, 573-4)

> [Then always with that serious voice of hers, devoid of any musicality, a little lower than one would have expected coming from her gentle little person, she told how women in England were totally different from here. ... She spoke simply, with little fervor, without any intention to surprise or make people laugh.]

During the fateful afternoon when Zeno is introduced into the Malfenti home, the serious and composed voice of Ada resounds in the elegant living room as a warning and a reproach to Zeno, who, in his desire to seduce, abandons himself to his bizarre and fanciful stories. Although his jokes eventually entice Ada to uncontrollable laughter, they procure him neither her love nor her understanding. Not only Ada's voice, but even her story of the English suffragettes seems a challenge to Zeno who entered that living room looking for '[la] salute morale e fisica per la santa monogamia' [moral and physical health, for holy monogamy (CdZ, 572)].

Since the beginning Ada, with her simple and healthy word, opposes herself to Zeno as the personification of the health to which he aspires.

> Io amavo la sua parola semplice, io, che come aprivo la bocca svisavo cose o persone perché altrimenti mi sarebbe sembrato inutile di parlare. Senz'essere un oratore, avevo la malattia della parola. (CdZ, 574)

> [I loved her simple word, I who, as soon as I opened my mouth, deformed things and people, for otherwise it seemed to me useless to speak. Without being an orator, I had the sickness of the word.]

Zeno's word, the symptom of his sickness, could have been cured by

Ada, whose health he had hoped to learn ('lei [...] m'avrebbe insegnata una vita d'intelligenza e di lavoro' [She ... would have taught me a life of intelligence and work] (CdZ, 592)]. The same qualities of seriousness and energy that Zeno already admired in her father now attract him to Ada, and, as in the case of Giovanni, spur a desire in him to resemble her. In Ada's shadow, Zeno could become the 'perfect' (i.e., finished) man who, leaving his sickness and shortcomings behind, would live like Giovanni Malfenti a virile life of struggle and victory. But Ada refuses to become his mammoth, and Zeno will have to recover in Augusta's shadow, from which he will keep telling and inventing endless stories as the symptoms and cause of his illness.

It is the angry voice of Ada that marks the end of Zeno's absurd courting. After finally declaring himself, Zeno ventures to attack the 'perfect' and 'easy' Guido by comparing him to a monkey, and he thus elicits an immediate reaction from Ada:

> Balzò in piedi sempre con il violino e l'arco in mano e mi soffiò addosso delle parole offensive. [...] Dimenticai le tante parole sdegnose ch'essa mi diresse, ma non la sua bella, nobile e sana faccia arrossata dallo sdegno e dalle linee rese piú precise, quasi marmoree, dall'indignazione. Quella non dimenticai piú ... (CdZ, 623-4)

> [She jumped to her feet still holding the violin and bow in her hands, and she blew offensive words at me. ... I forgot all the scornful words that she directed at me, but not her beautiful, noble and healthy face reddened by disdain, its lines made more precise, almost statuesque, by indignation. That I never forgot ...]

Nothing remains of Ada's words ('Io feci del mio meglio per dimenticarle e vi riuscii' [I did my best to forget them and I succeeded (CdZ, 623)]), but her face is engraved in Zeno's memory as if sculpted in marble, an image of his love and youth, a memory even more indelible since those traits will be destroyed by the progress of the illness. Ada's beauty silences her words and covers what could still hurt in the remembrance. Unlike those of Zeno, her words cannot 'cross time'; to them, the status of an 'avvenimento che si riallaccia agli avvenimenti' [event that connects with other events (CdZ, 813)] is denied. Thus, paradoxically, the freezing of Ada in a timeless image of beauty, her reduction to a fine porcelain object, constitutes as much of an effacement as the ravages of the Basedow disease.

Nonetheless, if not the words, the sound of Ada's voice keeps speaking to Zeno. During a visit after the birth of the twins, Zeno is the first to perceive a change in Ada, not through the decomposition of the precise lines of her face but through the unusual sound of her voice:

> – 'Sono belli, Zeno?' Restai sorpreso dal suono di quella voce. Mi parve piú dolce: era un vero grido perché vi si sentiva uno sforzo, eppure rimaneva tanto dolce. [...] ne fui commosso perché ve la scoprivo [la dolcezza] proprio quand'era rivolta a me. (CdZ, 784)

> [– 'Are they beautiful Zeno?' I was surprised by the sound of that voice. It seemed sweeter to me: it was a real cry because one could detect an effort, and nonetheless it remained so sweet. ... I was moved by it because I discovered [sweetness] in it exactly in the moment it addressed me.]

Later, on the occasion of a visit by Ada to Augusta, Zeno has his intuition confirmed:

> dinanzi alla stanza di lavoro di Augusta mi fermai perché sentii la voce di Ada. Era dolce o malsicura (ciò che si equivale, io credo) come quel giorno in cui era stata indirizzata a me. Entrai in quella stanza spintovi dalla strana curiosità di vedere come la serena, la calma Ada, potesse vestirsi di quella voce che ricordava un po' quella di qualche nostra attrice quando vuol far piangere senza saper piangere essa stessa. (CdZ, 786)

> [in front of Augusta's work room I stopped because I heard Ada's voice. It was sweet or uncertain (two things I believe to be equal) as on that day when it had been addressed to me. I entered that room driven by an odd curiosity to see how the serene, calm Ada could assume that voice that somewhat reminded me of one of our actresses when she wants to elicit tears without quite knowing how to cry herself.]

The woman that so 'coldly' rejected him no longer exists. That fearful eye, 'che freddamente esaminava cose e persone per ammetterle o respingerle' [which coldly examined things and people in order to accept or reject them (CdZ, 786)], is now disproportionately enlarged and emotionally moved. Ada is not Ada anymore. Her body has become a canvas on which the illness 'sapeva simulare tutte le emozioni' [could simulate all emotions (CdZ, 791)]. Ada, who so disliked Zeno's rhetorical exaggerations, is now paradoxically condemned to express every excess of feeling on her face, and to give her voice the hollow pitches of theatrical display. By a malice of destiny, or perhaps as a sort of Dantean *contrappasso*, the illness has forever altered the serious voice and disarranged the pure lines that had so contemptuously rejected Zeno. Now Ada's demeanour seems to promise everything and refuse nothing; her calm voice retains only the tones of the most endearing sweetness for Zeno.

If Augusta gave Zeno the opportunity to study and analyse the nature of true health, Ada offers him the possibility of articulating a philosophical system inspired by sickness, the Basedow disease: 'Mi parve ch'egli avesse portato alla luce le radici della vita' [It seemed to me that it brought to light the roots of life (CdZ, 789)]. In addition, Zeno himself becomes sick 'di una malattia lieve, ma lunga' [with a light but long illness (CdZ, 789)]. This sickness 'fu un pensiero dominante, un sogno, e anche uno spavento' [was a dominant thought, a dream, and even a fear (CdZ, 789)], namely the idea that 'the psychic perversions' that attacked Ada's nervous system would bring her in her illness to love the Zeno she had despised when healthy. But a change intervenes. Since Ada is no longer the bearer of a simple absolute health, she is also no longer accessible to Zeno's understanding. If Zeno earlier could have said, like Signor Aghios in 'Corto viaggio sentimentale': 'Ti conosco perché sei bella' [I know you because you are beautiful (1968: 158)], now he is obsessed by a need to interpret Ada's intentions, an obsession driven by the impossibility of doing so. Thus, while Augusta's health could not only be described but even learned, Ada's sickness, though capable of inspiring a philosophical reflection, cannot be known because it is defined by excess and uncertainty as her traits undergo constant unpredictable changes. It is in a mood, which Zeno defines as one of 'terror and hope,' that the subsequent relationship with Ada develops: 'Volevo baciare quegli occhi e quel corpo scheletrico?' [Did I want to kiss those eyes and that body all skin and bones? (CdZ, 811)].

As we will see, the relationship with Ada has become at this point more a question of mirroring than of desire: the terror is the encounter with one's self in the eyes of the other. Ada has become the actress, the symbiont who unexpectedly comes to contend for Zeno's place. The relation with this new Ada is potentially the most utopian moment in the novel, a moment that brings 'terror and hope,' as the coincidence of the desire for the other and the desire for oneself *as other* evokes a fullness far beyond the culturally sanctioned and consoling dream of an omnipotent mother.

In the dark parlor where Zeno and Ada meet for the first time alone after Guido's attempted suicide, Ada asks Zeno for the support of his fraternal love in the task of protecting Guido – namely to become, in her absence, Guido's mammoth. Zeno, who lived in the shadow of the finished man (Guido), waiting for his moment of strength, is explicitly asked by Ada to exchange places. Thus the unexpected association between Ada and Zeno begins. The pact, the promise of a silent complicity, has from the beginning a very ambiguous character for Zeno. The promise of support that Ada requests from him to help 'quel ragazzo' [that boy (CdZ, 814)] acquires, in the darkness of Ada's room, the tones of a love promise: 'non sapevo quello ch'ella volesse e che io desiderassi' [I did not know what she wanted and what I desired (CdZ, 812)]. Zeno's uneasy expectations are nonetheless soon disillusioned by Ada, allowing him to exit the uncanny dream lived in Ada's parlor and return, resigned and perhaps relieved, to reality:

> io stavo rassegnandomi a ritornare ad una vita molto ma molto comune, visto ch'essa non ci pensava di seguirmi in quella d'eccezione ch'io avevo sognata. (CdZ, 812)

> [I was on the way to resigning myself to returning to a life that was very, very common, since she was not even considering following me into the exceptional life I had dreamed of.]

Nevertheless, when he thinks of the conversation he had with her, Zeno comes to the realization that this fraternal relationship with the woman he used to love could offer something rarer than passion: 'dolcezza.' 'Tutto ciò era ben dolce, di un sapore raro in questa vita. Tanta dolcezza non avrebbe potuto darmi una vera salute?' [All this was indeed sweet, it had a quality rare to find in this life. Could so much sweetness have brought me true health? (CdZ, 815)]. But if this is the case, Ada will not play the unconscious mammoth; she like Carla is far from becoming a simple supplement to Augusta. From the vantage point of her sickness she is in fact able to read Zeno's soul, as he is dismayed to find out, since as he himself noted: 'Solo noi malati sappiamo qualche cosa di noi stessi' [Only us sick people know something about ourselves (CdZ, 651)], and, it should be added, *about others*. Unlike Augusta, who did not even know how health was made (CdZ, 651), the sick Ada, because of her sickness, gains a perspective on both her soul and Zeno's. Only her voice, with perhaps the exception of the psychoanalyst's, pierces through the fabric of Zeno's story and questions his narration, casting an unresolved doubt on his 'truths.'

It is once again in the dark living room of the Speiers's home that Zeno will see himself through Ada's eyes. After a second fake suicide attempt, Guido successfully if unwillingly has died, and Zeno, ostensibly in a last attempt to save his friend's reputation and patrimony, has missed his funeral, thus unleashing Ada's rage.

> Entrò vestita semplicemente di una vestaglia nera [...] giunse fino al tavolino a cui ero seduto e vi si appoggiò con le mani per vedermi meglio. [...] – 'Così hai fatto in modo ch'egli è morto proprio per una cosa che non ne valeva la pena!' Poi abbassò la voce come se avesse voluto tener segreto quello che mi diceva ... (CdZ, 859)

> [She entered simply dressed in a black robe. ... She reached the little table where I was seated and she leaned on it with her hands to get a better look at me. ... 'So you managed it in such a way that he died for something that wasn't at all worth dying for!' Then she lowered her voice as if she wanted to keep secret what she was telling me ...]

And in that low and affectionate voice that embraces their mutual mistake of not having loved Guido, Ada calls Zeno sweetly by name, thus recognizing him: – 'Povero Zeno! Fratello mio!' – [Poor Zeno! Brother of mine! (CdZ, 860)]. But this intimacy with Ada is certainly not what Zeno repeatedly imagined in his dreams. It is Ada's speech, though allegedly partly forgotten by Zeno, that dominates the concluding pages of the chapter:

> – 'Ed io ti scuso per non essere venuto al suo funerale. [...] Che ci avresti fatto tu al suo funerale? Tu che non lo amavi! Buono come sei, avresti potuto piangere per me, per le mie lacrime, ma non per lui che tu ... odiavi! [...] Ma neppure io seppi amarlo. [...] Ti sono grata di non essere intervenuto al funerale perché altrimenti non avrei neppur oggi compreso nulla. *Così invece vedo e intendo tutto.* Anche che io non l'amai ...' (CdZ, 859–60)

> [– 'And I excuse you for not having come to his funeral. ... What would you have done there? You who did not love him! Good as you are, you could have cried for me, for my tears, but not for him who you ... hated! ... But I as well was unable to love him. ... I am grateful to you for not having

attended the funeral because otherwise I would not have understood anything, not even today. Instead, in this way, *I see and understand everything.* Even the fact that I did not love him ...']

Before these accusations Zeno hides his face in his arm and in the sudden darkness sees

> che le sue parole avevano creato un mondo nuovo come tutte le parole non vere. Mi parve d'intendere anch'io di aver sempre odiato Guido e di essergli stato accanto, assiduo, in attesa di poter colpirlo. (CdZ, 860)

> [that her words created a new world as do all words that are not true. I seemed to believe myself that I too always hated Guido and that I remained next to him, assiduous, waiting to strike him down.]

It is useless to linger here and analyse (as the psychoanalyst will do) the truthfulness or falsity of Ada's interpretation; what is important to stress is how Ada takes up the privileged position of the interpreter: 'I see and understand everything,' she says, thus echoing in inverted form the initial 'Ricordo tutto, ma non intendo niente' [I remember everything but I understand nothing (CdZ, 535)] of Zeno. Ada's word intrudes into Zeno's narration and forces Zeno, as Carla's abandonment had already done, to confront himself. The shadow in which he had hidden has dissipated, leaving his profile exposed; perhaps it is a fictional profile, but no more fictional than the one proposed in his autobiography. As Zeno the fanciful conversationalist, the astute juggler of an 'uncertain' Italian language, the writer of a deceitfully playful but merciless narrative knows, words create new worlds, corrected ones, where truth is constantly renegotiated through the encounter with alternative realities.

Ada again escapes from Zeno's desire, but this time she does so by understanding him and calling him brother, by revealing his desire to him. Ada dominates the last pages of the chapter on the commercial association as an independent subject reified neither by her beauty nor by her sickness: 'nessuno guardandola avrebbe ricordata la malattia. Non c'era!' [nobody looking at her would have been reminded of her sickness. It was not there! (CdZ, 859)]. From this position she tells her version of the story, and this story, whether true or false, throws light on the 'uomo in abbozzo' who stood hidden in the shadow of the father, of Giovanni Malfenti, of Augusta and Guido, inspired by love and calculation, by a calculated love, by the ambiguous desire to protect and be protected. Ada does not simply act out this ambiguous truth in the fabula, *she knows it.*

After this dramatic conversation with Ada and her subsequent departure for Argentina the narration of Zeno's memories is interrupted. Zeno's first manuscript to Dr S. closes on Ada's voice wishing him farewell and urging him to remember: '– Addio, caro Zeno! Te ne prego, ricorda! Ricorda sempre! Non dimenticarlo!' [Farewell, dear Zeno! I beg you, remember! Always remember! Don't forget! (CdZ, 862)]
And again at the moment of embarking on the ship:

– Addio, Zeno, fratello mio. Io ricorderò sempre che non seppi amarlo abbastanza. Devi saperlo! [...] La giornata era torbida e fosca. Pareva che una sola nube distesa e niente minacciosa offuscasse il cielo. [...] Ada, dalla tolda del piroscafo, salutava agitando il suo fazzoletto. Poi ci volse le spalle. [...] La sua figurina elegante diveniva piú perfetta quanto piú si allontanava. (CdZ, 863)

['Good-bye, Zeno, my brother. I will always remember that I was unable to love him enough. You must know it! ...' The day was gloomy and dark. It looked like a single cloud, streched out and far from threatening, covering the sky. ... Ada, from the deck of the boat, was saluting, waving a handkerchief. Then she turned away from us. ... Her little elegant figure became more and more perfect in the distance.]

The scene slowly goes out of focus, blurred by the tears that fill Zeno's eyes. Ada, like Carla before and Teresina to come – the women that Zeno runs after and tries to reach in life and in dreams – has definitely turned her back to him. Neither mother, nor lover, nor wife, but simply Ada – she has carried in her voice a reproach and admonition that unites her and Zeno. And with the echo of her voice Zeno's narration ends, no longer able to console her or to exculpate himself.

'Ecco ch'essa ci abbandonava e che mai piú avrei potuto provarle la mia innocenza' [Now she was abandoning us and I would never be able to prove my innocence to her (CdZ, 863)]. In Zeno's language, to prove one's innocence and convince the other means to seduce, to conquer – that is, to subsume him or her in the economy of his own desire, in which no painful remainder is left hanging. Ada and Carla, however, break *this* symbiosis in an attempt to redefine it according to their own desire. Without the other, the 'uomo in abbozzo' is left without a narrative. All he can do now is to curl up in his shadow, a shadow that embraces both a faraway and dreamy infancy and the mists of old age, a shadow from which he is now almost indistinguishable.

Conclusions

How can the story of Zeno, the unfinished man, possibly conclude? Confronted with the expectation of meaning and resolution that comes with every narrative's end, Zeno makes recourse to an old, but by now tested delaying tactic. To evade any 'healthy' finality imposed on the word – as Dr S. will try to do – Zeno transforms 'the word [into] an event in itself' (CdZ, 574) that cannot be contained in any given temporal or significative chain. Two earth-shattering events are staged in the final chapter that put into a shadow, that is delay and distance, the literal end of the unfinished man: first of all, the apocalyptic explosion that carries away the whole world and Zeno with it; secondly, the dissolution of the narrative pact sustaining the novelistic genre. Rather than telling the end of his story, Zeno ends by writing about the impossibility of telling a truthful story and – by giving the boot to the psychoanalyst, the implicit reader of his memoires – the impossibility of interpreting such a story. Thus, with a playfully hybristic act, Zeno, the man of the future, ends narratively where all storytelling ends and biologically where the whole species is extinguished. In this universal hecatomb, his story once again concludes rhetorically in order not to conclude.

For this reason, Zeno's narrative strategies have far-reaching consequences, not only for the status of truth in the novel and for the invention of a new pact between writer and reader but for the ethical concerns that they raise. 'La narratività' – observes Savelli – 'non è presente direttamente ma in quanto possibilità negata, *fede trasgredita* o verità a cui l'accesso è impossibile' [Narrativity is not present directly but as negated possiblity, *a faith betrayed* or a truth to which access is impossible (1998: 77, emphasis mine)]. A faith is betrayed, but whose? Definitely, as Savelli observed, that of the reader, left searching for a narrative meaning. But betrayal as such is at the very core of the unfinished man's story, so much so that the failure to keep faith in his story is a way to hide the wreckage he left behind.

It is within this framework that 'L'uomo e la teoria darwiniana' can shed a new light on the final pages of *La coscienza*. 'Se l'uomo non avesse avuto l'anima inquieta,' Svevo wrote in the fable, 'egli sarebbe ancora il pacifico servo del Mammut e molti malanni sarebbero stati risparmiati alla nostra terra' [If man did not have a restless soul he would still be the servant of the peaceful Mammoth and many calamities would have been spared to our earth (UT, 640)]. Recapitulated in this sentence are the two movements contained in the fable: a look forward to the futureless future of a restless humanity, and *a regretful glance backward to a future contained in the past, in the other.* Not just an expression of Svevo's pessimism about the future of a restless humanity, the fable focuses upon the origin of such a future: the emancipation from the 'protection' of the mammoth as the breaking of the contract. Such a backward glance suggests, particularly in the last pages of *La coscienza*, that the virtuality of the Svevian man is better understood as an openess to the past than as an openess to the future. Seen in this light, Svevo's 'anxious hope for health' speaks of the fear of a futureless future and the hope contained in the past, in the return of the other, a return performed in the very act of writing and memory, the return of a faith transgressed.

The ending of *La coscienza* is organized around the progressive reversal of the fable of origin contained in 'La corruzione dell'anima.' In the last chapter, 'Psico-analisi' [Psychoanalysis], Svevo takes pleasure in inverting the progressive path of the man in search of an ever greater evolution. There Zeno regresses, from the consciousness of storytelling to the unconsciousness of the dreams pursued with Dr S., then from the solitary 'raccoglimento' [meditation] before an elemental and ahistorical nature along the banks of the Isonzo River to the affirmative unconsciousness of an animal health pursued in commerce, which finally leads him, a perversely modern amoeba, to rejoin with a last backward jump – 'traverso una catastrofe inaudita prodotta dagli ordigni' [through an unheard of catastrophe produced by lethal devices (CdZ, 895)] – the dust that predated the earth. The rhetorical effect of this movement is to collapse the future into the farthest past, reconnecting the 'mythical twins,' health and sickness (Savelli 1991: 476); thus do animal health and human sickness coincide, suggesting a new foundation of the human story beyond this sterile opposition.

* * *

As we know, after abandoning the cure, Zeno is separated by the outbreak of the war from his family, and, left alone in Trieste, starts speculating on every type of goods. 'Fu il mio commercio che mi guarí' [My commerce cured me (CdZ, 893)], declares Zeno proudly. But the buying and selling of goods, far from being the cure as Zeno seems to believe here, is but an effect of 'health.' At the roots of the resounding affirmation of health, 'Io sono guarito!' [I am healed! (CdZ, 892)], stands the emancipation from the other, the absence of any intersubjective dimension to self-definition: 'Non è per il confronto ch'io mi senta sano. Io sono sano, assolutamente' [It is not because of a comparison that I feel healthy. I am absolutely healthy (CdZ, 892)]. From Zeno's new Social-Darwinist perspective health is absolute and absolute health is amoral, the result of the animal freedom of losing oneself in the struggle, free of attachments and contracts, or, as in the case of Malfenti and Augusta, the result of naturalizing them to the point of invisibility. It is, in fact, a truly unattainable condition that finds its final fullfilment in the image of 'la terra ritornata alla forma di nebulosa [...] priva di parassiti e di malattie' [earth reverted to the status of a nebula ... freed from parasites and sicknesses (CdZ, 895)]. On the other hand, the comparison with the other is not just an insufficient proof of health, but, as the coupling of sickness and parasitism suggests, it *coincides* with sickness. *La coscienza di Zeno* is indeed the story of a disease (Saccone 1973: 66), the story of Zeno's dependence on the other, 'a genuine manifestation of sickness' – as Zeno once observed, commenting on his 'attachment' to Guido – 'or great goodness, two qualities that stand in very intimate relation' (CdZ, 751). The attachment to the other, whether symbiotic or parasitical, is the real name of Zeno's sickness.

'Perché voler curare la nostra malattia?' asks Svevo in a letter to Valerio Jahier, 'Davvero dobbiamo togliere all'umanità quello ch'essa ha di meglio?' [Why heal our sickness? Why take away from humanity its best part? (1966: 859)]. The final recognition that the disease is the cure introduces a potential reversal of the meaning of the sickness. The desire to heal, whether pursued through capitalist enterprise, a faith in progress, Social Darwinism, or psychoanalysis, is the very expression of the modern sickness. Paradoxically, Zeno's open-ended narrative, the escape from concluding the story, is one more materialization of this desire. But it is also the staging of the sickness, the unsuppressable remainder; that is, the return of time not as a pure quantity but as the terminally contaminated story of one's association with the other.

While enjoying the moment of 'vero raccoglimento' [true meditation] on the banks of the Isonzo, an understanding of life and sickness comes to Zeno inextricably bound up with the figure of the woman.

In mezzo a quel verde rilevato tanto deliziosamente da quegli sprazzi di sole, seppi sorridere alla mia vita ed anche alla mia malattia. *La donna vi ebbe un'importanza enorme.* Magari a pezzi, i suoi piedini, la sua cintura, la sua bocca, riempirono i miei giorni. E rivedendo la mia vita e anche la mia malattia le amai, le intesi! [...] Io, [...] ero stato accompagnato sempre dall'amore. [...] Da me la vita non fu mai privata del desiderio e l'illusione rinacque subito intera dopo ogni naufragio, nel sogno di membra, di voci, di atteggiamenti piú perfetti. (CdZ, 879; emphasis mine)

[In the midst of all that green, so delightfully radiant under the occasional rays of the sun, I was able to smile at my life and even at my sickness. *Woman played in both a very important part.* If only in pieces, her feet, her belt, her mouth, filled my days. And as I looked back on my life and my sickness I loved and understood them! ... I had always been accompanied by love. ... My life was never deprived of desire, and after every shipwreck illusions sprung up afresh for me in the dream of limbs, voices, and gestures still more perfect.]

The progression, piece by piece, towards a more perfect woman guarantees the survival of love – but which love, whose love? Zeno's smiling and satisfied prose sutures *a posteriori* the successive tears in the narrative, attempting to justify such wounds within the economy of a desire that feeds upon shipwrecks in order to be constantly reborn.

The dream of the buxom woman that Zeno reports in the immediately preceding pages illustrates the crowning of this movement towards greater perfection. In that instance, Zeno dreams of himself as an infant who sees above him, built on the roof of his parent's house, a brightly lit cage.

In quella gabbia non v'era che un solo mobile, una poltrona e su questa sedeva una donna formosa, costruita deliziosamente, vestita di nero, bionda, dagli occhi grandi e azzurri, le mani bianchissime e i piedi piccoli in scarpine laccate ... (CdZ, 870)

[In that cage, there was just one piece of furniture, an armchair, and on it a buxom woman was sitting; delightfully built, she was dressed in black, was blond, with big blue eyes, very white hands and her small feet in patent leather shoes ...]

The woman is like a small doll that the old man and the child dream of possessing 'ma nel modo piú strano: Era sicuro cioè di poter mangiarne dei pezzettini al vertice e alla base' [but in the strangest way: he was sure he could eat little pieces of it from the top and bottom (CdZ, 870)].

The woman in the cage is the 'donna a pezzi' [woman in pieces (CdZ, 520)] initially described by Zeno to the electricity doctor. Within a psychoanalytic interpretation she becomes an emblem of Zeno's 'sick love,' the counterpart to the illness of the last cigarette.[8] Like the last cigarette, the woman fetishized in her parts is the sign of the eternal return of male desire. At the same time, she is the whole – 'Tutto era lei' [She was everything (CdZ, 870)] – the guarantee of the plenitude of desire, the completion of that ideal to which Zeno gave expression while courting Ada: a better self, a lover and a second mother, this abstraction is both everything and a mere supplement in the struggle for a 'vita intera' [whole life]. The failed operation of 'costituirsi intero' (building oneself whole), stubbornly if unconvincingly pursued throughout the novel, finds a critical parallel and commentary in the construction of this woman. The liminal female apparition enclosed in a cage, like the declaration of absolute health, has the quality of a pastiche, fabricated and affected.

Read in the context of Zeno's reflection on the constructed quality of memory and writing, the dream of the delightfully built woman is an important apparition. Placed on the steep cliffs that mark the limits of the textual threshold, she is a siren that lures Dr S., and much criticism after him, in pursuit of an Oedipal truth. What is striking in the dream is its manneristic compendium of Zeno's 'sickness,' a mythological woman that everybody would like sooner or later to get a nibble at.

Thus, the 'funereal splendor' ['splendore funereo' (Saccone, 1973: 140)] of the woman, interpreted according to a psychoanalytic key as a warning to the dreamer of the danger that the final satisfaction of the Lacanian 'demand' involves – the release of desire in the quiet of death – acquires quite a different connotation. If the woman in the cage is dressed in mourning, this is worn for the death of a fetish. The woman in black reminds the reader of the recent mournful figure of Ada, and as such it bespeaks the death of the woman-object, that is the death of one form of male desire, a desire that deadens and destroys its object in order to prove its own existence. The encounter with Teresina, the last repetition in what was meant to be a perfect chain leading to the ideal woman, causes Zeno's unsinkable desire to have a new shipwreck, thus putting the lie to his dream of reconcilation.

Overtaken by the fear that the doctor might have indeed cured his desire, Zeno fondles Teresina, the adolescent daughter of a farmer, to find assurance that he is still 'sick,' namely that he can still desire a woman. The experiment pursued by Zeno is successful ('Grazie al cielo

Out of the Shadow of the Mammoth 199

non ero guarito ancora! Avevo cessata la cura in tempo' [Thanks to heaven I was not healed yet! I interrupted the cure in time (CdZ, 881)]), but his regret for the offence to Teresina's innocence ambiguously inaugurates the narration of the event.[9]

> L'esperienza che cercavo l'ebbi poco dopo e fu sufficiente per rassicurarmi, *ma non mi costò poco*. Per averla, *turbai e guastai* la relazione piú pura che avessi avuta nella mia vita. (CdZ, 880; emphasis mine)

> [A while later I had the experience I was looking for and indeed it reassured me, though *I paid for it dearly*. In order to obtain it I *upset and spoiled* the purest relationship that I have ever had in my life.]

The woman is not exactly the cigarette. Here the passage from one resolution to the next, from one life experiment to the other, always leaves a painful *après-coup*, a price to be paid, the other's subjectivity leaves an insuppressible trace.

Nevertheless, the narration continues on a Boccaccian note that seems to deny the survival of any remorse: – 'Quando ti dedicherai ai vecchi, Teresina?' – shouts Zeno after her, and Teresina, escaping the condition of passive object of Zeno's experiment, the fetishization of his desire, in turn objectifies Zeno and shouts back: – 'Quando sarò vecchia anch'io' – [– When will you begin to look at old men, Teresina? – [...] – When I will be old too – (CdZ, 882)]. Not only does Teresina 'rifiuta di farsi strumento terapeutico, oggetto mitico di risarcimento, di riduzione pedagogica' [refuse to be a therapeutic instrument, a mythical object of compensation, of pedagogical reduction (1982: 155)], as Mazzacurati notes, she threatens the man, in turn, with finitude. The other, far from being a passive mammoth, gives voice to her own desire. Not simply an 'allegory of alterity' or childhood that escapes 'l'orbita ciclica della genesi e dell'apocalisse della coscienza borghese, ammalata di sé' [the cyclical orbit of the genesis and apocalypse of the bourgeois consciousness, sick of itself (Mazzacurati 1982: 155)], Teresina is a woman, the latest and youngest, whose voice disrupts Zeno's monologue, throwing him from his Archimedean position on the metaphysical banks of the river back into the story. Embraced in a numinous light, the last woman turns her shoulder to Zeno, leaving him alone and old in the shadow.

> In quel momento, in qualche punto del cielo le nubi s'apersero e lasciarono passare dei raggi di sole che andarono a raggiungere Teresina che ora-

mai era lontana da me di una quarantina di metri e di me piú in alto di una decina o piú. Era bruna, piccola, ma luminosa! Il sole non illuminò me! Quando si è vecchi si resta all'ombra anche avendo dello spirito. (CdZ, 882)

[At that moment, the clouds opened somewhere in the sky and let through a few rays of sunlight which reached Teresina, who was now about forty metres away and ten or more metres higher than me. She was dark, small, but full of light! The sun did not shine on me! When you are old, you remain in the shadow no matter how witty you may be.]

'26 Giugno 1919 (*sic* 1915). La guerra mi'ha raggiunto!' [26 June 1915. War has reached me (CdZ, 882)]: with this notation the narration resumes. As always for Zeno the rhetorician, the word, like time, sutures all wounds, but in the narration, as in life, gaps keep opening that cannot be filled. Zeno can do nothing else at their borders than stop and continue the story under a new date or a new chapter, fictitious resumptions that seek to erase the always threatened and imminent end. After elaborating his Basedow philosophy, Zeno reflects on the necessity and ambiguity of contamination:

Già credo che in qualunque punto dell'universo ci si stabilisca si finisce col'inquinarsi. Bisogna moversi. La vita ha dei veleni, ma poi anche degli altri veleni che servono di contravveleni. Solo correndo si può sottrarsi ai primi e giovarsi degli altri. (CdZ, 789)

[I indeed believe that in whichever point of the universe one stood he would be polluted. One needs to keep moving. Life has certain poisons but then it has other poisons that work as counter-poisons. Only if one keeps running can one avoid the first and take advantage of the others.]

The endless repetition and correction of desire is the strategy that keeps pollution at bay. Cigarettes qualify as a poison that is a counter-poison. What about the women and the other symbionts in Zeno's associations? They are also both poisons to be guarded against *and* antidotes to be taken advantage of. But in this case running away will not avoid the pollution; there is no escape from the contamination with the other and her/his story, because contamination is the very name of the story.

Zeno is truthful when he states that 'woman had an enormous importance' in his life, but what that 'importance' could be escapes articulation. The only thing certain is that woman shares the scene with the dawning of understanding, or better understanding dawns on the scene of the other. Rather than a disembodied allegory of truth – the 'truth effect,' as Derrida termed it in *Éperons* – woman has a voice that tears the fabric of Zeno's discourse, questions it, and enacts a dialogic moment. In this gap Zeno could gain an understanding, because to speak of the other is the only way to understand oneself ('dirò di lui solo quanto possa giovare a ravvivare il ricordo di me stesso' [I will say about him only what could help with remembering myself (CdZ, 534)]). The word that the other pronounces or fails to pronounce is where Zeno's understanding both reveals and hides itself. Meaning is a textual effect contained in the unfolding of an intersubjective moment; it is an in-between.

But Svevo himself gives us a lead within the text to read his subject differently, beyond the opposition of health and disease, to read it in the context of a feared and desired contamination with the other and his/her story. Against psychoanalysis, a science where a sick subject is called to analyse his own sickness, Zeno proposes a science that by isolating the subject in single events of contamination forces him to say a truthful word:

> Mi ricordai con simpatia e commozione del mio passato lontano di chimico e di analisi vere: Io, un tubetto e un reagente! L'altro, l'analizzato, dorme finché il reagente imperiosamente non lo desti. [...] Qui, [...] tutto era verità. La cosa da analizzarsi era imprigionata nel provino e, sempre uguale a se stessa, aspettava il reagente. Quand'esso arrivava essa diceva sempre la stessa parola. (CdZ, 876)

> [I remembered with fondness and emotion my distant past like a chemist performing a true analysis: I, a tube and a reagent. The other, the analysed, sleeps till the reagent imperiously wakes it up. ... Here ... everything was truth. The thing to be analysed was imprisoned in the tube, and, always similar to itself, waited for the reagent. When this arrived the thing analysed always said the same word.]

How can we not think of Zeno at his point lying in his study searching for absolute immobility, waiting for a memory (a reagent) that would stir him up. As the analysed object which 'always resembles itself,' Zeno is imprisoned within himself as he laments at the beginning of his memoires: 'La mia vita non sapeva fornire che una nota sola senz'alcuna variazione' [My life could supply only one note without any variations (CdZ, 561)]. From this realization stems the desire for 'a more intense life,' the longing for 'becoming and dissolving like Napoleon and the wave,' the mixing with different reagents that will ensure such change.

The remembering old man with whom the novel opens is very much like the chemist who undertakes the task of recreating in writing the experiments that life had set out for him. Like the image of the infant that comes to him at rest, he is a virgin to analysis, and like that infant he is on the verge of being exposed to endless contaminations:

> Nel tuo seno – fantolino! – si va facendo una *combinazione* misteriosa. Ogni minuto che passa vi getta *un reagente*. Troppe probabilità di *malattia* vi sono per te, perché non tutti i tuoi minuti possono essere *puri*. (CdZ, 511; emphasis mine)

> [Mysterious *combinations* are at work within you child! Every passing moment brings to you *a reagent*. Too many possibilities of *sickness* are in store for you, since not all your moments can be *pure*.]

Life is the unfolding of all such combinations/contaminations. Zeno's science consists in the staging – Zeno's predilection for the theatrical form is a good point of departure for understanding the literary implications of this new science – and recording of the various reagents that poisoned and enriched his life. Although very similar to psychoanalysis, for Zeno the new science has one unbeatable advantage. Against the proliferation of discourse that characterizes both the 'talking cure' and Zeno the patient, in chemistry the analysed object once confronted with a reagent 'articulates always the same word.' The novel is structured on the subsequent reactions, in which the chapters are the recreation of each experiment. For this reason Zeno's knowledge is not cumulative, but always contingent, reactive. Each chapter stages Zeno's story as the contamination with a different other – man or woman matters not, for the ethic of symbiosis bypasses gender identity.

In the single experiments the story of Zeno manifests the potential to 'heal,' to coagulate into a meaning. But does it 'always utter the same word'? It is at this point, before reaching an answer elicited by the confrontation with the story of the other, that Zeno's narration repeatedly concludes. The word that, on the treshhold of death, escaped Zeno's father, is escaped by Zeno as the very treshhold of death. What remains consistent in the experiment is the fact that it is always the other, the reagent, that instigates the uttering of the word, for it is the word of the other that opens the possibility of meaning.

Every reagent is an active participant in the contamination and redefines the nature of the analysed object. The women in the novel are the most powerful reagents because they carry the germ of an alternative story. They are instigators of the word that has the potential to bring understanding to Zeno, to 'heal' him, or, as Zeno said after Carla abandoned him, to 'wean him.' In this sense, the staged experiment goes beyond the hopes of the scientist by bringing to the foreground the reagent as opposed to the subject/object of the experiment. It is at the point where the story of the woman could potentially start that the story of Zeno stops. His story happens in the antechamber of another story, heralding the birth of that story.

Zeno the actor strives for an ongoing contamination, for constant change in order to delay, in its very pursuit, understanding ('to see himself whole'). Zeno the 'chemist'/narrator understands his truth as the pursuit of this contamination: a possibility of healing/understanding that is inseparable from being poisoned by contact with the other. This is the insight contained allegorically in the fable of the man and the mammoth, a fable that is rewritten in each of the eight chapters of *La coscienza*, bringing forth in each of them a last word that is always the same: the word of the other, yet to be uttered.

Conclusion

If we follow for a moment Erich Auerbach's conception of Modernism as a 'modern realism,' one that attempts to represent reality at the level of experiential consciousness, Svevo's role in evolving a new literary form becomes visible. Emerging from the shadow of the nineteenth-century Realist and Naturalist traditions (Stendhal, Balzac, Flaubert, Zola), Svevo opened the modernist season early by staging the ongoing narrative construction and critique of his character's subjectivity. If, as Svevian criticism has frequently noted, 'la coscienza di sé come attività mistificante è il tema centrale dell'opera di Svevo' [self-consciousness as a mystifying activity is the central theme of Svevo's work (Benedetti 1984: 25)], what is most striking, and what disturbed an early reader like Debenedetti so, is that that theme involves a *complicity* between author and character. Herein lies Svevo's special place in the development of modernism.

The hermeneutic value of the 'deceiving activity' of the Svevian character as an 'errore necessario' [necessary error (Benedetti 1984: 126)] on the way to self-knowledge grants Svevo a Freudian insight: the so-called 'deception' – the lies, resistance, gaps, contradictions – coincides with the search for and unfolding of truth *as narrative*. Svevo challenges his reader to follow him on this tortuous narrative path, to participate in an activity that I have defined as contamination – the story of a consciousness becoming, through ongoing experimentation, symbiotic association and adaptation to the world and the other. Leaving behind the smooth, transparent surface of 'old' realist narratives, Svevo's modernist story adopts the form of a challenging interrogation, a request for interpretation – as Giulio Savelli has brilliantly shown in *L'ambiguità necessaria* – and finally for contamination.

This reading has interpreted the Svevian text as a representation of the 'shadow,' the textual in-between where the subject constitutes itself through an other, an intersubjective space where the telling of the self ambiguously coincides with the search for otherness. Therefore, this study has placed at the core of Svevo's poetic reflection not so much the anxious projection of the 'uomo in abbozzo' towards a future or an unspecified beyond, but rather a 'transversal' becoming, fittingly defined by Deleuze and Guattari as the 'creative involution' of a subject lost in contaminations with the other (1987: 238–9), the attempt, in Eduardo Saccone's words, to live two or more lives in one. In my analysis, the woman constituted the privileged site of this transformation, a shadow across time that embodies the modernist project 'to *interrupt* the modernity we live and understand [it] as a social, if not "normal" way of life' (Eysteinsson 1990: 6).

Through such writers as Gide, Conrad, and Pirandello, Fredric Jameson presents the representational universe of modernism as the coexistence of 'sealed subjective worlds,' the 'passage of ships in the night' (Jameson 1988: 350). We could argue that Svevo's obsessive focusing on the representation of consciousness constitutes his own formal expression of this 'monadic relativism.' But Svevo's single-mindedness has quite the opposite outcome. In fact, what the Triestine writer accomplished is the narrative dissolution of consciousness, portrayed in its endless opening up to the world and its infinite contaminations (in this way, no two modernist writers differ more radically than Svevo and Pirandello). Svevo chose to represent his subject in the dangerous process of becoming neither a subject, organic, unified, 'finished,' nor an objective linguistic phenomenon, but a discursive and existential 'abbozzo,' or sketch. By focusing on the shadowy in-between, the space of interpenetration of subject and world, the bond that ties the subject to his other, Svevo tells the story of consciousness as a story of parasitism, or, better, the granting of a reciprocity, *of symbiosis*. Svevo's story of the shadow, the night that envelops the closed modernist worlds, builds a textual bridge across those dark waters.

The textual experiment, the 'creative destruction' of the exemplary modernists, was a revolutionary and necessary breakthrough in the history of the novel. However, it is precisely that necessity that renders it less timely, less contemporary, than Svevo's quieter but equally revolutionary questioning of the nature of the subject, its consciousness, and its otherness.

Notes

Introduction

1 *La Guerre du feu* first appeared in installments in the magazine *Je sais tout* in July 1909 and was published as a book in 1911. It is intriguing to imagine Svevo using this book as a point of departure to write 'L'uomo e la teoria darwiniana.' If so, its date of composition should be moved from 1907, the year of the Wasmann conferences in Berlin, to at least 1909, if not 1911.

1: Between Darwinian Origins and Modernist Ends

1 'L'uomo e la teoria darwiniana,' in Svevo, *Opera omnia*, ed. Bruno Maier (1968: 637). Hereinafter cited in the text as UT, while 'La corruzione dell'anima' (1968: 641–3) will be cited as CA. The translations of the fables are mine.
2 Darwin, 'N Notebook,' 339.
3 'Fable donc: une allégorie disant ironiquement la verité de l'allegorie qu'elle est présentement ...' (Derrida 1987: 29; translation mine).
4 Renato Barilli is one of the first critics who recognized the centrality of the essays 'L'uomo e la teoria darwiniana' and 'La corruzione dell'anima' for a comprehensive understanding of Svevo's work. He defines them as 'il concentrato piú intenso della poetica di Svevo, e anche il suo piú maturo contributo di pensiero' [the most intense concentrate of Svevo's poetics and even his most mature intellectual contribution (1972: 41)]. Although the critic stresses the importance of the soul in Svevo's rewriting of the evolutionary tale, he fails to recognize how Svevo retraces the human 'leap' not to the appearance of the soul, but rather to the ability to maintain one, the ability to *resist* nature. For a reading of the various cultural models underlying

Svevo's history of humanity see Bouissy (1966: 209–29), who stresses the influence of Schopenhauer in Svevo's reading of Darwin; also Lavagetto 1986: 173–88.

5 Although 'La corruzione dell'anima' as well as 'L'uomo e la teoria darwiniana' are written in the wake of the ever-growing discourse that spans out of Darwin's *The Origin of Species* – the various hues of Darwinism, Social Darwinism, evolutionary theory – I will here concentrate my attention on the liaisons that the fable entertains with Darwin's founding reflection. The only exception will be the conference held in 1907 by the entomologist Erich Wasmann that explicitly spurred the writing of 'L'uomo e la teoria darwiniana.' For an account of the relation between Darwinian theory and its Social Darwinist interpretation in turn-of-the-century Italy, see Vadalà-Papale 1882.

6 For an opposing view, one that argues that cooperation and competition hold equal status in Darwin's thinking, see Gruber 1974: 54–5; 240–1.

7 In section 224 of *Human, All Too Human*, Nietzsche does attempt to draw a subtle if somewhat vague distinction between their concepts of struggle when he writes: 'the renowned struggle for existence does not seem to me to be the only point of view from which the progress or strengthening of an individual or a race can be explained' (1995, 3: 153–4).

8 For the co-presence of Darwin and Nietzsche in the Svevian fable see Magris 1976: 53–4. 'Quando Svevo scrive il suo saggio sulla teoria darwiniana, legge Darwin da una prospettiva nietzscheana. [...] Credo che Svevo sia stato un dei primi e dei pochissimi a capire [...] la portata e il significato della concezione nietzscheana del superuomo ...' [When Svevo writes his essay on Darwinian theory, he reads Darwin from a Nietzschean perspective. ... I believe that Svevo has been one of the first and one of the few people to understand ... the import and meaning of the Nietzschean idea of the superman].

9 For an extensive reflection on the relation between technology, the body, and 'the biosocial conditions of its production and reproduction,' see Haraway 1991: 21–42.

10 'ne sont pas seulement inassouvissables, elles son surtout fausses dans leur principe même. Par fausses, il faut entendre fictives and irréelles ... elles sont seulement figurées' (Rosset 1967: 67; translation mine).

11 Eduardo Saccone identifies the 'carattere senile' (senile character) of the Svevian protagonist 'nell'impossibilità di aderire completamente alla sua avventura; nella sua richiesta, nel suo desiderio di altro nel suo *riservarsi ad altro*' [in the impossibility of adhering completely to his adventure; in his request, in his desire for something else, in his *keeping himself in store for something other* (1995: 84)].

12 I am indebted to Keith Ansell Pearson for his reading of Nietzsche's reflection on the future and the trans-human condition in his book *Viroid Life*. He

writes: 'In his uncovering of the history of morality Nietzsche discovers that it is in his becoming sick, in his "blood poisoning," that human promise is to be found' (15).

13 I am borrowing this expression from Pearson's chapter in *Viroid Life*: 'Loving the Poison: The Memory of the Human and the Promise of the Transhuman.' According to Pearson, for Nietzsche sickness and decadence, rather than marking the end of a process, herald the promise of future overcoming. In his study of *La coscienza di Zeno*, Savelli suggests that Zeno's final healing, insofar as it is a healing of modernity's discontent, can be read as a postmodern moment, which he defines by quoting Lyotard as 'fine del lutto' [end of mourning (Savelli 1998: 139)].

14 A full account of his lectures can be found in Wasmann 1909.

15 Among the numerous critical readings of Svevo's work as a struggle of the individual against the levelling power of community, see Maxia 1977, Borghello 1977, Camerino 1996.

16 The leap puts once more in question the dictum: 'Natura non facit saltum'; this leap is the 'Ursprung,' the origin *as leap*, that stakes out man's path apart from the rest of the animal kingdom and guarantees the possibility of making a claim on the future.

17 The choice of the word *revolution* is very interesting at this point. In order to further his evolution – his forward movement – man has to overthrow the 'political system,' the polis established with the Mammoth. At the same time 'revolution' implies a course back to a starting point – 're-volvere' – a return to a previous position.

18 Pearson has argued that 'the genesis of the human is not only a technogenesis but equally, and just as importantly, a bio-technogenesis.' Similarly, evolution is not just a process of external complexification but could be understood equally well as a movement of internalization, of incorporation – 'evolution, like the egg, does not take place in the open air' (130).

19 According to de Man: 'the invention of the word man makes it possible for 'men' to exist by establishing the equality within inequality, the sameness within difference of civil society.' The question that rises in the current context would be: What if the other to be named is a woman? What if the first feeling upon encountering the other is not one of fear? To which chain of signification would this encounter give rise? See de Man 1979: 135–59.

20 For an overview of recent research in the field of biology that focuses on the centrality of symbiosis, see *Symbiosis as a Source of Evolutionary Innovation*, ed. Lynn Margulis and René Fester, 1991. Particularly relevant to our current study are the essays by Margulis, 'Symbiogenesis and Symbionticism,' and Maynard Smith, 'A Darwinian View of Symbiosis.'

21 This ability to take detours, to delay, is in fact the foundation of humanity's mastery over the rest of nature. It can be read as the willingness to *store energy,* as opposed to nature's incessant 'squanderings.' Consciousness, language, tool-making are all detours with respect to the immediate economy of adhering to a function (eating, killing, surviving). See Freud's reflections in *Beyond the Pleasure Principle* on the emergence of life as a detour from the primary experience of death: 'For a long time, perhaps, living substance was thus being constantly created afresh and easily dying, till decisive external influences altered in such a way as to oblige the still surviving substance to diverge ever more widely from its original course of life and to make ever more complicated *détours* before reaching its aim of death. These circuitous paths to death ... would thus present us today with the picture of the phenomena of life' (46).
22 Spivak 1988: 45. Even though Spivak drops any claim of originality for this formulation, since 'From Socrates through Nietzsche, philosophers have often wished to be midwives or mothers,' this reversal of Freud's model, as we shall see, does bear great consequences for a feminist reading of Svevo.
23 I am referring here to the definition of 'supplement' discussed by Derrida in *Of Grammatology,* 1976: 141–64.
24 Haraway, 1990: 144. In this passage, Haraway discusses the 'death of the subject' in the context of neo-Darwinian evolutionary theories, and eventually presents a feminist reassessment of the status of subjectivity through the fiction of primordial female communities. Starting from the recognition that in the realm of nature 'no unit, least of all the individual' is an autonomous 'rights-bearing subject,' but only 'a proximate means for the strategic ends of its own genes,' the question raised for a feminist critique and reassessment of these narratives of production and reproduction is the following: 'The imperative is to identify and replicate the "same" while holding the "other" at bay. But otherness is everywhere, masquerading as sameness. Altruism must be redefined in terms of the problematic investment in non-self: how can such a strategy yield a return on the self in the future? Which self?' (144–5). These considerations are of primary importance for an understanding of the Svevian preoccupation with 'altruism' as a strategy for constructing the self.

2: Of Artists, Women, and Jews

1 The critical discourse about modernism has contributed to reinforcing such a tension by retracing, on the one hand, the philosophical basis of the movement to an unprecedented crisis of subjectivity, and by elaborating, on the

other – particularly in English criticism – a canon dominated by 'the shadows of iconic individuals' (Eysteinsson 1990: 85).
2 For a discussion of the interlocking of power and gender in poststructuralist theory, see Miller 1986.
3 Debenedetti, 'Svevo e Schmitz' 1945: 27. Hereafter cited in the text as SeS; all translations are mine.
4 Debenedetti described the first Italian critical treatments of Svevo as the elaboration of 'una fotografia per tessera, in modo da poter subito rilasciare un documento di identità' [a passport picture, so that an identity card could be immediately issued (SeS, 28)].
5 Many are the considerations raised by this question. First of all, we could ask: who among the modernists unquestionably won a popularity contest?; and, secondly, we could point out the troubling implications of Debenedetti's argument: What does it mean to raise the question of an author's popularity in Fascist Italy? Maria Antonietta Grignani's reading of the use of the *plurale majestatis* in Debenedetti's essay as a way 'to declare the solidarity of the professional reader with the inclusive plural of the others, the unprofessional readers' (1990: 36) reinforces the sense that in writing 'Svevo and Schmitz' the critic was courting a historically ambiguous alliance.
6 For studies of Svevo's Jewishness and Jewish culture in turn-of-the-century Trieste, see among others: Levi 1964; Voghera 1955; Lavagetto 1989; Moloney 1973; and Schächter 1995. For the relationship between Jewishness and the concept of the misfit, see Camerino 1996.
7 'Nur die menschliche Praxis kann das Wesen der Menschen konkret zeigen' (Lukács 1962: 210; translation mine).
8 But even the initial title Svevo chose for his first novel, *Un inetto*, should stand as a warning. The ineptitude of *Una vita*, like the 'senility' in *Senilità*, points beyond the negativity it suggests towards another, perhaps opposite, perspective. The later Svevo teaches: What is called inept in one age will be the future of man in another. Following Macario's lecture to the weak Alfonso in *Una vita*, Svevian criticism has chosen to read such 'inferiority,' such passivity, also defined as 'sweetness,' through a Darwininan lense, anointing the Svevian subject in general as an 'inetto.' For interpretations relying on the concept of the 'inetto' as a crucial analytical tool, see Camerino 1996 and Baldi 1998. Even recently, Ulla Musarra-Schroeder (1994) and Victor Brombert (1999) refer to Svevo's character as an 'anti-hero,' thus implying once again his deficiency vis-à-vis the 'hero' of the realist and naturalist traditions, rather than focusing on his modernist *difference*.
9 See Grignani's insightful reading comparing 'Svevo e Schmitz' with the notes that prepared the essay. While focusing on Debenedetti's notes on

Senilità, she points out how Debenedetti 'poteva innescare un pionieristico o meglio profetico percorso d'analisi sulla focalizzazione interna del punto di vista [...]. Invece nel saggio Debenedetti amputa il *troppo* e il *vano*, articolando un giudizio lapidario sui due campi analogici chiave della *malattia* e del *destino* ...' [could have inaugurated a pioneering or even prophetic analysis of the internal focalization of the point of view. ... Instead in the essay Debenedetti amputates the *excessive* and *superflous* by articulating a concise judgment on the two key analogical fields of *sickness* and *destiny* ... (1990: 29; emphasis mine)]. Could a crucial insight into the modernist aesthetic have been left out of the essay just to satisfy a stylistic concern with the overall architecture of the piece? Or is this an act of political self-censorship? In either case, the reassuring rhetoric of sickness and destiny ends up taking the place, in the final published version, of the aesthetic 'excess,' what Debenedetti initially openly identified as Svevo's 'disconcerting timeliness.'

10 Michel David (1970) first put forward this interpretation, which was then pursued further by Cavaglion in 1982. The letter's in-depth study of Otto Weininger's reception in Italy is the major point of reference for my presentation of Weininger.

11 Quoted in Monk 1990: 313. Reacting to Weininger's views on women, Wittgenstein admits in a letter to a friend 'How wrong he was, my God he was wrong.' But nonetheless in the same letter he writes in a rather cryptical fashion: 'It isn't necessary or rather not possible to agree with him but the greatness lies in that with which we disagree. It is his enormous mistake which is great. I.e., roughly speaking if you add a ~ to the whole book it says an important truth.'

12 Anderson 1984: 175. Cavaglion, in *Otto Weininger in Italia*, ambiguously observes that 'La somiglianza tra Svevo e Weininger, dunque, si rivela oggettivamente poco persuasiva ma soggettivamente "impressionante" per chi, come Debenedetti, scorgerà nei tratti di questi due autori "un'irrefutabile aria di famiglia"' [The resemblance between Svevo and Weininger appears, therefore, objectively unpersuasive yet subjectively 'striking' for one who, like Debenedetti, will detect in the traits of these two authors "an irrefutable family likeness"' (209)]. As late as 1983, and still without any major objections having been raised, Svevian criticism has accepted Debenedetti's parallel between Svevo and Weininger (see Scandiani 1983).

13 From this perspective, we can now attempt to confront the meaning of the question of Svevo's popularity, as well as that of the popularity of Debenedetti, himself the author of *Amedeo* (the story of a listless adolescent – close relative of Alfonso Nitti and ironically another undeclared Jew). How could any right-minded Italian identify with such 'decadent' authors in the seventh

year of the Fascist era? Seen from beyond the looming historical catastrophy, Debenedetti's reference to 'popularity' has the feel of a perverse act of denunciation, perhaps even self-denunciation.

14 Triestine society at the turn of the century is traditionally described as intensely misogynyst. But it should be noted how one of the texts quoted by Cavaglion to support his statement, *Trieste nei miei ricordi* by Giani Stuparich (1948), depicts a quite different picture. Stuparich gives fair, if not lengthy, recognition to the contribution of women to the arts and expressly praises the independent spirit of Triestine women. Scipio Slataper's epistolary, written between 1909 and 1915 and published in 1958 as *Alle tre amiche*, is another eloquent testimonial of the status of women as privileged interlocutors.

15 Although Scandiani's article takes its point of departure from an important statement within the scope of this study, 'La donna è specchio e riflesso di tutta la problematica sveviana' [The woman is mirror and reflection of the entire Svevian problematic (551)], Scandiani limits her brief analysis to the feminine types of the wife and the lover. Furthermore, Scandiani underlines Svevo's affinity with Weininger in his representation of women in the first two novels ('basti pensare ai tratti violentemente misogini con cui sono disegnate le figure di Annetta in *Una vita* e di Angiolina in *Senilità*,' [it suffices to think of the violently misogynistic traits with which Annetta in *Una vita* and Angiolina in *Senilità* are drawn (552)] only to conclude that in the *Coscienza di Zeno* 'proprio quando Svevo viene a conoscenza di Weininger ... i tratti misogini vengano senz'altro attenuati e ridimensionati' [precisely when Svevo comes to know Weininger ... the misogynistic traits are definitely played down and reduced (553)].

16 In 'Etica della dolcezza: la vocazione di Svevo tra moderno e postmoderno' [Ethic of Sweetness: Svevo's vocation between Modernism and Postmodernism], Mauro Buccheri recognizes the centrality of the 'ethic of sweetness' to Svevo's oeuvre, but curbs his insight with the conclusion that 'l'incontro definitivo con l'altro e con l'utopia della mitezza è rinviato ad una testualità che forse sorgerà oltre e fuori dell'opera sveviana, nella storia e nel soggetto futuri' [the definitive encounter with the other and with the utopia of mildness is postponed to a textuality that perhaps will emerge beyond and outside Svevo's work, in history and in the subject of the future (Buccheri 1995: 68–9)], thus negating the intersubjective space won by the Svevian subject *in its textuality*.

17 This fable was sent to Letizia on 20 December 1911. Contini acutely identifies in it the furthest frontier of Svevo's reflection when she observes: 'Attraverso l'intonazione tradizionale e l'apparente innocenza della favola moralistica, un discorso nuovo e una concezione totalmente in crisi

dell'universo irrompono nella pagina, indipendentemente dalle capacità di controllo dell'autore' [Through the traditional intonation and the seeming innocence of the moralistic fable, a new discourse and a conception of the universe totally in crisis break through the page, independently from the author's capacities of control (1979: 136)]. Contrary to Contini, we maintain that Svevo was fully conscious and in control of the implications of his reflection. Contini herself hints at these implications when she speaks of the pedagogic intent of a fable written for the young daughter: 'il problema cioè di dare un'autentica alternativa di libertà al nuovo personaggio femminile che vede crescere accanto a sé' [that is, the problem of giving an authetic alternative of freedom to the new female personage he sees growing beside him (137)].

18 In Horkheimer and Adorno we find the following articulation of the idea: 'The rights of man were designed to promise happiness even to those without power. ... The thought of happiness without power is unbearable because it would then be true happiness' (1988: 172).

3: Between Darwinism and Dreams

1 In an analysis that focuses on literary self-consciousness in the *Coscienza di Zeno*, Gregory Lucente (1986: 157) hints *en passant* to such an interpretation of *Una vita*: 'Although the narrative of *Una vita* is often flat and listless, the literary collaboration at its center serves to focus the psychological development of the proudly obstinate yet helpless main character in a doubly revealing "literary" light.'

2 See Langella 1992: 173. Langella concludes that 'Alfonso non ammette definizioni esaustive; nel senso lato e inclusivo egli è *colui che non sa*: non sa agire [...] non sa comprendere' [Alfonso does not allow an exhaustive definition; in the more general sense he is *the one who does not know*: he does not know how to act ... he cannot understand (186)]. But, as I will argue in this essay, his situation is even more complex, since Alfonso can indeed act, but more often chooses not to; he has a keen ability to analyse his feelings and actions but more often revels in self-deception.

3 *Una vita*, in Svevo, *Romanzi*, ed. Mario Lavagetto (1993: 3). Hereafter cited in the text as UV; all translations are mine.

4 For another pointed reading of this exordium that equally stresses the innovative use of the letter as a 'document' see Tancredi 1971: 55–83. In her analysis, the cultural alibis of the alienated petit bourgeois intellectual pose as a rejection of city life.

5 For a study of Balzac's influence on *Una vita*, see D'Antuono (1986: 121–40),

who draws a comparison between the protagonists of Svevo and Balzac's novels as small-town intellectuals (123–7), and Langella 1990: 13–59.

6 Before collaborating with Annetta, Alfonso encounters a truly humble disciple: the mousy Lucia, daughter of Alfonso's landlady. Alfonso's Italian lessons to Lucia introduce on a smaller stage the search of a dialogue, no matter how degraded, with the other. With Lucia, Alfonso tries to satisfy his intellectual ambition, frustrated sensuality, and search for recognition by pursuing the ambiguous Svevian desire 'd'imparare insegnando' [to learn by teaching (UV, 61)]. On her side, the socially and intellectually inferior Lucia enters the abusive lessons with a mixed desire for love, social advancement, and equality, the desire 'd'ammirarsi vicendevolmente' [to admire each other (UV, 63)]. Somewhat inverted – Annetta is socially superior, culturally if not intellectually inferior to him – and greatly complicated by the subtle mirroring of the two characters, Alfonso's relationship with Annetta will nevertheless revolve around these same motives. For a study of the *mise en abîme* between Alfonso's story and various secondary plots, see Benedetti 1993.

7 For Pampaloni 'Alfonso Nitti è un "teorista," e lo Svevo è il romanziere dei "teoristi," perché il vero tema del suo narrare non è la rappresentazione, ma la ricerca di una definizione dell'autenticità della vita' [Alfonso Nitti is a "theorist" and Svevo is the novelist of "theorists," because the true theme of his narrative is not representation, but the search for a definition of life's authenticity (1980: 100–29)]. But we could object that it is exactly the search for a definition that determines, above all in Alfonso's case, the distance from the realm of authenticity. The only possible authenticity is that belonging to the narrator through his consciousness of the overwhelming presence of inauthenticity.

8 Such a description will eventually constitute a misleading cliché for Annetta. Surprised by the daring of Alfonso's kisses – it is only on the occasions of these 'surprises' caused by Alfonso that the narrator takes up her point of view – she reflects that 'si sentiva di nuovo sicura accanto a quel ragazzo. Era stata proprio questa qualità di ragazzo che l'aveva portata con lui tanto innanzi. Che cosa aveva da temere da quella timidezza personificata?' [She felt safe again next to that boy. It had been exactly his boyishness that carried her so far. What did she have to fear from that personified timidity? (UV, 139)].

9 A similar destiny had already befallen early on the 'dear and beautiful letters' of the mother as they were removed from the privacy of Alfonso's nostalgic dream. '[Maller] gli porse una carta che Alfonso riconobbe derivante dalla bottega del Creglingi. Vi gettò un'occhiata ed erano proprio i cari car-

atteri della madre. *Arrossì; si vergognava di quella brutta scrittura e di quel brutto stile.* C'era in lui qualche cosa di offeso per quella lettera resa pubblica' [Maller handed him a paper that Alfonso recognized as coming from Creglingi's shop. He threw it a glance and he saw indeed the dear characters of his mother. *He blushed; he felt ashamed of that ugly handwriting and of that bad style.* Something in him was offended by that letter being made public (UV, 13–14; emphasis mine)]. The purity and goodness of the dream returns as a miserable stammering on the lips of the mortified clerk. Once exposed to the public gaze, the letters are reduced to a crumpled piece of common paper, an object to be ashamed of. Further on, the letter will go through a further vulgarization by becoming 'due paginette delle sue zampe di mosca' [two little pages of her fly scribblings (UV, 94)].

4: The Crying of the Statues

1 Rousseau, 'Pygmalion,' 1226. See the discussion of this brief 'scène lyrique' in de Man 1979: 160–87.
2 Bárberi Squarotti, 356–65. Squarotti suggests a parallel between Emilio and Pygmalion when he points out how Emilio's fantasy of a 'donna ideale' is achieved by negating the reality of woman.
3 Italo Svevo, *Senilità*, in *Romanzi*, ed. Mario Lavagetto (1993: 335). Hereinafter cited in the text as S; all translations are mine.
4 Cf. *La Coscienza di Zeno*. In a daydream, Zeno changes the features of the woman to lend her the qualities of fine porcelain: 'Un sogno pericoloso perché può conferire nuovo potere alle donne di cui si sognò e che rivedendo alla luce reale conservano qualche cosa delle frutta, dei fiori e della porcellana da cui furono vestite' [A dangerous dream because it can give a new power to the women whom you dreamed about, so that once you see them in the daylight they keep something of the fruit, flowers and porcelain that decorated them (CdZ, 578–9)]. Balli's representation is founded on this very reification of the woman.
5 For discussions of point of view in the novel see Palumbo 1976, Saccone 1977, and Benedetti 1991. Palumbo puts the narrator, the ironic 'coscienza di Svevo,' at a higher level than the character, from which he oversees the reconstitution of meaning through the shifting perspectives of the story. Benedetti agrees with Saccone that 'il predominio del punto di vista di Emilio è innegabile' [the predominance of Emilio's point of view is undeniable (205)], but then proceeds to analyse crucial instances in which the thoughts of Amalia (and Balli) emerge in the story. See Baldi 1998 for a comprehensive analysis of the narrative perspective in the novel.

6 Miceli-Jeffries observes how the figure of the woman can play a double role: 'da una parte opera come oggetto di desiderio, di possesso e di piacere o felicità, e dall'altra come processo di autoidentificazione e di scoperta da parte dei protagonisti' [on the one hand, she functions as an object of desire, possession and pleasure or happiness, and, on the other, as a process of self-identification and discovery (1990: 353)].
7 See Benedetti 1991 for a detailed analysis of all the instances in which Amalia's thoughts are narrated.
8 For a structural analysis of the *incipit* of the novel, see Guglielminetti 1964: 135–7.
9 Correctly, Biasin reads *Senilità* as 'uno studio in forma romanzesca della comunicazione umana, della problematicità della parola' through which unfolds 'la critica serrata di Svevo alle falsità del linguaggio' [a study in novelistic form of human communication, and the problematicity of the word ... Svevo's stringent critique of the falsities of language (Biasin 1984: 137)].

5: Leading the Pedagogue by the Hand

1 'Prima pagina scritta nella nuova stanza 30–9–99,' in 'Pagine di diario e sparse,' Svevo 1968: 816. My analysis of biographical documents will be in line with Contini's work on Svevo's *Epistolario*, in which she strives to identify 'su scala ridotta e verificare in vitro lo spiegarsi dei procedimenti di costruzione sveviani' [on a reduced scale and verified *in vitro*, the unfolding of Svevian strategies of construction (1979: 16)].
2 For a different interpretation of the play that marginalizes the importance of woman see Saccone 1977.
3 The disorder that invests the relations between sexes parallels the disorder of time that Giovanni wants to heal with the process of 'ringiovanimento.' The endless symbiotic and imitative associations pursued by Svevo's characters suggest a desire to reverse sexual positions in a way similar to those of age. Just as we can speak of Svevian characters as 'vecchi giovani' and 'giovani vecchi' (Saccone 1977), so may we imagine 'uomini donne' and 'donne uomini.'
4 'Cronaca della famiglia' in a letter to Livia dated 12 Agosto 1897, in *Epistolario* 1966: 66. Hereinafter abbreviated in the text as 'Cronaca.'
5 'Diario per la fidanzata' in Svevo, *Racconti, saggi, pagine sparse*, ed. Bruno Maier (1968: 784). Hereafter abbreviated in the text as 'Diario.'
6 Nietzsche, 'Schopenhauer als Erzieher,' 337. Translation is mine. The original passage reads as follows: 'Und das ist das Geheimniss aller Bildung: sie verleiht nicht künstliche Gliedmassen, wächserne Nasen, bebrillte Augen ...'

7 For studies on the importance of education in Svevo, see Ricciardi 1972; and Saccone 1977. Ricciardi's study analyses the education of the Svevian character as a failed attempt to rebuild the mythical 'whole' man of the European bourgeoisie. Saccone's essay, focused on a reading of *Senilità*, puts into question the very concept of *Bildung* in Svevo, defining Emilio's education as 'una educazione alla realtà' [education to reality].

8 See Debenedetti, 1945: 68.

9 Similarly, Amalia does not know any education; she does not *grow out of* her love-experience, but she is instead 'terminally' cured of it and thereby returned to her grey essence. 'Fra poco egli sarebbe ritornato a lei per *guarirla dei sogni* che aveva spiati' [Soon he would have come back to her *to cure her of the dreams* that he had overheard (S, 394; emphasis mine)]; 'Egli si vedeva accanto Amalia *guarita, assennata*, ridivenuta capace di sentire il suo affetto' [He saw himself next to Amalia *healed, sensible*, again able to feel his affection (S, 478; emphasis mine)].

10 Among the few studies that comprehensively deal with the figure of the woman in Svevo's work see Schächter 1989. While maintaining that Svevo's sympathetic representation of women superseded the prejudices of the turn of the century male, Ettore Schmitz, Schächter does not move beyond listing the social stereotypes of the time. More relevant to our study is Scandiani, 'Svevo, Weininger e la donna,' (1983: 551–8). Although I do not agree with Scandiani's reading of Svevo's attitude towards woman as torn between open misogyny and admiration, I subscribe to the main premise of his study: 'Nella donna prende corpo uno dei tanti sintomi, e forse il piú decisivo, di un piú generale malessere dell'uomo nei confronti della stessa esistenza' [The woman embodies one of the many symptoms, and perhaps the most decisive one, of a more general uneasiness in man towards his own existence (551)].

11 'La novella del buon vecchio e della bella fanciulla,' in Svevo, *Racconti, saggi, pagine sparse*, 1968. The story was first published by Morreale in a collection including 'Vino generoso,' 'Una burla riuscita,' 'La madre,' and 'Il vecchione' in 1929. Hereafter cited in the text as NB.

12 Magris discusses the connection between old age, 'inettitudine,' and writing in Svevo's last narratives. Old age, being the 'libertà dall'obbligo di attestare a se stessi e agli altri il proprio valore, la propria capacità e vitalità' [freedom from the obligation to attest to oneself or to others one's value, ability, and vitality], supersedes the oppositions used to explicate Svevo's work (e.g., action/contemplation, age and youth), becoming not just 'il volto dell'inettitudine bensì della vita stessa' [the face of ineptitude but rather of life itself (1985: xxvii)].

13 See for a similar reading Saccone 1998:112.
14 For a study of the the ontologically weak element that childhood shares with old age in Svevo's late writings see Heyer-Caput 1991: 44–63. Similar considerations, though treated more from the perspective of the role of writing in the late Svevo, are raised *en passant* by Chegia 1991: 57–72.
15 'La morte' in Svevo 1968: 252; hereafter cited in the text as M.
16 Infancy already appeared as a forewarning of death with 'i bimbi rosei che ballano nel sole' [the rosy children who dance in the sun] by Amalia's deathbed. This image has an illustrious antecedent in Dante's vision of the last *beati*, the souls of the baptized children: a foreshadowing of the poet's regression before history, and, more painfully for him, before the word.
17 According to P. N. Furbank, this short story is the last piece Svevo worked on before the car accident that caused his death: 'On the day they were to leave for home he was still in the middle of writing when Livia called him to say the car was waiting. The fragment he had been working on was later published as "La morte"' (1966: 150).
18 'Corto viaggio sentimentale,' in Svevo, *Racconti, saggi, pagine sparse*, 1968:160.

6: Out of the Shadow of the Mammoth

1 Italo Svevo, *La coscienza di Zeno*, ed. Mario Lavagetto (1993: 751). Hereafter cited in the text as CdZ. All translations are mine.
2 In the large body of critical literature studying the stucture of the novel see Mazzacurati 1982: 37–49; Contini 1983: 98–105; Benedetti 1984.
3 The uncanny glances of the various doctors intersect and refract one another throughout the novel. See Cavaglion 1985: 305–24; and Olive Lalanne 1993.
4 My reading here differs from that of Contini 1979 and Savelli 1998. Contini maintains that Guido's appropriation on an existing fable 'è ancora un bluff di Guido, indizio della vanità e del puerile esibizionismo che farà parte del suo destino' [is another bluff of Guido's, a sign of his vanity and childish exhibitionism (137)]. Savelli sees in Zeno's commentary a coincidence between the judgment of both character and implicit author on Guido as superficial and fatuous. 'Si può affermare con sicurezza che Zeno è in grado di comprendere la mente di Svevo e di apprezzarla, e che Guido, in quanto non è capace di stimare la differenza tra questa e la propria, la apprezza senza davvero comprenderla' [We can state with certainty that Zeno is able to understand Svevo's mind and to appreciate it, and that Guido, being unable to evaluate the difference between the author's and his own mind appreciates it without really understanding it (114)]. But why should we be

so sure? The fact is that Zeno can narrate neither Guido nor himself with objectivity.

5 The 'Hymn to life' sung by the dying has an echo in the later 'hymn' to the successful struggle occasioned by the sight of Guido's misery and self-pity over his financial ruin. About the losers, Zeno wonders: 'Perché non muoiono e vivono tacendo?' [Why don't they die and live in silence?], and he continues: 'E invece simpatica la gioia di chi ha saputo conquistarsi una parte esuberante del commestibile e si manifesti pure al sole in mezzo agli applausi. L'unico grido ammissibile è quello del trionfatore' [It is instead likeable the joy of he who was able to conquer the greater part of the goods and demonstrate this in the open surrounded by applause. The only admissible cry is the one of the winner (CdZ, 834)]. We have come a long way from the meek Alfonso. Even if Zeno is still no Darwinian in his actions, when disparaging the fallen Guido or declaring his health in the concluding pages of the novel, he becomes a ruthless proponent of the survival of the fittest.

6 Psychoanalytic interpretations see in Augusta the representative of the father, the embodiment of the law, while Ada is read on different occasions as the instance of the mother (Jonard 1969), or of the father (Rosowsky 1970; Robinson 1970). Availing himself of Lacanian theory, Saccone sees in Ada 'una mitica e mostruosa, padre *e* madre, madre fallica' [a mythic and monstrous father *and* mother, a phallic mother (Saccone 1973: 96)]. While recognizing the insights of these interpretations, my point of reference in the pre-Oedipal economy of symbiosis disperses the hierarchy of the father/ the law. All characters, as I will argue, occupy both the active and passive position in the association, independently from their gender. Woman in Augusta's case is the mammoth, but Carla and Ada, far from being mammoths, become the 'donne in abbozzo.' Interestingly, *all* the male characters eventually occupy the strong but finished position of the mammoth.

7 In his essay 'The Uncanny' [1919], Freud comes to this definition of the term: '... for this uncanny is in reality nothing new or alien, but something which is familiar and old-established in the mind and which has become alienated from it only through the process of repression' (1955b: 241). In light of this definition, Freud is able to understand the implications of Schelling's previously quoted definition: the uncanny is 'something which ought to have remained hidden but has come to light.' In our present context, the appearance of a double in the subjectivity of the woman gives rise to an uncanny feeling in the male subject, whose body, instead of having remained hidden in the shadow of the mammoth, the reified body of the other, has been brought to light. Thus, it is not the appearance of the other's subjectivity but the man's sight of his own body that is uncanny.

8 From this perspective, all the women in the novel would constitute endless metonymic substitutions of that first and last ideal that has to remain unreachable in order to guarantee its repetition, namely, as Saccone noted in his *Commento a Zeno*: 'un ritmo il cui fine dovrebbe essere quello di preservare il desiderio' [a rhythm whose end should be that of preserving desire (141)], the desire 'di avere e conservare un desiderio insoddisfatto' [to have and retain an unsatisfied desire (140)]. The chain of Freudian *Verschiebungen* that invests the woman – Zeno's limping from Ada, to Alberta, to Augusta, to Carla, and then to Augusta, and to Ada again – remains indistinguishable within this interpretative framework from the chain of 'last' cigarettes. To again use a Lacanian formulation, the woman is the phallus, meaning, at a symbolic level, that her subjectivity is both generated and destroyed by the same process of signification that is constitutive of Zeno's subjectivity.
9 We should note that many of Zeno's recollections are organized according to this rhetorical strategy: they are introduced by regrets that the narration of the story itself will try to dissolve, or at best reduce. Cf. the stories of his relationships with his father and Carla.

Bibliography

Works by Italo Svevo

Unless otherwise indicated, the source for Svevo's short works is Bruno Maier, ed., *Opera Omnia*, vol. 3, *Racconti, saggi, pagine sparse* (Milan: dall'Oglio, 1968).

Novels

Una vita [1892]. In *Romanzi*, ed. Ferdinando Amigoni. Turin: Einaudi-Gallimard.
Senilità [1898]. In *Romanzi*, ed. Nunzia Palmieri. Turin: Einaudi-Gallimard.
La coscienza di Zeno [1923]. In *Romanzi*, ed. Arrigo Stara. Turin: Einaudi-Gallimard.
Il vegliardo [1995]. Ed. Giuseppe Langella. Milan: Vita e pensiero.

Plays

Terzetto spezzato [1912]. In *Commedie. Opera Omnia*, ed. Bruno Maier. Vol. 4. Milan: dall'Oglio.
La rigenerazione [1926]. In *Commedie. Opera Omnia*, ed. Bruno Maier. Vol. 4. Milan: dall'Oglio.

Short Stories

'Una lotta' [1888]. In *I racconti*, ed. Giacinto Spagnoletti. Milan: Rizzoli. 1988.
'Lo specifico del dottor Menghi' [1903].
'La novella del buon vecchio e della bella fanciulla' [1926].

Unfinished Short Stories

'Argo e il suo padrone'
'Corto viaggio sentimentale' and 'Corto viaggio sentimentale' in 'Appendice seconda'
'Diario di bordo'
'La morte'
'Orazio Cima'
'In Serenella'

Essays

'La corruzione dell'anima'
'Del sentimento in arte'
'Ottimismo e pessimismo'
'Per un critico' [1887]
'L'uomo e la teoria darwiniana'

Other Works

'Cronaca della famiglia [1897]. In *Epistolario. Opera Omnia*, ed. Bruno Maier. Vol. 1. Milan: dall'Oglio.
'Diario per la fidanzata'
'Pagine di diario e sparse'
'Profilo Autobiografico'

Correspondence

Carteggio con J. Joyce, V. Larbaud, B. Crémieux, M.A. Comnène, E. Montale, V. Jahier, ed. Bruno Maier. Milan: dall'Oglio, 1965.
Epistolario. In *Opera Omnia*, ed. Bruno Maier. Vol. 1. Milan: dall'Oglio 1966.
Lettere a Svevo. Diario di Elio Schmitz, ed. Bruno Maier. Milan: dall'Oglio, 1973.

Secondary Sources

Almansi, Guido. 1972. 'Il tema dell'incesto nelle opere di Svevo,' *Paragone* 23 (264): 47–60.
Anderson, Mark. 1984. 'Otto Weininger in Italia.' *Modern Language Notes* 99 (1). (Italian issue, January): 172–5.
Ara, Angelo, and Claudio Magris. 1982. *Trieste. Un'identità di frontiera*. Turin: Einaudi.

Auerbach, Erich. 1974. 'The Brown Stocking.' In *Mimesis*, trans. Willard R. Trask. Princeton, NJ: Princeton University Press, 525–53.
Baldi, Guido. 1998. *Le maschere dell'inetto: Lettura di 'Senilità.'* Turin: Paravia.
Balzac, Honoré de. 1927. *Louis Lambert.* In *Oeuvres Complètes de Honoré de Balzac.* Vol. 31. Paris: Louis Conard.
Bárberi Squarotti, Giorgio. 1989. 'La donna ideale: Svevo, D'Annunzio, non senza Leopardi.' *Lettere Italiane* 41 (3): 356–65.
Barilli, Renato. 1972. *La linea Svevo-Pirandello.* Milan: Mursia.
Bazlen, Roberto. 1970. *Note senza testo.* Milan: Adelphi.
Bebel, August. 1971. *Woman under Socialism.* New York: Schocken.
Beer, Marina. 1979. 'Alcune note su Ettore Schmitz e i suoi nomi.' *Contributi Sveviani.* Trieste: Lint, 11–30.
Benedetti, Carla. 1984. *La soggettività nel racconto: Proust e Svevo.* Naples: Liguori.
Benedetti, Laura. 1991. 'Vivere ed essere vissuti: Amalia in Svevo's *Senilità.*' *Italica* 68 (2): 204–16.
– 1993. 'I riflessi di sé nelle storie degli altri: Alcuni sdoppiamenti sveviani.' *Narrativa* 4: 73–86.
Benedetti, Laura, Julia Hairston, and Silvia Ross, eds. 1996. *Gendered Contexts: New Perspectives in Italian Cultural Studies.* New York: Peter Lang.
Benjamin, Walter. 1969. 'The Image of Proust.' In *Illuminations*, edited and with an introduction by Hannah Arendt. New York: Schocken, 201–15.
– 1977. 'Schicksal und Charakter.' *Illuminationen.* Frankfurt am Main: Suhrkamp, 42–9.
Biasin, Gian Paolo. 1984. 'Un *Deo Gratias* qualunque: Svevo, il linguaggio, il sapere.' *Italica* 61 (2): 134–46.
Bini, Daniela. 1978. 'Senilità e salute, ragione e istinto, scrittura e vita in un "buon vecchio" e in una "bella fanciulla."' *Forum Italicum* 12 (3): 351–68.
Biondi, Marino. 1990. 'Trieste in Svevo.' *Il ponte* 46 (12): 67–86.
Borghello, Giampaolo. 1977. *La coscienza borghese – Saggio sulla narrativa di Svevo.* Rome: Savelli.
Bouissy, André. 1966. 'Les fondaments idéologiques de l'oeuvre d'I.S.' *Revue des études italiennes* 12: 209–45, 350–73; 13 (1967): 23–50.
Brombert, Victor. 1999. 'Italo Svevo, or the Paradoxes of the Antihero.' In *In Praise of Antiheroes: Figures and Themes in Modern European Literature 1830–1980.* Chicago: University of Chicago Press, 54–69.
Buccheri, Mauro. 1986–87. '*Senilità* di Italo Svevo o l'"avventura della differenza."' *Rivista di studi italiani* 4–5 (1–2): 85–108.
– 1995. 'Etica della dolcezza: La vocazione pedagogica di Svevo tra moderno e postmoderno.' In *Italo Svevo tra moderno e postmoderno*, ed. Mauro Buccheri and Elio Costa. Ravenna: Longo, 63–79.

Butler, Judith. 1987. *Subjects of Desire*. New York: Columbia University Press.
Camerino, Giuseppe Antonio. 1996. *Italo Svevo e la crisi della Mitteleuropa*. Milan: Istituto di propaganda libraria.
Cary, Joseph. 1993. *A Ghost in Trieste*. Chicago: University of Chicago Press.
Cavaglion, Alberto. 1982. *Otto Weininger in Italia*. Rome: Carucci.
– 1985. 'L'igenista vecchio (Figure di medici nella *Coscienza di Zeno*).' *Letteratura Italiana Contemporanea* 15: 305–24.
Chegia, Silvia. 1991. 'La costellazione Zeno: La grande vecchiaia tra inettitudine, scrittura, eros e morte.' *Il Cristallo* 33 (2): 57–72.
Contini, Gabriella. 1979. *Le lettere malate di Svevo*. Naples: Guida Editori.
– 1980. *Il quarto romanzo di Svevo*. Turin: Einaudi.
– 1983. *Il romanzo inevitabile: Temi e tecniche nella 'Coscienza di Zeno.'* Milan: Mondadori.
– 1996. *Svevo. La scrittura e l'interpretazione*. Palermo: Palumbo.
Cornell, Drucilla, and Adam Thurschwell. 1987. 'Feminism, Negativity, Subjectivity.' In *Feminism and Critique*, ed. Seyla Benhabib and Drucilla Cornell. Cambridge: Polity Press, 143–62.
Darwin, Charles. 1974. 'N Notebook.' In *Early Writings of Charles Darwin*. Transcribed and annotated by Paul H. Barrett, in *Darwin on Man*, by Howard Gruber. New York: Dutton, 329–60.
– 1985 [1859]. *The Origin of Species*. London: Penguin.
D'Antuono, Nicola. 1986. 'Balzac e Georges Ohnet: due fonti e alcuni aspetti del romanzo *Una vita*.' In *Amore e Morte in 'Senilità e altro su Svevo*. Salerno: Pietro Laveglia editore, 121–40.
David, Michel. 1970. *Psicoanalisi nella cultura italiana*. Turin: Boringhieri.
de Beauvoir, Simone. 1974. *The Second Sex*. New York: Vintage.
Debenedetti, Giacomo. 1945. 'Svevo e Schmitz.' In *Saggi Critici*. Rome: O.E.T., 27–85.
– 1967. *Amedeo*. Milan: All'insegna del pesce d'oro.
– 1971. *Il romanzo del Novecento*. Milan: Garzanti.
de Certeau, Michel. 1988. 'Spatial Stories.' In *The Practice of Everyday Life*. Berkeley: University of California Press, 115–30.
de Lauretis, Teresa. 1976. *La sintassi del desiderio*. Ravenna: Longo.
Deleuze, Gilles. 1993. 'Rhizome Versus Trees.' In *Deleuze Reader*, ed. Constantin V. Boundas. New York: Columbia University Press.
Deleuze, Gilles, and Felix Guattari. 1986. *Kafka: Toward a Minor Literature*. Minneapolis: University of Minnesota Press.
– 1987. *A Thousand Plateaus: Capitalism and Schizophrenia*. Minneapolis. University of Minnesota Press.
de Man, Paul. 1979. *Allegories of Reading*. New Haven, CT: Yale University Press.

- 1986. 'The Rhetoric of Temporality.' In *Blindness and Insight*. Minneapolis: University of Minnesota Press.
Derrida, Jacques. 1976. *Of Grammatology.* Baltimore: Johns Hopkins University Press.
- 1979. *Spurs: Nietzsche's Styles/Éperons: Les Styles de Nietzsche.* Chicago: University of Chicago Press.
- 1987. *Psyché. Inventions de l'autre.* Paris: Galilée.
De Sanctis, Francesco. 1883. *Il darwinismo nell'arte.* Naples: Stabilimento Tipografico dei classici italiani.
Dombroski, Robert S. 1995. '*La coscienza di Zeno* ai confini della modernità.' In *Italo Svevo tra moderno e postmoderno*, ed. Mauro Buccheri and Elio Costa. Ravenna: Longo, 139–47.
Eysteinsson, Astradur. 1990. *The Concept of Modernism*. Ithaca, NY: Cornell University Press.
Fava Guzzetta, Lia. 1991. *Il primo romanzo di Italo Svevo: Una scrittura della scissione e dell'assenza.* Messina and Florence: Casa Editrice G. D'Anna.
Foucault, Michel. 1986. 'Of Other Spaces.' *Diacritics* 16: 22–7.
Freud, Sigmund. 1955a. 'Femininity.' *New Introductory Lectures (1932). The Standard Edition*, ed. James Strachey. Vol. 22. London: Hogarth, 112–35.
- 1955b [1919]. 'The Uncanny.' *The Standard Edition*, ed. James Strachey. Vol. 17. London: Hogarth. 217–52.
- 1990. *Beyond the Pleasure Principle.* New York: W.W. Norton.
Furbank, P.N. 1966. *Italo Svevo: The Man and the Writer.* Berkeley: University of California Press.
Gallop, Jane. 1987. 'Reading the Mother Tongue: Psychoanalytic Feminist Criticism.' *Critical Inquiry* 13: 314–23.
Ghidetti, Enrico. 1992. *Italo Svevo: La coscienza di un borghese triestino*. Rome: Editori Riuniti.
- 1993. *Il caso Svevo: Guida storica e critica.* Bari: Laterza.
Gilman, Sander. 1986. *Jewish Self-Hatred: Anti-Semitism and the Hidden Language of the Jews.* Baltimore: Johns Hopkins University Press.
Grignani, Maria Antonietta. 1990. 'La poesia combatte col rasoio: dall'avantesto al racconto critico.' *Autografo* 7 (n.s. 19): 19–37.
Gruber, Howard. 1974. *Darwin on Man: A Psychological Study of Scientific Creativity.* New York: Dutton.
Guglielminetti, Marziano. 1964. *Struttura e sintassi del romanzo italiano del 900.* Milan: Silva.
Haraway, Donna. 1990. 'Investment Strategies for the Evolving Portfolio of Primate Females.' In *Body/Politics Women and the Discourses of Science*, ed. Mary Jacobus, Evelyn Fox Keller, and Sally Shuttleworth. New York: Routledge, 139–62.

- 1991. *Simians, Cyborgs, and Women: The Reinvention of Nature.* New York: Routledge.
Harvey, David. 1990. *The Condition of Postmodernity.* Cambridge, MA, and Oxford: Blackwell.
Heyer-Caput, Margherita. 1991. 'Infanzia e vecchiaia: Dimensioni privilegiate della letteratura del "raccoglimento" nell'ultimo Svevo.' *Yearbook of Italian Studies* 9: 44–63.
Hoberman, John. 1995. 'Otto Weininger and the Critique of Jewish Masculinity.' In *Jews and Gender: Responses to Otto Weininger,* ed. Nancy Harrowitz and Barbara Hyams. Philadelphia: Temple University Press, 141–53.
Horkheimer, Max, and Theodor Adorno. 1988. *Dialectic of Enlightenment.* New York: Continuum.
Irigaray, Luce. 1985. *This Sex Which Is Not One.* Ithaca, NY: Cornell University Press.
Jacobus, Mary. 1986. *Reading Woman: Essays in Feminist Criticism.* New York: Columbia University Press.
Jameson, Fredric. 1988. 'Cognitive Mapping.' In *Marxism and the Interpretation of Culture,* ed. Cary Nelson and Lawrence Grossberg. Houndmills, Basingstoke, Hampshire, UK: Mcmillan Education, 347–57.
Jardine, Alice. 1985. *Gynesis: Configurations of Woman and Modernity.* Ithaca, NY: Cornell University Press.
Jeuland Meynaud, Maryse. 1985. *Zeno e i suoi fratelli: La creazione del personaggio nei romanzi di Svevo.* Bologna: Patron.
Johnson, Barbara. 1989. 'Gender Theory and the Yale School.' In *A World of Difference.* Baltimore: Johns Hopkins University Press, 32–41.
- 1998. *The Feminist Difference: Literature, Psychoanalysis, Race and Gender.* Cambridge: Harvard University Press.
Jonard, Norbert. 1969. *Italo Svevo et la crise de la bourgeoisie européenne.* Paris: Les Belles Lettres.
Kofman, Sarah. 1985. *The Enigma of Woman.* Ithaca, NY: Cornell University Press.
Lacan, Jacques. 1977. 'The Function and Field of Speech and Language in Psychoanalysis.' In *Écrits.* New York and London: Norton, 30–113.
- 1977. 'The Mirror Stage.' In *Écrits.* New York: Norton, 1–7.
Lalanne, Olive. 1993. 'Svevo et le savoir médical.' *Revue des études italiennes* 39 (14): 1–4.
Langella, Giuseppe. 1990. '*Una vita* di Italo Svevo e il romanzo francese dell'Ottocento.' *Novecento* (Cahiers du CERCIC) 12: 13–59.
- 1992. '*Una vita* e il *Dizionario dei sinonimi*: per una revisione della categoria sveviana dell'inettitudine.' *Letteratura italiana contemporanea* 13 (35): 171–89.
Lavagetto, Mario. 1986. *L'impiegato Schmitz.* Turin: Einaudi.

- 1989. *La gallina di Saba*. Turin: Einaudi.
- 1993. 'Introduzione' to Italo Svevo, *Romanzi*, ed. Mario Lavagetto. Turin: Einaudi-Gallimard, ix–lxxix.

Lefebvre, Henri. *Critique of Everyday Life*. Vol. 1. London: Verso.

Le Rider, Jacques. 1993. *Modernity and Crises of Identity: Culture and Society in Fin de Siècle Vienna*. New York: Continuum.

Leroi-Gourhan, André. 1993. *Speech and Gesture*. Cambridge: MIT Press.

Levi, Eugenio. 1964. 'Italo Svevo e l'anima ebraica.' In *Il lettore inquieto*. Milan: Il Saggiatore, 177–92.

Lucente, Gregory. 1986. 'The Genre of Literary Confession and the Mode of Psychological Realism.' *Beautiful Fables*. Baltimore: Johns Hopkins University Press, 156–76.

Lukács, Georg. 1971. 'Erzählen oder beschreiben?' *Probleme des Realismus I*. Band 4. Neuwied and Berlin: Hermann Luchterhand, 197–242.

Magris, Claudio. 1976. 'Svevo e la cultura tedesca a Trieste.' *Il caso Svevo*, ed. Giuseppe Petronio. Palermo: Palumbo.
- 1985. 'La scrittura e la vecchiaia selvaggia.' Introduction to *I racconti*, by Italo Svevo. Garzanti: Milan, xix–xxxviii.
- 1988. 'Things Near and Far: Nietzsche and the Great Triestine Generation of the Early Twentieth Century.' In *Nietzsche in Italy: Stanford Italian Review*, ed. Thomas Harrison. Saratoga, CA: Anma Libri, 293–99.

Margulis, Lynn. 1991. 'Symbiogenesis and Symbionticism.' In *Symbiosis as a Source of Evolutionary Innovation*, ed. Lynn Margulis and René Fester. Cambridge: MIT Press, 1–14.

Marx, Karl. 1978. 'Theses on Feuerbach.' In *The Marx-Engels Reader*, ed. Robert C. Tucker. New York: Norton, 143–5.

Maxia, Sandro. 1977. *Svevo e la prosa del 900*. Bari: Laterza.

Maynard Smith, John. 1991. 'A Darwinian View of Symbiosis.' In *Symbiosis as a Source of Evolutionary Innovation*, ed. Lynn Margulis and René Fester. Cambridge: MIT Press, 26–39.

Mazzacurati, Giancarlo. 1974. '3 Progetti di analisi per 3 micro-strutture sveviane (*Una Vita*).' *Forma e Ideologia*. Naples: Liguori, 219–66.
- 1982. 'Teresina, la luce, l'apocalisse di Zeno.' In *Il secondo Svevo*. Ed. Francesco Paolo Botti, Giancarlo Mazzacurati, and Matteo Palumbo. Naples: Liguori, 136–56.

Miceli-Jeffries, Giovanna. 1990. 'Per una poetica della senilità: la funzione della donna in *Senilità* e *Un amore*.' *Italica* 67 (3): 353–70.

Miller, Nancy K. 1986. 'Arachnologies: The Woman, the Text and the Critic.' In *The Poetics of Gender*, ed. Nancy Miller. New York: Columbia University Press, 270–96.

Minghelli, Giuliana. 1994. 'In the Shadow of the Mammoth: Narratives of Symbiosis in *La coscienza di Zeno.*' Modern Language Notes 109.1: 49–72.
Moloney, Brian. 1973. 'Svevo as a Jewish Writer.' *Italian Studies* 27: 52–63.
– 1986. 'Plot and Sub-plot in Italo Svevo's *Una vita.*' *Association of Teachers of Italian Journal* 48: 92–6.
Monk, Ray. 1990. *Ludwig Wittgenstein: The Duty of Genius.* London: Jonathan Cape.
Musarra-Schroeder Ulla. 1994. 'Italo Svevo e la modernità europea.' In *Italo Svevo: Scrittore europeo.* Atti del convegno internazionale Perugia (18–21 March 1992), ed. Norberto Cacciaglia and Lia Guzzetta Fava. Florence: Olschki, 153–60.
Nabokov, Vladimir. 1970. *Speak Memory*. New York: Pyramid Books.
Nägele, Rainer.1987. *Reading after Freud.* New York: Columbia University Press.
Nietzsche, Friedrich. 1972. 'Schopenhauer als Erzieher.' In *Unzeitgemässe Betrachtungen I–III*, ed. Giorgio Colli and Mazzino Montinari. Berlin: Walter de Gruyter, 333–423.
– 1973. *Beyond Good and Evil.* London: Penguin.
– 1974. *The Gay Science.* New York: Vintage Books.
– 1975. *Twilight of the Idols.* London: Penguin.
– 1978. *Thus Spoke Zarathustra.* New York: Penguin.
– 1994. *On the Genealogy of Morality.* New York: Cambridge University Press.
– 1995. *Human, All Too Human.* In *The Complete Works of Friedrich Nietzsche*, ed. Ernst Behler. Vol. 3. Stanford, CA: Stanford University Press.
Palumbo, Matteo. 1976. *La coscienza di Svevo.* Naples: Liguori.
Pampaloni, Geno. 1980. 'Italo Svevo narratore: da *Una vita* a *Senilità.*' In *Italo Svevo oggi*, ed. Marco Marchi. Florence: Vallecchi, 100–29.
Pasolini, Pier Paolo. 1992. *Petrolio.* Turin: Einaudi.
Pearson, Keith Ansell. 1997. *Viroid Life.* London: Routledge.
Pittoni, Anita. 1968. *L'anima di Trieste. Lettere al professore.* Florence: Vallecchi.
Ricciardi, Mario. 1972. *L'educazione del personaggio nella narrativa di Italo Svevo.* Palermo: Flaccovio.
Robinson, Lillian S. 1978. 'On Reading Trash.' *Sex, Class, and Culture.* Bloomington: Indiana University Press, 200–22.
Robinson, Paula. 1970. 'Svevo: Secret of the Confessional.' *Literature and Psychology* 1: 101–14.
– 1971. '*Senilitá*: The Secrets of Svevo's Weeping Madonna.' *Italian Quarterly* 55: 61–84.
Rosny ainé, Joseph Henry. 1994 [1911]. *La guerre du feu.* Brussels: Labor.
Rosowsky, Giuditta. 1970. 'Théorie et pratique dans *La coscienza di Zeno.*' *Revue des études italiennes* 16: 49–70.

Rosset, Clément. 1967. *Schopenhauer: Philosophe de l'absurde*. Paris: Presses Universitaires de France.
Rousseau, Jean-Jacques. 1961. 'Pygmalion.' In *Oeuvres complètes*, ed. Bernard Gagnebin and Marcel Raymond. Vol. 1. Paris: Gallimard.
– 1964. *Discours sur l'origine et les fondements de l'inégalité*. In *Oeuvres complètes*, ed. Bernard Gagnebin and Marcel Raymond. Vol. 3. Paris: Gallimard.
Saba, Umberto. 1988. *Tutte le poesie*. Milan: Mondadori.
Saccone, Eduardo. 1973. *Commento a Zeno*. Bologna: Il Mulino.
– 1977. *Il poeta travestito*. Pisa: Pacini.
– 1995. 'Antinomie e correzione.' In *Italo Svevo tra moderno e postmoderno*, ed. Mauro Buccheri and Elio Costa. Ravenna: Longo, 81–92.
– 1998. 'Il giorno e la notte. Riflessioni sulla *Novella* di Svevo.' *Modern Language Notes* 113.1: 108–20.
Savelli, Giulio. 1990. 'Ultima sigaretta, eventi e storia nella *Coscienza di Zeno*.' *Modern Language Notes* 105.1: 87–104.
– 1991. '"Ogni riferimento è puramente casuale": il lettore nel finale della *Coscienza di Zeno*.' *Strumenti critici*. Vol. 3 (September): 457–77.
– 1998. *L'ambiguità necessaria: Zeno e il suo lettore*. Milan: Francoangeli.
Scandiani, Giuseppe. 1983. 'Svevo, Weininger e la donna.' *Humanitas* 4: 551–8.
Schächter, Elizabeth. 1989. 'Schmitz, Svevo and Sexuality.' In *Moving in Measure: Essays in Honour of Brian Moloney*, ed. Judith Bryce and Doug Thompson. Hull, UK: Hull University Press, 133–51.
– 1995. 'The Enigma of Svevo's Jewishness: Trieste and the Jewish Cultural Tradition,' *Italian Studies* 50: 24–47.
Schopenhauer, Arthur. 1988. *Die Welt als Wille und Vorstellung*. Zürich: Haffmans Verlag.
Scott, Joan. 1988. 'Gender: A Useful Category of Historical Analysis.' *Gender and the Politics of History*. New York: Columbia University Press, 28–50.
Slataper, Scipio. 1954. *Scritti politici*. Milan: Mondadori.
– 1958. *Alle tre amiche*. Milan: Mondadori.
– 1966. *Il mio Carso*. Florence: La Nuova Italia.
Spivak, Gayatri Chakravorty. 1983. 'Displacement and the Discourse of Woman.' In *Displacement: Derrida and After*, ed. Mark Krugnick. Bloomington: Indiana University Press, 169–95.
– 1988. 'Unmaking and Making in *To the Lighthouse*.' In *Other Worlds: Essays in Cultural Politics*. New York: Routledge, 30–45.
Stuparich, Giani. 1948. *Trieste nei miei ricordi*. Milan: Garzanti.
Tancredi, Marida. 1971. '*Una vita* di Svevo.' *Angelus Novus* 21: 55–83.
– 1973. 'La fede di Argo.' *Problemi* 38: 414–21.

Vadalà-Papale, Giuseppe. 1882. *Darwinismo naturale e darwinismo sociale.* Turin: Loescher.

Voghera, Giorgio. 1955. 'Presenza e spirito ebraici nella letteratura triestina.' *L'osservatore politico-letterario.* 21(3): 18–31.

– 1980. *Gli anni della psicoanalisi.* Pordenone: Studio Tesi.

Wasmann, Erich. 1909 [1907]. *The Berlin Discussion of the Problem of Evolution.* London: Kegan Paul, Trench, Trubner.

Weininger, Otto. 1906. *Sex and Character.* New York: G.P. Putnam's Sons. Originally published as *Geschlecht und Charakter* (Vienna: W. Braumüller, 1903).

Weiss, Peter. 1984. *The Persecution and Assassination of Jean-Paul Marat as Performed by the Inmates of the Asylum of Chareton under the Direction of the Marquis De Sade.* New York: Atheneum.

Wilden, Anthony. 1969. 'Death, Desire, and Repetition in Svevo's *Zeno.*' *Modern Language Notes* 84(1): 98–119.

Wittig, Monique. 1990. 'Homo Sum.' *Feminist Issues* 10(1): 3–11.

– 1984. 'The Trojan Horse.' *Feminist Issues* 4(2): 45–50.

Wlassics, Tibor. 1971. 'Sulla "Novella" di Svevo.' *Nuova antologia* 2046: 248–55.

Index

Adaptation, 4, 12; as crystallization, 4, 20, 27; happiness of, 19–21; in Darwin, 22–3; potentiality vs., 26, 38; in the end of *La coscienza*, 32
Adorno, Theodor, 72, 214n18
Almansi, Guido, 146
Anderson, Mark, 212n12
Ara, Angelo, 8ff, 14
Auerbach, Erich, 204

Baldi, Guido, 211n8, 216n5
Balzac, Honoré de, 52, 204; *Louis Lambert*, 77–8, 83–4
Bárberi Squarotti, Giorgio, 216n2
Barilli, Renato, 95–6, 99, 207n4
Bazlen, Roberto, 10–14
Bebel, August, 130, 158
Beckett, Samuel, 48
Beer, Marina, 6, 59–60, 67
Benedetti, Carla, 163, 204, 219n2
Benedetti, Laura, 109, 115, 215n6, 216n5, 217n7
Benjamin, Walter, 47
Biasin, Gian Paolo, 217
Bildungsroman, 74, 93
Bini, Daniela, 139
Biondi, Marino, 7

Borghello, Giampaolo, 209n15
Bouissy, André, 208n4
Brombert, Victor, 211n8
Buccheri, Mauro, 101, 213n16
Butler, Judith, 42

Camerino, Giuseppe Antonio, 209n15, 211n6
Carocci, Alberto, 51
Cary, Joseph, 7
Cavaglion, Alberto, 66–7, 69, 212nn10,12, 219n3
Chegia, Silvia, 219n14
Conrad, Joseph, 205
Contamination, 4–8, 12; symbiosis as, 4–6, 14, 43, 66, 204; anxiety of, 5, 57, 62–3; and modernism, 5, 13–14, 16–18, 62–3, 101, 204–5; woman as site of, 5, 16–18, 65, 200–3; Deleuze and Guattari on, 43; intersubjectivity as, 45; and pedagogy, 131–3, 136–7; and psychoanalysis, 201–3
Contini, Gabriella, 144, 162, 213n17, 217n1, 219n2

D'Annunzio, Gabriele, 55

Dante Alighieri, 62, 219n16
D'Antuono, Nicola, 214n5
Darwin, Charles, 11, 17f, 21, 75, 208; and *The Origin of Species*, 22–6; 27, 29ff, 38; on symbiosis, 41
Darwinism, 15, 34, 78; Social, 12, 93, 96, 196; the ethic of, 94, 98; in *Una vita*, 93–101; critique of, 43; 'metaphysical darwinism,' 60; and the poetics of naturalism, 94–5; in *La coscienza*, 31, 177
David, Michel, 212n10
Debenedetti, Giacomo, 5, 13, 67, 88, 94, 204, 211nn3, 4, 5, 9, 212nn12,13, 217; 'Svevo e Schmitz' ('Svevo and Schmitz'), 49–59; on Svevo and naturalism, 50–2; on Svevo and modernism, 50–1, 211n9; on the aesthetic of symbolic unity, 51–2; and Lukàcs's critique of modernism, 52; on symbiosis in Svevo, 53–5; on Fascist aesthetic, 55–6; and Jewish self-hatred, 57, 63–4; on femininity in Svevo, 58–9, 64; on Svevo and Weininger, 57–9, 63–4
de Certeau, Michel, 13f
de Lauretis, Teresa, 128
Deleuze, Gilles: minor literature, 13; creative involution, 16, 42–3, 205
de Man, Paul, 40, 209n19
de Moré, Charles Albert, 9
Derrida, Jacques, 18, 44, 66, 122, 125, 180, 201, 210n23
De Sanctis, Francesco, 94
de Staël, Madame, 83
Dombroski, Robert, 17
Dostoyevski, Fyodor, 9

Eliot, T. S., 48

Ethic of *dolcezza* (sweetness): and symbiosis, 71, 75, 98, 213n16; as inferiority and weakness, 72, 99, 147; as dreaming in *Una vita*, 75, 80; and pedagogy in *Senilità*, 136; and health in *La coscienza*, 190; 213n16
Evolution, 18; and the idea of progress, 23–4; Nietzsche on, 24–5; as resistance in Svevo, 28–9; theory of (in *La coscienza*), 31–4; as *pause* in Svevo, 35–6; through symbiosis, 39–43; critique of, 43
Eysteinsson, Astradur, 16, 47, 57, 205, 210n1

Fable of the Man and the Mammoth, 4–6, 10, 34–45, 72, 128, 147–8; as critique of progress, 43–4; in *Una vita*, 80, 84, 89; in *Senilità*, 111; in *La coscienza*, 162–3, 165, 167–71, 173, 178–80, 184, 187, 194–5
Fascism, 12, 55–6
Fava Guzzetta, Lia, 82, 87, 96f
Fester, René, 209
Feuilleton, 4; Svevo on the, 87–8; in *Una vita*, 89, 92–3; the ethics of, 93–4
First World War, 9; myth of cleansing struggle, 12
Flaubert, Gustave, 204
Foucault, Michel, 10
Frescura, Attilio, 13
Freud, Sigmund, 61f, 64, 86, 119, 210nn21, 22, 220n7
Furbank, P. N., 219n17

Gall, Franz Joseph, 135
Gallop, Jane, 159
Ghidetti, Enrico, 3
Gide, André, 205

Gilman, Sander, 61
Grignani, Maria Antonietta, 211n9
Gruber, Howard, 208n6
Guattari, Felix: minor literature, 13; creative involution, 16, 43, 205
Guglielminetti, Marziano, 217n8

Haraway, Donna, 39f, 44, 208n9, 210n24
Harvey, David, 46, 48
Hegel, Georg Wilhelm Friedrich, 40, 42
Heyer-Caput, Margherita, 219n14
Hoberman, John, 71
Hofmannsthal, Hugo von, 125
Horkheimer, Max, 72, 214

Il convegno, 49–50
Inetto, 5, 29, 48, 52; Debenedetti on the, 51–3; and Lukács's *menschliche Gestalt*, 52; and the Fascist aesthetic, 55–6; as Jew and woman, 58–9; critique of, 75, 84, 211n8

Jacobus, Mary, 59
Jameson, Fredric, 17, 205
Jardine, Alice, 47
Jeuland Meynaud, Maryse, 5
Jewishness: and modernism, 5, 51, 57–9; and femininity, 58–9, 72
Johnson, Barbara, 66, 73, 92–3, 121
Jonard, Norbert, 220n6
Joyce, James, 7, 48f, 61

Kafka, Franz, 48
Kofman, Sarah, 119
Kraus, Karl, 61

Lacan, Jacques, 159, 164
Lalanne, Olive, 219

Langella, Giuseppe, 75, 99, 214f
Lavagetto, Mario, 13f, 63, 75, 88, 95f, 133, 175, 207n4, 211n6, 216n3, 219n1
La voce, 13, 61
Lefebvre, Henri, 7
Le Rider, Jacques, 72
Leroi-Gourhan, André, 26
Levi, Eugenio, 211n6
L'indipendente, 61
Locke, John, 121
Lucente, Gregory, 214n1
Lukács, Georg, 52, 57, 211n7

Magris, Claudio, 8ff, 14, 16, 208n8, 218n12
Maier, Bruno, 207n1, 217n5
Marat, Jean Paul, 21, 26
Margulis, Lynn, 209n20
Marx, Karl, 130, 147
Maxia, Sandro, 209n15
Mazzacurati, Giancarlo, 74ff, 88, 199, 219n2
Miceli-Jeffries, Giovanna, 217n6
Miller, Nancy, 211
Modernism, 5; and race, 6, 57–9; and contamination, 5, 13–14, 16–18, 62–3, 101, 204–5; Italian, 14; and Svevo, 16–18, 32, 48, 50, 204–5; and the figure of the woman, 16–18, 47–8, 62; and modernity in *La coscienza*, 32; symbiosis and rhetoric of struggle in, 47–9; the artist in, 46–9; and Jewishness, 51, 57–9, 62; Italian Fascism and the resistance to, 55–6; and *Una vita*, 92–3, 101
Modernity, 4, 15, 47–8; and Svevo, 16; and the *uomo in abbozzo*, 32; and Weininger, 61
Moloney, Brian, 82, 211n6

Monk, Ray, 212n11
Montale, Eugenio, 73f
Musarra-Schroeder, Ulla, 211n8
Mussolini, Benito, 55

Nabokov, Vladimir, 34, 43
Natural selection, 12, 21; human desire and, 23, 29; cooperation vs., 34
Naturalism, 78; and Darwinism, 94-5, 100-1
Nietzsche, Friedrich, 18, 27f, 29, 32, 34, 38, 46-7, 53, 60, 122, 125, 134, 156, 209, 217; on Darwin, 22-5, 208n8

Palumbo, Matteo, 118, 121, 126
Pampaloni, Geno, 215
Pasolini, Pier Paolo, 98
Pearson, Keith Ansell, 34, 42-3, 208-9
Pedagogy: and symbiosis/contamination, 74, 131-3, 172; and women, 129-34, 136-7; and seduction, 133-7, 139-40, 173-4, 180-1; as cure, 136, 144-5; vs. biology, 134-6; anxiety of position in, 141-4, 147; and death, 148, 150-5; and psychoanalysis, 158-60, 164
Pirandello, Luigi, 205
Pittoni, Anita, 8 passim
Plato, 133
Proust, Marcel, 47, 50

Ricciardi, Mario, 218n7
Robinson, Lillian, 92
Robinson, Paula, 110, 220n6
Rosny aîné, Joseph Henry: *La guerre du feu*, 3-4, 207n1
Rosowsky, Giuditta, 220n6

Rosset, Clément, 30, 208n10
Rousseau, Jean-Jacques, 40, 102, 126, 216n1

Saba, Umberto, 6ff, 11, 13
Sacchetti, Franco, 81
Saccone, Eduardo, 25, 74ff, 99, 101, 110, 114f, 119, 165, 170, 179, 183, 196, 198, 205, 208n11, 216 passim
Savelli, Giulio, 32, 163, 165, 194f, 204, 209n13, 219n4
Scandiani, Giuseppe, 67, 68, 213n15, 218n10
Schächter, Elizabeth, 211n6, 218n10
Schmitz, Elio, 74
Schmitz, Ettore, 3f, 6, 43, 49, 51, 72, 74, 84f, 99; on marriage, desire, and pedagogy, 127-33; 155, 157, 218n10
Schopenhauer, Arthur, 29, 75, 99, 130, 207n4, 217n6
Slataper, Scipio, 8, 12ff, 213n14
Solaria, 51
Smith, Maynard, 209n20
Spencer, Herbert, 24
Spivak, Gayatri Chakravorty, 210n22
Stein, Gertrude, 61, 63
Stendhal, 52, 204
Strength and weakness, 4; dialectic of, 21, 24-5, 48
Struggle for existence, 4, 21; rhetoric of, 12, 47; as metaphor in *The Origin*, 22, 24; Nietzsche on, 22, 24; Svevo on, 27-8, 84; in Hegel, 40; ethic of (in *Una vita*), 84-5, 94-101; in *La coscienza*, 172, 177
Stuparich, Giani, 213n14
Svevo, Italo, 3ff, 5; pseudonyms and Italian/Jewish identity, 6-7, 10, 48, 51, 59; and the Italian language,

13; on human origins, 18–21, 34–40; and modernism, 16–18, 32, 48, 50, 204–5; on struggle for existence, 27–8, 84; Italian reception of, 49; and Weininger, 57–60, 63–4, 66–71, 212f; and the representation of women, 16–18, 44–5, 66–72, 156–60; and misogyny, 66–71; on the *feuilleton*, 87–8; and psychoanalysis, 159

- *Una vita* (*A Life*), 3, 29f, 54, 57, 63, 72, 73–101, 215n9; Trieste in, 7; literary models in, 87–8, 91–2; point of view in, 88; mirroring between narrator and characters in, 88–90; modernism in, 92–3, 101; critique of realist and naturalist character in, 95–7; critique of Social Darwinism and naturalism in, 100–1
- *Senilità* (*As a Man Grows Older*), 54, 58–9, 74, 101, 102–6, 148, 169, 218n12; Trieste in, 7; conflicting aesthetics in, 104–5; narrative point of view in, 108–9; symbiosis and art in, 110–11, 116–19; woman and truth in, 121–5; pedagogy and seduction in, 130, 133–7, 139–40
- *La coscienza di Zeno* (*Confessions of Zeno*), 122, 128, 132, 148, 156, 160, 161–203, 216; modernism and the critique of modernity in, 31–4, 49, 54, 57; Weininger in, 67–71; psychoanalysis and symbiosis in, 163–5, 201–3; the figure of the woman in, 196–203
- Other works: 'Argo e il suo padrone' ('Argo and his master'), 158; 'Una burla riuscita' ('The Hoax'), 74, 175; 'La corruzione dell'anima' ('The Corruption of the Soul'), 5,

27, 33, 35, 162, 195, 207n4; as myth of origin 15, 18–23; 'Corto viaggio sentimentale' ('Short Sentimental Journey'), 155–8, 189; Appendix to 'Corto viaggio sentimentale,' 88, 93–4; 'Cronaca della famiglia' ('Family Chronicle') 129–31; 'Del sentimento in arte' ('On Sentiment in Art'), 147; 'Diario di bordo' ('Log Book'), 53, 71, 171, 180; 'Diario per la fidanzata' ('Diary for the Fiancé'), 45, 84, 99, 131–2; *Epistolario* (*Correspondence*), 49, 136, 196, 217n1; 'Una lotta' ('A Struggle'), 97; 'La morte' ('Death'), 134, 148–55, 158, 219nn15, 17; 'La novella del buon vecchio e della bella fanciulla' ('The Story of the Good Old Man and the Beautiful Girl'), 133, 138–48, 154f; 'Orazio Cima,' 64, 71, 98; 'Pagine di diario e sparse' ('Diary Notes and Other Fragments'), 17, 43, 73, 92, 140, 159; 'Per un critico' ('For a Critic'), 83; 'Profilo autobiografico' ('Autobiographical Profile'), 73, 137; *La rigenerazione* (*Rigeneration*), 127–8, 145; 'In Serenella,' 124; 'Lo specifico del dottor Menghi' ('Doctor Menghi's Formula'), 148; *Terzetto spezzato* (*Broken Trio*), 129; 'L'uomo e la teoria darwiniana' ('Man and Darwinian Theory'), 3, 5, 128, 162, 167f, 179, 194–5, 207n1 (Intro), n1 (Ch. 1), 4, 208n5; as myth of origin, 15, 17f, 27–30, 34–42, 39–40; *Il vegliardo* (*The Venerable Old Man*), 144, 156

Symbiosis, 7, 12, 14, 168–71; allegory

of, 4, 18, 39; Darwin on, 41–2; ethic of, 6, 72, 101; and modernism, 16–18, 46–8; Deleuze and Guattari on, 16, 42–3; and birth of subjectivity, 34–5; and evolution, 39; as reflection/recognition, 42, 189; Debenedetti on Svevo and, 53–5; psychoanalysis and, 66, 163–5; as *dolcezza*, 71, 75, 98; as artistic collaboration, 74, 110–11, 116–26; as parasitism, 163, 177, 193, 196

Tancredi, Marida, 214n4
Tedeschi, Steno, 61
Tommaseo, Niccolò, 7ff
Tolstòj, Lev, 52
Trieste, 6ff; history of, 8 passim; human geography of, 10–11; as a city in *abbozzo*, 12; and rhetoric of racial purity, 12; misogyny in, 66–7

Uomo in abbozzo (unfinished man), 4f, 14; 28–9, 75, 132, 205; and Nietzsche's 'preparatory human beings,' 29; and Schopenhauer's contemplator, 29–30; as defined by the pause, 30, 84; origins of (in *Una vita*), 84, 95f, 99; limits of, 31–4, 162–3, 168–9; critique of (in 'L'uomo e la teoria darwiniana'), 37–8, 44; as critique of realist and naturalist character, 54, 95–7; and Fascism, 55–6; like woman and child, 89–90, 147–8, 185; in *La coscienza*, 162–3, 165–70, 180, 184, 192f

Vadalà-Papale, Giuseppe, 208n5
Voghera, Giorgio, 211n6

Wagner, Richard, 112, 114
Wasmann, Erich, 34, 39, 208n5, 209n14
Weininger, Otto, 60–66, 135–6, 212nn10, 11, 12; and the anxiety of contamination, 5, 62–3; Debenedetti on, 57–9, 63; *Geschlecht und Charakter*, reception of, 60–1; against modernism, 61–2; on genius, 62–3; on Jews and women as parasites, 62; on bisexuality and contamination, 65–6; and Svevo, 57–60, 63–4, 66–71, 212n12, 213n15
Weiss, Peter, 21
Wilden, Anthony, 128
Wittgenstein, Ludwig, 61, 212
Wlassics, Tibor, 142–3 passim
Women: and modernism, 5, 17–18, 46–8, 64, 205; as symbionts, 4–5, 44–5, 122–3, 126, 200–3; and Jews, 58–9, 72; Svevo and the representation of, 66–72, 157–60; and aesthetic representation in *Senilità*, 104–10, 119–26; and psychoanalysis, 119, 158–60; and pedagogy, 129–34, 136–7, 156–60; and truth, 121–3; and friendship, 156; in *La coscienza*, 196–203

Zola, Emile, 204